Advance praise for *A Ministry S*

Forty years as a pastor's wife should be an immediate ticket to sainthood. Lisa is a survivor and a thriver who has mined wise lessons from tricky terrain. This story of God's grace in a life, a marriage, and a church will comfort the hurting and unsettle the comfortable. Thanks, St. Lisa!

—Phil Callaway
Best-selling author of twenty-five books
Host, *Laugh Again Radio*

Lisa Elliott has created the essential handbook for anyone seeking to enter public ministry. I wish I had read it years ago! If you want to not only survive but thrive as you serve God and others, this book is a must-read!

—Cheryl Weber
Host, *100 Huntley Street*

As a former minister's wife, I read through *A Ministry Survival Guide* and felt like I was reliving a checklist of shared experiences from my twenty-five years in pastoral ministry. Lisa nailed it with openness and honesty on her adjustments, challenges, and places of brokenness in her journey to survive the demands of being a minister's wife.

This book is not just a survivor guide; it is a rich mentoring resource. Referencing biblical mentors gives a solid base to Lisa's practical tips and leadership principles. Young minister's wives who are at times yelling "Help!" will find enough encouragement, inspiration, and clear direction in this book to help them in their journey.

—Margaret Gibb
Executive Director, Women Together

Is it unorthodox to highlight almost *every* line as it speaks to me!? Sitting in my sunshine-filled backyard with birds a chirpin', I read the inside of Lisa's heart poured out onto the pages before me—from her pointed questions that challenged me, to her calls to action that provoked me into acting and responding by looking deep within my own heart. *A Ministry Survival Guide* was especially validating to me as a woman with over (ahem!) fifty years of living out my calling in the ministry of music arts. Relating. Laughing. Reflecting. You will experience all of this and more as you devour this valuable tool for all women in ministry penned by my friend and gifted writer, Lisa Elliott.

—Marlene O'Neill
Award-winning concert, stage, and studio vocalist

This book is a wonderful summary of a lifetime of learnings that will be a gift to many who will read it for years to come. It's written to ministry spouses but it's a gift to every woman who loves Jesus and loves His Church and loves her husband and loves her family and isn't sure there's enough of her to go around.

Throughout the book, Lisa offers wisdom from biblical mentors, but in the sharing of her own story—the good and the hard of it—she is herself a gentle mentor. I haven't had the pleasure of meeting Lisa in person (yet), but I feel like I've met a friend. A wise, kind, honest, funny, and generous friend. She welcomes us into this book, and her life, the way I imagine she would welcome us into her home: with a big hug and a fresh cup of coffee. Likely a double-double.

—Sharol Josephson
National Director, FamilyLife Canada

As a young pastor's wife new to ministry, I read through *A Ministry Survival Guide* feeling as though I was sitting across from Lisa in her living room with a coffee in hand, listening to her recount the Lord's faithfulness through her time in ministry. Lisa's vibrant relationship with the Lord, experience, and practical insights are a huge encouragement. Reading how the Lord has not only allowed her to survive but thrive in this extraordinary calling has blessed my heart. It has acted as a reminder for me to keep fixing my eyes on the founder and perfecter of my faith, and by doing that I know that he will allow me to do the same.

—Rachel Rohr
Pastor's wife

How much we needed this book sixty-two years ago when we began our pastoral ministry. How often we wondered, "Are we the only ones who have faced this kind of pain?" Lisa, a gifted storyteller, has given an abundance of help and guidance to those in ministry. You are either laughing or crying with her. She is real and honest through and through.

Journey with Lisa as she encourages you with her personal stories, practical advice, biblical mentors, and Bible study for personal replenishment of biblical truths. Here is a book chuck full of personal stories of ministry, marriage, family, and so much more. We would encourage all Christ-followers to read it and be bathed in Lisa's abundance of scriptures. Lisa's hope is that we don't just survive the challenges of life but thrive in them, bringing glory to our Saviour Jesus, King of Kings.

—Pete and Shirley Unrau
Founders and directors of Oasis Retreats (1999–2011)

In *A Ministry Survival Guide*, we are impressed with Lisa Elliott's honest vulnerability as she shares many of the realities of her experiences of genuine ministry. While she at times paints a picture of ministry that is painfully real, she is able to balance it with positive responses using a plethora of biblical references to aid in dealing with the challenges that so often arise. She does a masterful job of presenting many practical steps, giving hope and support to those in leadership roles in the ministries to which they have been called.

—Don and Dawn Howard
Forty-five years of pastoral and intentional interim ministry

Lisa has captured well her journey through the refining fire of being a pastor's wife. She has allowed the Lord to prepare her as a holy vessel to be poured out for Him and ministers to the wives of God's shepherds from that deep place. Through descriptive imagery and the lens of her story of life in ministry for forty years, Lisa extends an invitation to explore that ministerial life with her, to grieve in the pain and sorrow but also to rejoice in the joys and successes. Words of life, hope, and nourishment ring out from every page. Whether or not you're in ministry, Lisa's stories and practical principles from her heart will help you thrive and grow through the challenges of life.

—Arlene Borg
Ministry Coordinator, One Way Ministries

Reading *A Ministry Survival Guide* makes me want to sit down with Lisa for a coffee or enjoy a long walk together. I experienced a wide range of emotions as I took it all in. I can see my sister, sister-in-law, and my mom; all pastors' wives with similar stories to tell. Lisa shares a wealth of situations that I could resonate with and relate to in my own life as a pastor's kid and woman in ministry. Lisa's stories brought back so many family memories of ministry life—the good, the bad, and the ugly. It's real. It's authentic. And it's encouraging. And above everything, God's provision and sustaining grace shines through it all.

—Beth Rawn
Transformational life coach, lay leader, and pastor's kid

"There's absolutely nothing wrong with claiming your territory and putting up a No Trespassing sign when necessary," writes Lisa Elliott in her book, *A Ministry Survival Guide*. Although she's referring to guarding her marriage, setting boundaries is only one of the topics she covers in this relevant and practical read. She openly shares from personal experience the joys and sorrows of ministry life, weaving Scripture and dashes of humour throughout. Lisa unwraps very helpful ideas to not only survive but thrive in a life of ministry. As a ministry leader, I highly recommend this book. I gleaned many helpful suggestions from its pages, and I know you will, too.

—Ruth Coghill
Author of *The WOW Bible Study Series*
and *Unborn, Untold: True Stories of Abortion and God's Healing Grace*

In her book, *A Ministry Survival Guide,* Lisa gives us an authentic look behind the curtain of ministry life. She tells stories that make you smile, make you angry, make you cry, and make you believe that regardless of how tough things can get, there's always a way forward. She's a mentor and lover of Jesus who through her adversity has grown stronger and more resilient. She has much to teach us all.

—Cam Taylor
Transitional Leaders Network and author of *Detour* and *Between Pastors*

Since I'm not the wife of a pastor, I wondered at first if this book would appeal to me. I had barely stepped into Chapter One, though, and I found myself riveted (and nodding). Lisa Elliott doesn't hold back. She shares wholeheartedly, sometimes humorously, and is always honest about how she's coped over her years in ministry. From losses to heartache, to well-meaning people, to dealing with critical spirits, Lisa doesn't gloss over anything. Instead she speaks frankly yet humbly about how the Lord has been at work, moulding and making her who she has become. There is no bragging in this book. But there is raw reflection and a beautiful, encouraging attitude towards the God of both the mountain and the valley. This book celebrates both.

—Glynis Belec
Author of *Cancer: No Laughing Matter, But it Helps!*

A
Ministry
SURVIVAL
GUIDE

Straight from the Heart

Lisa Elliott

Printed in Canada

Print ISBN: 978-1-4866-2176-7
eBook ISBN: 978-1-4866-2177-4

Word Alive Press
119 De Baets Street, Winnipeg, MB R2J 3R9
www.wordalivepress.ca

Cataloguing in Publication may be obtained through Library and Archives Canada

CONTENTS

We remember before our God and Father your work produced by faith, your labor prompted by love, and your endurance inspired by hope in our Lord Jesus Christ.

—1 Thessalonians 1:3

ACKNOWLEDGEMENTS

Where would I be today without the Lord's provision of fellow sojourners? He's put many on my path to help and encourage me with all He's called me to do. The publishing of this book has been no exception.

To begin with, I'd like to thank each one of you who has touched, invested, and impacted my life throughout the years. I haven't enough pages to write about each of you. Whether or not you recognize yourself in this book, hopefully I've expressed my gratitude directly to you at the time of our divinely appointed intersection. The Lord has used your influence, advice, and encouragement to play an integral part in all that I am today. You've left footprints on my heart, and I will never be the same.

Next, I'd like to thank my Word Alive Press team. I'm humbled at your willingness to come alongside me, again, to bring my stories to life. You've not only offered professional advice, you've made a rich investment in my life and ministry for over a decade now. Thank you for believing in me enough to produce three works, from the depths of my heart, to touch the hearts and lives of God's people. Thank you also for graciously offering a safe place for my heart to land with my blog, Straight from the Heart. Finally, thank you for the confidence you've instilled by including me as part of the team.

Thank you to my heart-friend, Shelly Esser. Thank you for always taking the time you didn't always have, to not only read my work in progress but read my heart in between the lines. Your sacrifice of love has not gone unnoticed. Thank you for asking me the heart-questions. The Lord knew my heart would need your probing in just the right places to prompt me to produce the words He'd already placed there. Your ceaseless encouragement has allowed me to flourish in ways I could never have imagined. While our heart-nership predominantly takes place through emails, it goes well beyond words. For that, I'm thankful.

A special thanks to my sister-by-heart, Jamie Trudeau. You have faithfully invested in my life for more years and in more ways than I can count. Some of them are woven into these pages. Thank you for selflessly listening to, praying over, and holding my heart, allowing me to process the Lord's working in my life. Thank you for sharing in my greatest joys and taking the risk to join me in my deepest sorrows. Your gift of friendship reminds me daily, twice on Sundays, just how far and wide and high and deep is the love of God.

Thank you to my precious now-adult children: Natalie, Jacob, and Erin. Where have the years gone? I recognize now more than ever just how gracious and generous God has been to loan you all to me. Thank you for your grace as I've fumbled my way through life as a ministry mom. You've contributed to this book in more ways than you could know. I'm eternally grateful for the invaluable lessons I've learned through each of you. I'm so thankful the Lord stopped me in the church foyer that perspective-changing day. That timely encounter let me know how important it was to enjoy, not endure, you in a season that, looking back, seems all too short. I'm so thankful that I learned to stop and smell the roses while they were in bloom. And bloom you have! Each one of you, right where the Lord has you planted. You've made my life worth living in every single moment.

An added thank you to my son, Ben, who while no longer here on earth still speaks today. I wouldn't be the author I am without the pain and grief that initiated it all. It is now part of my eternal hope as I anticipate our great family reunion.

Thank you to the love of my life and partner in ministry, David Elliott. What would my life be without you? Perhaps it's a funny question to ask, seeing as this book wouldn't be relevant without you. Nor would any of the other aspects of who I am today if it weren't for the life and calling we share. I'm thankful the Lord intercepted my path to put you on it and redirect my steps. I couldn't ask for anyone better to share this crazy life with. Not only have you faithfully stuck with me for the past forty years, you've cheered me on as I've heeded the Lord's personal call upon my life. Even in moments when our life hasn't made any sense, you've helped me to make sense of it because it's the journey we've been on *together*. I wouldn't trade it for anything!

Finally, to the Author of my life, You are my life. You are my source of inspiration. You are the Living Word. Thank You for writing Your Word upon my heart.

To him who is able to keep [me] from stumbling and to present [me] before his glorious presence without fault and with great joy—to the only God [my] Savior be glory, majesty, power and authority, through Jesus Christ our Lord, before all ages, now and forevermore! Amen.

—Jude 24–25

FOREWORD

When my mom told me she was writing a third book, it was easy to get on board and support her with enthusiasm! I've always valued both her writing and her life insights. We often joke about how I'm living out her life twenty-five years behind her. The resemblance is undeniable and a bit uncanny at times, but the gift of having someone who has been there and done that is invaluable.

For this reason, I have believed since day one that this book, while inspired by her life in ministry, primarily as a pastor's wife, would be a resource for women from all walks of life. I thought of countless friends and women alike who would read my mom's words and be encouraged by her insights.

"It's like the book just wrote itself," she told me.

As she shared her stories, trinkets, and tips learned along the way, as well as a wealth of discerning wisdom, I hung from her every word. Many times I chuckled to myself at the relatable humour, while other times I held my breath to capture the lump in my throat before it could get away on me.

You see, I have lived the past thirty-three years with a front row view to all that you now hold in your hands. Truly, I've been witness to a majority of the daily sagas of my mom's life. I have witnessed firsthand many of her experiences, joys, and heartaches.

I've watched as she and my dad raised four children, aged five and under, with no family nearby. I've watched them pack us all up and move us more times than I can count on one hand, while somehow instilling strong roots and security in us no matter where we landed. I've watched them juggle work, time at home, volunteering their time, and loving anyone who landed on our doorstep over the years.

I've felt them tend to our broken bones, broken spirits, and broken hearts, all the while helping us to rebuild stronger. I've watched as they lived through every parent's worst nightmare, the suffering and death of their child, burying one child and only days later watching another hop on a plane to travel the country and make roots in another part of it. I've felt them long-distance love each of us, no matter where life has taken us, cheering us on so loud that it's as though we're still six under one roof.

I've watched as waves of depression struck and tsunamis of hope swept through—as they've faced grief and ministry and parenting and marriage, using their hardships to lay down stones of counsel for those walking similar paths.

If you asked my mom, she might point out that, as her oldest "guinea pig" child, I've been a privy spectator (and at times involuntary participant) to her short-comings, inadequacies, and failures. However, if you were to ask me, I'd give you a different perspective. In these less than glamorous moments, which are part and parcel of any family life, I have witnessed the birth of the strength, wisdom, beauty, and warmth you will come to know.

It is possible that my mom has lived the opposite of a flawless, unscathed life, as her story is certainly marked with scars, wounds, and imperfections. Rather, the per-fection I perceive is in her raw vulnerability. It's in her willingness to be transparent, to admit her unashamed reliance on Jesus, and to kneel at His feet in surrender. It's in watching her rise again only by His strength, thereby showcasing His undeniable power in her life. I see perfection in her heart because she is an imperfect woman who has devoted her life to placing her unwavering trust in a perfect God.

Buckle up, folks: you are now riding shotgun to the inner workings of my mom's heart, and to a life completely given over to Jesus.

As you sift through the pages of my mom's heart, don't be surprised if you, like me, are moved to both tears and laughter as she unveils many of her own breathtak-ing and outrageous moments in life and ministry—moments when the private and public lines of living become blurred and ministry is revealed as an all-encompass-ing lifestyle rather than a superficial Sunday obligation.

This book is more than just a crash course in how to navigate ministry, but rather how to thrive in the places you have been called to minister. My mom's stories come straight from the heart and her counsel comes straight from the Word of God. Her wisdom has come with the painstaking cost of personally living through the good, the bad, and the ugly. All of it is planted in a biblical perspective that *"in all things God works for the good of those who love him, who have been called according to his purpose"* (Romans 8:28).

I haven't lived with my immediate family for over a decade now. They have since lived in several homes I have never called mine. I've also made home elsewhere with my own growing family. Even still, there's something comforting about the feeling of coming home. Home is the deep connection I share with the people who fill it, the ones with whom I feel safe to be myself. I truly believe that home is where the heart is, as the popular saying goes. Reading this book is like coming home.

I trust that as you enter into the realm of my mom's heart, ushering you toward the heart of God, you will experience the comfort of home. May the words in this book encourage, inspire, and motivate you, fixing your eyes on Jesus, just as they have done for me.

It's an honour to be living my mom's life twenty-five years behind her, raising four kids in another province. I'm ever thankful for her heart, which houses Jesus, who will lead us all safely home.

Straight from the daughter's heart,

—Natalie Friesen (née Elliott)

WELCOME
TO MY *Heart*

Dear Friend,

Welcome to my heart. I'm so glad that you're here! I've been looking forward to this time with you for quite a while. Help yourself to your favourite beverage and nestle into a comfortable chair by the crackling fire built by our heavenly Father.

What I want to entrust to you has been held safely in this sacred place, deep within the sanctuary of my heart. Priceless principles, timeless truths, and invaluable lessons mined from over forty years of experience as a pastor's wife and woman in ministry—a vast treasury of riches untold.

Lean in closely. You won't want to miss what I have to say.

It's possible that you've come broken, wounded, wondering, wandering, or simply curious. No matter. Whatever it is that's brought you here, you are welcome. We are all sojourners on this road, after all. Whether you're a pastor or a pastor's wife, someone in ministry or in a Christian career, a mentor or a young mom, preparing for ministry or experiencing the twilight years of faithful service, you will find valuable resources right here as we tour the chambers of my heart.

Before we begin the tour, I want to make you aware that what you are about to explore is a work in progress. You're bound to uncover cluttered corners, sort through piles of unfinished business, discover imperfections, and observe significant renovations. I'm not going to excuse any of it. The Lord is still at work here. He's in the process of accomplishing all the good He started, promising to *"carry it on to completion until the day of Christ Jesus"* (Philippians 1:6). For that I am humbly grateful.

We will definitely enjoy some laughter as we identify our different yet strangely similar life and ministry experiences. No doubt we will also shed some tears along the way. However, whether what I share with you puts a smile on your face or forms a lump in your throat, my prayer is that our hearts will find a deep connection, that you will find safety, validation, encouragement, and hope to live out your calling in whatever form it takes.

Perhaps you're asking some of the same things I have as you've faced the unique challenges of ministry. Questions such as: How do you find yourself without getting lost in others' expectations? How do you make your family a priority when ministry calls? How do you persevere when you feel like giving up? How do you recognize God's blessings when your vision is obstructed by the burdens you bear?

I may not have all the answers you're looking for. However, one thing is certain: by the time we're through, you won't feel alone in whatever it is you're facing.

Together we will explore some of the very real needs, challenges, heartaches, and personal issues that ministry life presents. We'll unlock the secrets for preserving a private life in the spotlight of public ministry. We'll discover the essence of being true to who God has created us to be. We will learn the importance of fortifying our marriage and see the special part we each play. We will learn the fine art of balancing family and ministry. We will identify some warning signals on the dashboard of our hearts to help us prevent burnout. We will understand the value of blooming where we're planted, even while transplants ominously loom.

Rather than joining the ranks of the walking wounded, we will learn how to become wounded healers. We will bear witness to the growth that takes place through personal challenges. We will realize the importance of a godly support system. We'll recognize that all good gifts come from the Father of lights. And most importantly, we'll see how essential it is to nurture a vibrant relationship with the Lord, the Keeper of our hearts.

At strategic intervals, you will discover *Survival Tips* that invite you to sit with your thoughts. There's no rush. I encourage you to pick up a journal and journal along. Take all the time you need to ponder and process your own personal journey. Be assured of my prayers on your behalf as you do.

The *Biblical Mentors* sections will offer insightful principles to help us navigate life on this side of heaven. Abraham, Hagar, the Virtuous Woman, Elijah, Ruth and Boaz, David, Mary and Elizabeth, and Jesus Himself will lead us by their example. The Hebrews Hall of Faith will show us how to be resilient. John the Baptist and my own son, Ben, who now also cheers from the heavenly grandstand, will demonstrate the and-then-some-ness of our God. Listen closely and you'll hear the saints in glory cheering us on in the race we're running.

For those of you who are looking for further encouragement and insight from God's Word, feel free to use the Bible study at the end of the book to probe *Deeper into the Heart of God*. Allow His love letter to penetrate your heart as you search the recommended scripture and answer the questions provided. Discover for yourself the simple yet profound and timeless truths and apply them to your life. Better yet, invite others to join you to study and discuss together, as iron sharpens iron. Experience the joy of synergy that comes with journeying alongside others.

It's my prayer that the lessons, principles, and examples I share from my own experience alongside insights from God's Word will help you to thrive, not merely survive in this extraordinary life you've been called to.

Now, *"May these words of my mouth and this meditation of my heart be pleasing in your sight, Lord, my Rock and my Redeemer"* (Psalm 19:14).

Chapter One

LEARNING TO LIVE YOUR
Private Life IN PUBLIC

STEPPING INTO THE SPOTLIGHT OF PUBLIC MINISTRY CAN MAKE FOR A TRICKY manoeuvre. Orientation can be disorienting. There is much to navigate, such as facing our fears, overcoming our inadequacies, hurdling the expectations and opinions of others, choosing friends, setting boundaries, discovering who God created us to be, and being true to live out our calling. It's especially delicate where nurturing and maintaining a sense of privacy is concerned.

How much of your private life should be exposed? Who's watching? What are they expecting? How does one guard against public opinion? Should the opinions of others matter? How is it possible to keep any semblance of sacred? How does one live a private life in public?

The irony of this chamber of my heart is that I'm taking a risk by exposing it.

The Best Made Plans

A funny thing happens when we give the Lord complete control of our lives. He takes it!

I committed my life to Christ when I was fifteen and recommitted it to Him when I was seventeen, after a year of soul-searching. My plan had been to pursue my Early Childhood Education degree at community college—that is, until the Lord used a day-late registration fee to stop me in my tracks and set me on a new course, literally. That's when I first learned that I could make all the plans I wanted, but it was the Lord who directed my steps (Proverbs 16:9).

Before I knew it, I was registering at Bible college for a four-year Bachelor of Religious Education, majoring in Camping and Christian Education. I figured I'd pick up where I left off with my own plans once the four years were over.

In my second year, however, the Lover of my soul introduced me to the man who would become the love of my life. He put David Elliott on my path. I was his orientation group leader when we met. Appropriate, given that there was a lot of reorientation going on in both of our hearts and lives.

David was a Bachelor of Sacred Music major. He had been accepted into the program with a saxophone and a few tunes he tinkered at on the piano. His original plan had been to go into engineering at a prestigious university on a football scholarship… until the Lord stepped in and redirected *his* path.

I wrapped up high school after Grade Twelve, whereas David completed Grade Thirteen. That put me a year ahead of him in my program. However, I lagged well behind him in my infant faith. God used him to help me work through foundational truths. He shared his love of God and his love of God's Word with me. He even shared his prayer journal from when he was a young teenager. He pointed out the sections when he had prayed for God's pick of a helpmate. How amazing to think that *I* was the answer to his prayers!

The camping major and the music flake. Here we were thinking that we'd build a campfire and have a singsong when, in fact, the Lord had plans that neither of us could have imagined. He used a summer internship at David's home church to extend his call to pastoral ministry. From that summer onward, I joined him in ministry at every opportunity I had.

Called from the privacy of our own lives, the Lord brought us into the public spotlight. We spent many of our weekly dates ministering to a group of teenagers. There was certainly no privacy there! Come to think of it, our relationship hardly knew anything outside of public ministry.

Three and a half years later, David graduated with a B.Th. I had graduated a year earlier with my B.R.E., along with the prospect of obtaining my MRS. That's right. I was soon to be a pastor's wife—whatever that was.

If only my friends could see me now! But wait, they were about to. My private life was about to go public.

> **Trust the Lord's leading.** If you're actively seeking God's will for your life, at some point or another you can expect Him to step onto your path and redirect your plans. I can assure you that it's only because He's got hope and a plan for your future (Jeremiah 29:11). It far exceeds anything you could think or imagine (Ephesians 3:20) and it's all for your good (Romans 8:28). Trust His leading. Trust His timing. Trust His ways. *"Trust in the Lord with all your heart and lean not on your own understanding; in all your ways submit to him, and he will make your paths straight"* (Proverbs 3:5-6). How has the Lord interrupted or intercepted your plans? How have those plans turned out for your good?

Great Expectations

I entered the church foyer that morning in my usual Tigger-like fashion, bouncing from one person to the next, meeting and greeting and laughing and carrying on as if I had no care in the world.

If people only knew.

Truth be told, most Sundays I would have preferred to remain in my husband's office until the church service began. Sometimes I did.

My outgoing personality deceived people into thinking I was a natural extrovert when in reality I was merely a social introvert. It took me years to discover it for myself! Regardless, week by week I put all insecurities aside and rose to the challenge of foyer life.

One Sunday morning, I nonchalantly thrust myself into a conversation between the chairman of the board's wife and someone I'd never met. My friend reined me in and lovingly wrapped her arm around my shoulder. Then, with a glint in her eye, she introduced me to the woman standing in front of her.

"And *this* is our pastor's wife," she said in mock apology.

I gasped in shock at the implication of her comment. "Please don't hold it against him," I said.

We all laughed. Little did the newcomer know, however, that I was being sincere.

What makes a pastor's wife any different than a plumber's wife or an electrician's wife? As far as I was concerned, pastors' wives weren't any different than the average Sue in the pew. They just happened to be married to the pastor.

It's not like there's a pastor's wife training school. And there isn't any manual entitled *Pastor's Wife Conduct for Dummies*—although it might be helpful! From what I could tell, there was no mould. If there was, I didn't fit into it.

Thankfully, I didn't have any preconceived notions of what a pastor's wife should be. And most of the time my ignorance worked in my favour.

I learned quickly that expectations were unavoidable. Some were unwritten while others came prepackaged: dress codes, behaviour, church attendance, ministry involvement. Whether fully exposed or behind closed doors, dealing with others' expectations wasn't easy.

I knew the chairman of the board's wife well enough to know that her verbal jibe that day in the church foyer hadn't been intended as an insult or to embarrass me. The complete opposite was true. She loved that I was who I was.

In fact, several years later, when we transitioned to a new church, my friend's parting words turned out to be more of a gift than I could have guessed.

"Never stop being who you are," she said.

What great advice! I was going to need it for all the years to come.

When all is said and done, you've got to be who you is, 'cuz if you ain't who you is, you is who you ain't. Ain't that the truth?

Survival Tip ─────────────────────────

Stay true to who God created you to be. Do you know who you are? Who has God created you to be? List some of your character traits. What are your passions? What makes you uniquely you? Self-awareness helps you to ward off the expectations of others. Expectations are to be expected, after all. All the more reason to know who God created you to be and what He expects of you. Micah 6:8 says, *"He has shown you, O mortal, what is good. And what does the Lord require of you? To act justly and to love mercy and to walk humbly with your God."* What have others expected of you? Are these expectations realistic? How do they line up with what you sense the Lord expects of you?

Keeping It Real

It was a blessing and bonus to sit under my husband's preaching from week to week. I was amazed at how the Lord moved him aside and spoke personally to me through the solid biblical truth he presented. I even responded to an altar invitation one Sunday without my husband giving one!

Between the impactful preaching of the Word and promptings by the Holy Spirit. It was always a good idea to have some Kleenex on hand. I'd long since discovered that my heartstrings were attached to my tear ducts. I could always tell when the Lord was at work because my heart would be moved and my tears would be activated.

After my weekly ladies Bible study, my husband commonly asked how the study went. A look of confusion would wipe over his face when I reported, "It was great! We went through several boxes of Kleenex."

"And that's your idea of a good time?" he'd comment.

I recognized that God created me to *"rejoice with those who rejoice; mourn with those who mourn"* (Romans 12:15). I learned that this wasn't something to be ashamed of.

The Lord has, in fact, used my tears for His purposes. My tears have given others permission to shed their own. My tears have been sown into the hearts of others as I've walked alongside them in their pain. I've shed tears of joy while listening to many share of the work that the Lord is doing in their hearts. I've made rich investments in others' lives simply through offering the gift of my tears. As a result, my legacy at every church we've pastored has been a box of Kleenex in each pew.

Authentic Christianity is what the church was intended for, in my books—to be real with one another, bearing with one another, loving one another, comforting one another, teaching one another, and all the other one anothers in between. The bottom line is that we need one another.

None of us should be ashamed or embarrassed by who God has created us to be, tears or not. There's a place in the body of Christ for each of us. With this simple truth in mind, I determined to be authentic in my faith and true to the One who created me in His very own image—with no apology.

Survival Tip

> **Discover your spiritual gifts.** God created you as a part of His body, the church (1 Corinthians 12:27). Consider taking a spiritual gift test. It's also fun and insightful to explore personality tests such as the Enneagram. Other tests come in colours and letters and even animals. People will confirm and affirm you in your gifting. As 1 Corinthians 1:5–7 tells us, *"For in him you have been enriched in every way... Therefore you do not lack any spiritual gift as you eagerly wait for our Lord Jesus Christ to be revealed."* What part of the body are you? You'll know as you consider what enlivens your spirit and gives you a sense of joy and purpose. List some of those things. They are the gifts that come naturally in a supernatural way.

Celebrity Life

Being put on a pedestal always caught me completely off-guard. I thought idolizing was reserved for those on the magazine covers I'd browse as I waited in the grocery store line.

Speaking of grocery stores, one particular day after I started having children, I walked into one on a mission. I hoped to get in and out unscathed—that is, keep my head down, grocery list in hand, check items one by one, and plough my way through with singular focus. This was, after all, my once-a-week outing without the kids. Mommy's hour out! I wanted to make the best use of my time of freedom. And the clock was ticking.

As I entered the fresh produce section, a woman from our church stopped me in my tracks, right by the sour grapes. Her face turned as pink as the ripened grapefruit in the next aisle. But, surprisingly, not because I'd just about ran her over, flattening her like a banana split… with a cherry on top.

"I guess I just didn't picture ever running into my pastor's wife in a grocery store," she said, turning a deeper shade of rosy apple.

My likely premature but sorrowfully impulsive response was, "Well, I'm heading for the toilet paper aisle next! We use Cottonelle, by the way." Then, with a wave and a smile, I darted past the cauliflower and around the corner.

At this rate, I figured I'd be dodging paparazzi before I knew it!

The next time you go grocery shopping, make sure you take a good look around. You never know who might "turn-ip."

And then there was the time when an unsuspecting friendly neighbour, new to our church, found out we were campers.

"Where do you go camping?" was her innocent question.

"If I told you, I'd have to kill you."

I didn't want to be completely rude, so I gave in. I immediately regretted it, especially when we discovered my friend and her family on the campground beach, having made sure to schedule their holiday for the same week as us.

I suppose my friend took me more seriously when she spotted us—beach chairs turned away from the crowd, time-off ballcap pulled a little further down, holiday reading pulled a little further up, dark sunglasses dawned for special effect… and a Do Not Disturb sign posted at my side.

Finding my privacy didn't have to be offensive. However, a fence wouldn't have been a bad idea.

Set social boundaries. Ministry can be challenging in that your and your spouse's work world is the one you also have to socialize in. It's important, therefore, to seek out friendships outside your church or find others in ministry who understand your need to be off-duty. Settings where you're not the only one asked to give the blessing over the food. We all need friends with whom we can relax and be ourselves. Even Jesus had friends with whom He could let His hair down and put His feet up. We read of friends like Mary, Martha, and Lazarus, for instance, in Luke 10:38–42. Who are some of these friends for you? How would you describe a setting that allows you to be yourself?

Bad News Travels Fast

"So what does your husband do?"

This is a typical question when we're getting to know someone. Even as a young pastor's wife, I wasn't naïve enough to realize that bad news travelled fast.

My answer usually came with my head down, hand sliding across my mouth to muffle my words: "He's a pastor." All the while, I'd just hope the person asking either wouldn't hear or wouldn't care.

In one scenario, my newfound friend replied, "A what?"

Are you kidding me? She didn't know what a pastor was? How great was that? Dare I tell her and completely blow my cover?

I'd just made a fresh batch of chocolate chip cookies. Hot out of the oven. As we sat enjoying them along with a cup of tea, we carried on in our getting-to-know-you questions and answers.

"Pastor is another word for minister," I politely responded.

"What's the difference between a pastor and a priest?"

I gave her the best answer I could, indicating that they're different names used in different denominations to give a title to someone who shepherds a flock of God's people.

One question led to another until she finally asked, "What is a Christian anyway?"

I nearly choked on my cookie. I knew the Bible told me to always be prepared to answer everyone who asks us to give the reason for the hope we have (1 Peter 3:15). Nonetheless, I was completely unprepared!

I quickly excused myself to go and change a diaper that suddenly needed changing—or not—all the while praying, "O God, O God, O God. What do I say now?" I wanted to be able to share Jesus as naturally as I breathed, but suddenly I was short of breath. The Lord eased my pounding heart and assured me that He'd give me the words.

Once I gathered myself together, I headed back downstairs, trying not to appear as flustered as I felt.

"Share what you know," the Lord whispered to my heart.

I told my newfound friend how I had come to know Jesus as my personal Saviour and Lord. Then I explained the good news of the Gospel, using the analogy of the cookies she'd been enjoying.

"I could sit here and list all the ingredients I used to make them," I said. "I could demonstrate the process by which to mix and measure them, and the temperature I set the oven at to bake them. I could even eat them in front of you to show you how delicious they are. But until you've tasted them for yourself, there's nothing I can convince you of."

Before the cookies were gone, right there in my family room, toys strewn all over the floor, children playing in the background, she prayed to invite Jesus to come into her life. She had tasted and she'd seen that the Lord, He is good!

Survival Tip

> **Use your public position for God's good.** There's no need to be ashamed of your position or that of your spouse's. In fact, it could be just the open door you've been waiting for! You certainly don't have to be ashamed of the Gospel, because it's the power of God that brings salvation to everyone who believes (Romans 1:16). What are the things you know about the Lord? What have you experienced in your walk with Him? What's your story? Be assured that when you're willing to be used, the Lord will give you the words to say (Matthew 10:19). Besides, no one can refute what God has done in your life. Rather than hiding in the shadows, watch for open doors of opportunity. Who knows where those opportunities may lie? How has the Lord used your public position for His kingdom building?

Under the Watchful Eye

Most Sundays my children sat in the pew with me while my husband took his place on the platform.

I turned my head for a moment. That's all the time it took for my son Benjamin, three at the time, to shift one chair further away from me. We didn't have the traditional wooden pews that would've made it easy for me to slide over unawares. When he realized he had gotten away with it, he shifted over to another chair. His eyes never left mine as he shuffled his little bottom over one more time.

The next thing I knew, he was moving ahead to the next pew.

I was in a dilemma. Did I remain in my seat with my other two children and allow Benjamin to continue to move, or should I dodge for him? Rather than interrupt the service in progress, drawing even more unnecessary attention to myself, I chose to remain in my seat.

As Benjamin inched closer and closer to the front pew, he looked over his shoulder and gave me an impish grin. There he sat all by himself, swinging his little legs back and forth. Now and again he'd glance back at me.

Following the service, a woman approached me and said, "You'd better get a handle of that boy while he's young, or else you're in for it when he's a teenager!"

I understand that it takes a village to raise a child, but is the church family given surrogate rights? Are the pastor's children declared public property?

I wish I could say that was the only incident when someone had a better way of rearing my children than I did.

On another occasion, our daughter Natalie, only two years old, got out of my reach and, before I knew it, headed up to the front of the church. Thankfully, her dad was only giving some announcements. When he saw Natalie approaching, he picked her up.

"Whose little girl is this?" he said. "Her parents need to learn how to control their child!"

Most, knowing exactly whose child this was, laughed. We're not sure how impressed any visitors in the congregation that morning were with this whole scene. And I didn't wait around long enough to find out.

Survival Tip

> **Seek to please the Lord above anyone else.** It may feel as though you're always under the watchful eye. Really, you are. However, it's not the watchful eyes of those around you that you need to be concerned about. The Lord is also watching: *"For the eyes of the Lord range throughout the earth to strengthen those whose hearts are fully committed to him"* (2 Chronicles 16:9). Seek to please Him above all else. When have you felt watched? How did you handle yourself? How does it change your behaviour to know that the Lord is watching you?

Friend or Foe

For someone accustomed to effortlessly making friends everywhere I went, I wasn't prepared for how that translated into ministry. It didn't take long to learn to tread lightly where making them was concerned.

I dared not play favourites! Others were watching. I needed to be careful with what I said and to whom I said it. Who to trust? That was the question. I learned to be wise and discerning as people warmed up to me. The last thing I wanted was to be considered a feather in somebody's Sunday bonnet. At times it felt like congregants expected me to be a carrier pigeon. Destination: Pastor David Elliott.

At times I wondered at the sudden awkwardness between me and thought-to-be friends—that is, until I learned about some sort of decision made at the board level that I hadn't been aware of but nonetheless would still be held accountable for. It got especially dicey when I privately and lovingly confronted a friend only to have it he held against me or my husband's ministry. How does one recover from friends who leave the church disgruntled or angry after years of your investment?

Of course, there were things I held confidentially in my ministry bank. One friend endearingly called me the Vault. I took it as the compliment it was intended to be. There were things I often wish I didn't know. Things no one would ever know that I knew. And I prayed that my knowing wouldn't interfere with the friendships I sought to maintain.

Let's just say that being a ministry wife isn't exactly the best way to make friends. It can be lonely at the top.

All I wanted were friends who didn't associate me with what my husband did or what position I held. I wanted friends who'd accept me because of me rather than what I could do for them. Friends that would simply be my friend. I was grateful when I was able to find some.

Survival Tip —

> **Choose your friends wisely.** God created us for relationship. We need each other. However, we need wisdom in choosing those to whom we can entrust ourselves. As much as we'd love to think we can share our hearts with everyone, sadly not everyone is trustworthy. It's important to find one or two others with whom we can share our personal burdens. Perhaps test the water with small confidences before sharing more significant ones. It's called "selective vulnerability." One way to build relationships on a meaningful level is to bring the Lord into them. Invite Him into your conversation. Tell others what the Lord is up to in your life. List some of your closest friends. How did they earn your trust? Furthermore, how confidential are you? How can you better earn the trust of others?

The Volunteer Employee

"*Some of us* don't get paid to do this," she blurted out at me.

"You think I do?" Well, that would have been my *mild* reply. But I was too taken aback to speak.

Thankfully, I was able to muster up some self-control. This is one fruit of the Spirit I've learned is essential in ministry. My restraint also likely saved my husband's job on more than one occasion.

What on earth would have possessed this woman to believe that I was paid to do what I was doing? Did she really think I was a fringe benefit on the payroll? Did she think I was paid for my involvement at the church? Even if I was, the thought that money would be my motive for service was perhaps the worst insult I could have ever received. What a way to sap the joy out of serving Jesus! Besides, my husband didn't get paid near enough for what *I* did! If he did, we'd enjoy an early retirement!

It was enlightening, not to mention somewhat disturbing, to discover how others perceived my spiritual act of worship, even those I thought I knew and assumed knew me better.

What other occupation includes an employee's spouse in the interview process? Through the years, I've sat through many interviews at my husband's side, answering questions such as "So, what will *you* do for us?" Experience gradually taught me an appropriate way of answering that didn't boast of all I'd done or was capable of doing, but neither led them to believe I was at their disposal It's never been easy to differentiate between when personal life ends and ministry life begins.

Who knew that my years of experience as a receptionist would come in handy as a pastor's wife? It was nothing to receive several phone calls a week asking me for the time and place of such-and-such event or the phone number for such-and-such person. I was tempted to answer the phone with, "Directory Assistance. For which parishioner please?" One year I asked my husband if I could join in on the fun of Secretary's Day, seeing as I did her job from my home.

Not knowing came in handy. Ignorance was bliss. That's the reason I stopped receiving weekly bulletins. Besides, what I didn't know couldn't hurt anyone.

Don't get me wrong. I believe the pastor's wife plays a vital role in her husband's ministry success. The good news is I haven't got him fired yet!

Survival Tip ——————————————————

> **Use prayerful discretion.** People will make assumptions about your ministry involvement. They may question your motives. They may assume you know more than you do. When have these scenarios played out in your life? Don't hold it against them. Rather, use prayerful discretion when responding to these assumptions. Between you and your spouse, determine what's important for you to know and not know. When people come to you with questions, and they will come, graciously answer what you can. Otherwise direct traffic to the church office or those who may know better than you. It's okay not to have all the answers.

Straight from the Heart

While it definitely presented its challenges, being a pastor's wife also opened up a plethora of opportunities for me to discover my gifts and my place within the body of believers. Leading, coordinating, encouraging, exhorting, and teaching… I grew and learned as I went.

And as I learned to embrace my public-private life, the Lord made it even more public by putting me on a platform—literally.

I always considered that my calling transcended church walls. However, I wasn't prepared to face what that calling would entail, much less as a public speaker! Wasn't He aware that I had failed public speaking? As much as I'm a talker, there's a big difference between speaking in public and public speaking. It is, after all, one of the top fears people identify.

Regardless, I couldn't escape the Lord's call.

I highlighted the verses in my Bible as they jumped off the page:

The Spirit of the Sovereign Lord is on me, because the Lord has anointed me to proclaim good news to the poor. He has sent me to bind up the brokenhearted… to comfort all who mourn, and provide for those who grieve… to bestow on them a crown of beauty instead of ashes, the oil of joy instead of mourning, and a garment of praise instead of a spirit of despair.

—Isaiah 61:1–3

Bind up the brokenhearted? Comfort all who mourn? Provide for those who grieve? What kind of call was this?

My feelings of not-enough-ness were overwhelming. The fear of failure and rejection gripped my heart and paralyzed me. Not to mention the suffocating dread that overcame me at the thought of putting myself out there to make a public fool of myself—and charging an admission fee!

I could take you back to the place where it all began. My sixth-grade teacher made a public spectacle of me in front of the class. And to think, it was all over the misspelling of the word neighbour…

Her cutting words—"How can you be so stupid?"—bore deeply into my memory.

My schoolmates took it from there. "Stupid" was their new label for me. From that day forward, my fear of rejection stepped into the spotlight. Who wants to be made a fool of, especially in front of their peers?

It's amazing how one word can haunt you for the rest of your life, isn't it? It didn't matter that my husband, faithful friends, and many others affirmed my teaching ability, including the Lord Himself.

I presented more excuses than Moses at the burning bush. "Who am I?" "What will I tell them?" "I can't speak." "I can't do it!" "You've got the wrong person."

Beyond my fear of inadequacy was my fear of disappointing the Lord. Greater still was the regret I'd experience if I didn't respond to His call upon my life. I certainly didn't want to miss out on being part of His plan. With my simple yes, the Lord gave me His assurance and a promise. As He worked in my heart, He'd plant His Word there that, in turn, could be spoken into the hearts of others.

After much prayerful labour, my speaking ministry was birthed, Straight from the Heart. My writing ministry came on its heels. My delivery was based upon Romans 15:18, which tells us, *"I will not venture to speak of anything except what Christ has accomplished through me…"*

Just to be sure, He laid an entire series of messages on me on the topic of overcoming inadequacy, featuring none other than my friend Moses. I referred to my notes often! However, realizing that the pressure was off me and my performance, and instead put onto the Lord and His glory, made me feel a lot better.

When all was said and done, the biggest hurdle I had to jump was me.

Survival Tip

> **Face your fears.** It's easy to listen to inner voices of defeat that haunt us from our past. Those voices are even more believable when we're vulnerable, tired, or fearful. What are some of your fears? What experiences in your past have stifled God's call upon your life? Nobody talks to you more than you talk to yourself. So tell yourself the truth. Here's the truth: the Lord wouldn't choose you if He didn't think He could use you. 2 Corinthians 12:9 says, *"But he said to me, 'My grace is sufficient for you, for my power is made perfect in weakness.' Therefore I will boast all the more gladly about my weaknesses, so that Christ's power may rest on me."* Based upon this truth, what is one thing you can do to overcome one of your fears today?

Making Your Mess Your Message

Perhaps the most public display of my private life took place the year our eighteen-year-old son Ben battled leukemia. What started out as a personal crisis drew public attention beyond the scope of my imagination.

You never know what God will use to get His message out to a hurting world. I certainly hadn't expected that He'd use the most traumatic experience of my life to proclaim His glory to the ends of the earth! But He did.

> *I waited patiently for the Lord; he turned to me and heard my cry. He lifted me out of the slimy pit, out of the mud and mire; he set my feet on a rock and gave me a firm place to stand. He put a new song in my mouth, a hymn of praise to our God. Many will see and fear the Lord and put their trust in him.*
>
> —Psalm 40:1–3

It was challenging to live our lives in front of a live audience. At the same time, there was strange, divine comfort that came as others, including complete strangers, joined our journey of faith. Our church family stepped it up to provide what seemed to be a bottomless well of practical support. Previous churches where we'd ministered encouraged us with cards, gifts, phone calls, and prayer. A network of cyber support flooded our inboxes.

After Ben died, the ripples continued. If I thought the Lord had stretched me beyond my comfort zone when He'd called me into the spotlight as a speaker, the floodlights shone upon me in my messy vulnerability.

Then He did something I could never have expected. He turned my mess into a message of hope.

Unique speaking opportunities opened up to me and welcomed my grieving heart to the platform: the Starlight Children's Foundation, nurses conferences, a workshop for oncology students, radio and television interviews, and more. I didn't fully understand how a heaping pile of brokenness and tears could minister to anyone.

Then someone told me that the fact that I was still standing, much less speaking, was hope personified. That changed everything.

The Lord turned my message of hope into articles for *Just Between Us*, a publication for women in ministry, a monthly blog, and two books in which my family's complete story is told: *The Ben Ripple: Choosing to Live through Loss with Purpose* and *Dancing in the Rain: One Family's Journey through Grief and Loss.*

The Lord also opened up a ministry my husband and I could lead together. GriefShare became our staple in every church we pastored after Ben's death. Not only were we able to find healing for our grieving hearts and broken family, but we were able to witness other grieving people come to know the Healer Himself.

Believe me when I tell you that there is hope for the journey when we allow the Lord to turn our mess into a message for His glory.

Survival Tip

> **Allow God to turn your misery into ministry.** It can be a humbling experience to know that God uses us, not only in spite of ourselves but in our most vulnerable and painful moments. We all have a story. The choice is whether we choose to wallow in it or use it for the glory of God, however He chooses to use it. It doesn't have to be from a speaking platform or by writing a book. It can be as simple as sharing over a cup of coffee with a friend, or praying for someone in crisis, or listening to someone share their pain, or writing an encouragement note, or meeting someone's practical need. We read in 2 Corinthians 1:3–4, *"Praise be to the God and Father of our Lord Jesus Christ, the Father of compassion and the God of all comfort, who comforts us in all our troubles, so that we can comfort those in any trouble with the comfort we ourselves receive from God."* When is a time in your life when God turned your misery into ministry?

My Not-So-Secret Identity

As I sat amongst the women in the Bible study group, the question went around the table: "Can you please tell us a bit about yourself?" We had barely begun our ministry at this new port of call, so I figured I could tell an endless number of things about myself. Or so I thought.

Each woman took a turn sharing who they were. When it got to me, before I could open my mouth, the leader of the group said, "We all know who *you* are! *You're* the pastor's wife!"

Thankfully, by this point in our ministry, my years of experience at warding off others' preconceived notions gave me the wisdom to respond with care. Without being rude, as quickly and graciously as I could, I replied, "You are correct. I am the pastor's wife. However, that's not my identity."

I went on to share a bit more about myself. I told them about my love of writing and speaking and ministry beyond the church walls. I told them about my love of sharing my faith and hanging out with new believers. I disclosed that my greatest ministry was my ministry to my family, and especially to my husband, their pastor

What the Lord's called us to do is not our identity. It's simply a role He allows us to fulfill to teach us lessons, build our character, and make us into the best version of who He created us to be as His children. Ultimately, we discover who we are when we find our identity in Him.

Survival Tip

> **Find your identity in Christ.** There's a reason God created you. It's because He wants to use *you.* So don't try to be someone you're not. When He created you, He said, "It is *very* good!" You're the only one who can be you. You are a very intentional creation of God, fashioned in His image. He is intimately acquainted with you. You are His workmanship, created to do good works (Ephesians 2:10). You're a child of the King of kings (John 1:12, Romans 8:14–16, Galatians 3:26). You are precious and honoured in His sight (Isaiah 43:4). You are loved beyond measure by the Author of Life. Rejoice in who you are, because He takes great delight in you and rejoices over you with singing (Zephaniah 3:17). You were fearfully and wonderfully made (Psalm 139). Write out all of the above verses, inserting your own name. I would encourage you to go online and watch the Father's Love Letter.[1] Close your eyes and bask in the love He has for you as you listen for His heartbeat.

---

1   Visit www.fathersloveletter.com

I'm a Survivor

For years, my family and I set aside an hour a week to check out of life as we knew it. With munchies in hand, we'd each nestle into a comfy chair and tune into the television reality show *Survivor*. The show aired the night before my husband's day off. So we affectionately called it Survivor Night.

For those unfamiliar with the show, each season a new group of castaways is dropped off on a tropical island in the middle of nowhere with only a backpack containing a few essential items. The goal of the game is to see who will "outwit, outplay, and outlast" the others to become the sole survivor, winning a million dollars.

While the show isn't everyone's cup of tea, I have a strange connection to it. Throughout each season, I grow to appreciate the players' endurance and stamina as they bear up under extreme weather conditions and compete in gruelling challenges. I feel the pain of defeat in their losses and rejoice with them in their victories. I see them carefully build alliances only to be blindsided by those they thought they could trust. I weep with them when their families arrive for a reward, realizing how valuable those relationships are. I identify with their efforts, struggles, and frustrations as they fight to survive against all odds.

During every single episode I say to myself at some point, often out loud, "I could never do that!" Until I finally realized I *have* done that! That's when it occurred to me that the reason I find such a connection to the game is that *ministry* is a lot like *Survivor*.

You see, I'm a survivor. Not merely a sole survivor but a *soul* survivor. What the castaways play out in front of a camera for forty days, I've lived for forty years before a live audience called the church. At times it's felt like I've had a spotlight on me, my marriage, and my family. I've been scrutinized and reviewed by critics. I've fumbled through unrehearsed lines and unscripted scenes, most of it unedited.

While I may not win a million dollars at the end of it all, my reward is waiting for me in glory. I find assurance in what 2 Timothy 4:8 tells us:

> *Now there is in store for me the crown of righteousness, which the Lord, the righteous Judge, will award to me on that day—and not only to me, but also to all who have longed for his appearing.*
>
> —2 Timothy 4:8

Survival Tip

Rise to the challenge. The game of *Survivor* is full of challenges. These challenges test endurance, stamina, and skills that push the survivors to their physical, mental, and emotional limit. Likewise, your endurance will undoubtedly be put to the test in ministry. You will be pushed to your limit. There will be moments when you doubt you have what it takes to accomplish what God has called you to do. You're not alone. He will never leave you or forsake you (Hebrews 13:5). The Lord's desire is that you not only survive, but thrive in what He's called you to do. He never calls you without equipping you. As 2 Peter 1:3 says, *"His divine power has given us everything we need for a godly life through our knowledge of him who called us by his own glory and goodness."* Why not take some time right now to recommit your ministry to Him?

Living in the spotlight gives way for interesting perceptions and unwarranted opinions, as well as spoken and unspoken expectations. But there are ways to keep a semblance of the sacred. Honesty is necessary, but full disclosure is an option.

We can triumph over our fears, failures, and inadequacies as we trust the One who calls, equips, and empowers us to serve Him. By His grace, we can turn our weaknesses into strengths. With the confidence He offers us, we can stay true to our calling while knowing that He doesn't make mistakes.

Finding our identity in the Lord and understanding not only who we are but Whose we are trumps who others think we should be. And instead we are given the freedom to be all that God created us to be.

Just like Jesus, we must live our lives to please an audience of one—the One who knows us best and loves us most, with no conditions.

Straight from the Father's Heart

Whatever you do, work at it with all your heart, as working for
the Lord, not for human masters, since you know that you will receive
an inheritance from the Lord as a reward. It is the
Lord Christ you are serving.
—Colossians 3:23–24

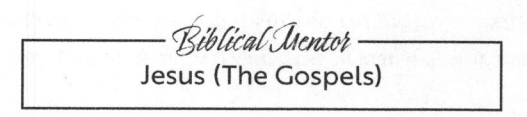

Biblical Mentor
Jesus (The Gospels)

"What would Jesus do?" This is a profound question we all need to ask, especially where public ministry is concerned. Jesus gives us the perfect example. When it comes to living a public-private life, He knows best. So as you step into the spotlight of public ministry and guard your privacy, follow in His steps.

Knowing who you are alleviates the need to prove yourself. People will always have their say, speculations, and opinions when it comes to your public performance. It was one of the challenges Jesus perpetually faced (Matthew 16:14–16).

Fortunately, Jesus knew who He was. Throughout the Gospel of John, Jesus publicly yet humbly declared who He was and still is today: the Bread of Life (John 6:35), the Light of the world (John 8:12), the Door (John 10:9), the Good Shepherd, (John 10:11), the Way, the Truth, and the Life (John 14:6), and the true Vine (John 15:1). Because He knew who He was, there was no need to prove Himself to others.

Likewise, when we know who we are in Christ, there's no need to prove ourselves to anyone. We need to trust not only in who Jesus says He is but in who He says we are. We *are a chosen people, a royal priesthood, a holy nation, God's special possession, that [we] may declare the praises of him who called [us] out of darkness into his wonderful light"* (1 Peter 2:9).

Retreating gives you the strength to advance. Jesus was on public display everywhere He went. His presence and performance were in constant demand. Therefore, He retreated on a regular basis not only for privacy but also for power. We read about the tug-of-war between His public and private life time and time again in the Gospels.

Here are a few examples.

When Jesus heard what had happened, he withdrew by boat privately to a solitary place. Hearing of this, the crowds followed him on foot from the towns.

—Matthew 14:13

Very early in the morning, while it was still dark, Jesus got up, left the house and went off to a solitary place, where he prayed. Simon and his companions went to look for him, and when they found him, they exclaimed: "Everyone is looking for you!"

—Mark 1:35–37

At daybreak, Jesus went out to a solitary place. The people were looking for him and when they came to where he was, they tried to keep him from leaving them.

—Luke 4:42

By retreating, Jesus was empowered by His Father and could better give and serve those to whom He had been sent. He encouraged His disciples to do likewise in a scene that unfolds in Mark 6:30–46. He also encourages those of us who follow Him to do the same today.

Privacy and publicity need wise discernment. There are several instances when Jesus requested that those He healed keep the miracle He performed quiet. He was able to discern when to keep His public life private. It was the excited recipients of His miracles that couldn't keep quiet about them.

In one instance, *"He gave strict orders not to let anyone know about this…"* (Mark 5:43)

Jesus needed to discern between keeping public ministry public or private. So must we. Finding the balance between private and public exposure keeps us humble—just like Jesus. Luke 2:52 is a good verse to keep handy: *"And Jesus grew in wisdom and stature, and in favor with God and man."*

Asking good questions puts the responsibility where it belongs. By asking good questions, Jesus deflected attention and responsibility off Himself. He not only asked good questions; in good Jewish form, He answered people's questions with a question. It put the responsibility back on those who needed to take responsibility for their actions.

A few of His questions found in the Gospel of John are:

- "What do you want?" (John 1:38)
- "Why do you involve me?" (John 2:4)
- "Do you want to get well?" (John 5:6)

Good questions! Take some time to ask them of yourself.

Pleasing your heavenly Father is what is expected of you. Jesus never measured up to people's expectations, and He didn't try. The religious leaders were always watching Him, criticizing Him, and scrutinizing His every step. But He had one mission in mind: to please His heavenly Father.

Just think how much freedom He permitted Himself by keeping this focus: *"For I have come down from heaven not to do my will but to do the will of him who sent me"* (John 6:38).

Just as Jesus lived up to the expectations of His heavenly Father, so must we as we follow in His steps and learn to live a private life in public.

Chapter Two

FORTIFYING YOUR *Marriage* IN A BROKEN WORLD

THE PLACE IN MY HEART WE'RE ENTERING IS RESERVED AND PRESERVED FOR THE love of my life and partner in ministry. There's always room for improvement to make a good thing better. For this reason, this area is always under construction.

The foundation is under constant review to ensure its durability. Forces have to be united in efforts to protect and defend. Threats are real. Personalities have to be strong to withstand the challenges of ministry.

Therefore, there is always a chance of conflict. If you put that all under one roof, things could become tense in a hurry. One certainly doesn't want the sun to go down on simmering anger (Ephesians 4:26), especially on a Saturday night!

Mutual investments are of the utmost importance. Trust is essential. Communication is critical. Full disclosure is vital. Teamwork is always the best option.

Two are better than one, because they have a good return for their labor: If either of them falls down, one can help the other up. But pity anyone who falls and has no one to help them up. Also, if two lie down together, they will keep warm. But how can one keep warm alone? Though one may be overpowered, two can defend themselves. A cord of three strands is not quickly broken.

—Ecclesiastes 4:9–12

Building a Shelter in a Time of Storm

It was the middle of June and we were newly married. Given that we were poor college graduates, camping seemed like an inexpensive yet romantic way to spend a few nights of our honeymoon. We were setting up the two-man tent we'd just purchased when it happened—our first marital fight. He thought it should go one way. And I was pretty sure it went another.

Later that night, shivering in our sleeping bags on our flimsy groundsheet, it happened again—our second marital fight. I was cold and had finally found a warmish chunk of real estate on the cold, hard ground when he wanted me to move over closer to him. He'd have to come my way if he wanted any warmth against my cold shoulder.

Thankfully, the sun rose again the next morning and we were able to move into our day, excited about its prospects.

Several years and four children later, we were a little more prepared and, thankfully, a little more understanding of each other.

Camping became one of the highlights of our summer experience. My husband and I would send the kids on firewood gathering missions while we painstakingly set up our now twelve-man tent. There were always a few tense moments as we set things up, but we'd learned a lot more about working together since our honeymoon.

Then there was the big blue tarp. We'd each take a corner and, treating it like a parachute, try to get as much air beneath it to drape it over our tent. Just thinking about it makes me sweat! Next we had to tack it down and hoist it up with four long adjustable metal stakes. People would stop and stare in awe.

One night as we crawled into our sleeping bags, it rained. And it rained. And it rained some more. Thunder rolled, shaking our foundation—adding to the bowling alley effect of our sleeping quarters.

Thankfully, the kids had fallen asleep quickly after their full day of beach activity. David and I must've eventually fallen asleep, too, at some point. I know this because we were awakened by a large crash and the feeling of something more than our sleeping bags suddenly weighing upon us. That's when we realized, in our sleepy stupor, that the tarp had fallen and crushed the tent we were nestled beneath.

The strobe of the lightning allowed us to at least make our way outside of our sleeping bags. We groped around on our knees, gasping for the air we suddenly felt deprived of. We finally found the zipper that held us "safe and secure" inside the thin layer of canvas, fumbled with it, and desperately made our escape.

If I wasn't claustrophobic before then, I was now.

There was only one thing to do in the middle of the night as we stood in the downpour in our pyjamas. We had to prop up the monster tarp and somehow manage to rebuild the tent.

The soggy state we found ourselves in was nothing compared to the fear that struck me with every bolt of lightning. There my husband stood, holding up the metal rods turned electricity conductors. Silhouetted against the flashing lightning for special effect, he looked just like Hercules. He certainly was, and still is, my hero. He's living testament to Ephesians 5:25, which says, *"Husbands, love your wives, just as Christ loved the church and gave himself up for her."*

By God's grace, we've made it through all kinds of storms since that fateful night. The good news is that we've lived to tell about them all!

Survival Tip _____

> **Build your marriage on a sure foundation.** Storms come in all shapes and sizes: health crises, burnout, financial pressure, ministry stressors, and church conflict, to name a few. What are some of the storms you've faced? Remember, the Lord is your shelter. He's your refuge. As Proverbs 18:10 reminds us, *"The name of the Lord is a fortified tower; the righteous run to it and are safe."* How has the Lord brought you through each storm you've faced? What are some of the lessons you've learned in the midst of the storm?

Leaving and Cleaving

My mother-in-law graciously gifted me her thirty-five-year-old wedding dress. I wore it with dignity and love on my wedding day. My mother and I refurbished it beautifully to give it some new life and make it my own. The finished product suited the occasion well.

If a picture's worth a thousand words, our wedding photo said it all. David and I took centre stage. I stood on my newlywed husband's right and his mother stood on his left, clinging to his arm. Should I have felt threatened?

Two becoming one took some time. It was hard to find the balance between our twosome, in its attempt to become a onesome. For example, for several years our holidays included an annual walk-and-bawl session. Clarification: *we* walked, *I* bawled. When would we come to an understanding that as much as I loved his parents, I didn't cherish the thought of spending our only two weeks of holidays with them? I felt that I shared him enough as it was.

Looking back now, I'm very thankful we spent the time we did with my in-laws, as this was our children's opportunity to get to know their long-distance grandparents. But at the time it didn't feel like much of a thanks offering.

It took a lot of open, honest, and sometimes frustrating conversation before we fully heard each other's hearts and understood our pure intentions. We eventually came up with a holiday plan that worked for both of us. It included not only claiming a piece of our summer vacation but also reworking some of the festive holidays, like Christmas, Easter, and Thanksgiving, typically spent with my side of the family. This helped us keep some of these special times to ourselves to make our own family memories.

Thankfully, we came to an understanding of what it meant to, as they say, cut the apron strings. It didn't mean that we were cutting ourselves off from our parents or extended family. Simply, we needed to leave and cleave. We were a cord of three strands, bound by God's Holy Spirit and braided together with our parents' blessing as we became one in Him.

Survival Tip _____

> **Embrace your differences.** We need each other, differences included! You were created to be different. We all have different opinions, gifts, abilities, passions, personalities, and even different approaches to life. There's nothing wrong with that. God *"created them male and female and blessed them"* (Genesis 5:2). And as Roman 12:6 says, *"We have different gifts, according to the grace given to each of us."* Differences are meant to enhance our relationship, not to be competitive or combative. Maximize your spouse's potential by being their number one cheerleader. Praise, don't poke, especially in public. In what ways are you and your spouse different? How has that created conflict? Make a list of ten things you love about your spouse. Make a list of ten things you contribute to your marriage in all of your uniqueness.

Private Property; Trespassers Will Be Prosecuted

Perhaps it was our spiritual gifting, or maybe it came through personal experience, but whatever the reason we recognized the need to connect with newcomers looking for a place to connect. Therefore, for years, and in every church we ministered in, we hosted a newcomers group, often in our home, as was our joy and privilege. With each group, my husband put together a getting-to-know-you quiz. In response to the questions, each member took turns guessing which answers belonged to which participants.

One of the questions asked was "What brought you to this church?" Answers varied from "A friend brought me" to "I found your website" to "I'm new to town and was driving by when I saw this church." My own answer may have given me away, or at least I hoped it would: "I came to this church because I'm in love with the pastor." It usually lightened the mood amongst nervous strangers.

I've found all kinds of creative ways to claim my stakes and protect my property. You see, while other newlyweds were fighting over which way to hang the toilet paper and which end of the toothpaste tube to squeeze, we stepped onto the frontlines of spiritual warfare in full-time ministry. I, therefore, quickly learned the necessity of putting on the armour of God each day as I took my place on His battlefield to protect our marriage. After all, Mark 10:9 says, *"Therefore what God has joined together, let no one separate."*

I've learned that danger lurks in places where you'd least expect it, and the church is no exception. Call it my insecurities, having been raised in a single-parent home, or just call it a wise precaution. Either way, experience has taught me to never let my guard down when my marriage is concerned.

Together, my husband and I came up with some strategies to help protect it. To name a few, David was not to be left alone with women or drive them anywhere, at least not without me. We opted for any opportunity to minister *together.* We stopped answering the phone on our day off to preserve the Sabbath. We eventually stopped responding to emails for the same reason.

Threats sometimes arose that infringed on our family time, days off, holidays, and special occasions. Some church members weren't shy about dropping by unannounced. For added effect, phone calls and emails that called for my husband's immediate attention imposed themselves on us outside of "office hours." Funerals, weddings, and crises didn't always conveniently fit into our workaday world.

We needed to set our own boundaries and unplug from computers and cell phones from time to time. We had to take the time we needed to get away from the ministry stressors that never went away.

Additionally, over time we learned that the best place to talk about church issues was outside our home. We made an especially conscious decision not to bring any church discussion inside our bedroom. There were enough daytime hours devoted to that.

There's absolutely nothing wrong with claiming your territory and putting up a No Trespassing sign when necessary. It's healthier for all of us.

Survival Tip

> **Guard your marriage tenaciously.** We need to build safeguards to protect our marriage vows. Listen to your gut instinct and never assume "it will never happen to you." Proverbs 4:23, 25–27 tells us, *"Above all else, guard your heart, for everything you do flows from it… Let your eyes look straight ahead; fix your gaze directly before you. Give careful thought to the paths for your feet and be steadfast in all your ways. Do not turn to the right or the left; keep your foot from evil."* Be open and honest about concerns or red flags. We need each other's sixth sense to alert us to danger. Set social boundaries. Guard your time off. Take days off and holidays without guilt. Claim your privacy. All of these are essential in maintaining a healthy ministry marriage. What measures have you put in place to protect your relationship? If you haven't already, come up with a protection plan together.

Coffee Mates

I didn't like coffee—and everyone knew it, as a coffeemaker wasn't on any of our guests' gift lists when our wedding came around. My poor newlywed husband had to resort to instant coffee and powdered cream.

Out of desperation for a decent cup of coffee, he eventually purchased a small coffeemaker—and one day he invited me to share a cup with him. He fixed me up a triple-triple, otherwise known as a coffee milkshake. How could I not like it?

However, it wasn't until my third pregnancy that coffee became a big attraction to me. The smell of freshly brewed coffee wooed me to the coffee hour Bible study room. From that point on, coffee was on the menu.

Not only was I not a big fan of coffee when we were first married, I also wasn't a big fan of mornings. However, as my love for coffee grew, so too did my love for the morning. Both because I was in love with the person I shared them with.

To this day, by the time I get down the stairs on a typical morning, my husband already has the coffee on as I fumble my way to the coffee pot. My favourite mug is out of the cupboard waiting for me. That's if he hasn't already fixed my coffee up for me.

For the record, I'm now down to a double-double.

Then we take our places on adjacent couches. Or, weather permitting, out on our backyard swing. We spend the next hour or so together, separately, both of us holding our Bibles in our laps as we read. We're usually not reading from the same part of the Bible, so we take the time to share the insights that stand out to us. The inspiration we receive cross-pollinates.

Finally, we pray together. We entrust our marriage, family, and ministry to the One who has called us to serve Him.

I wouldn't trade this time for anything. There's nothing more special than to share all that God is doing in our individual lives—together! I'm blessed to be his helpmate and thankful to be married to my coffee mate.

Survival Tip

> **Do your best to connect every day.** It's important to make intentional time to connect every single day. Find a time that suits you the best. It could be first thing in the morning over coffee or at the end of the day once the kids are in bed, or maybe some other time during the day. Once a day, a day a week, a month a year, set the world aside and focus solely on each other and your marriage. It's not hard for ministry to seep into our conversation, scheduling, and family activity, so it's essential to tune out the church to better tune into each other. Put your phone away. Give your mate your undivided attention. Think about how this might enhance your relationship. Consider going for a daily prayer walk around your neighbourhood. Share with each other what the Lord is speaking through His Word to your heart. How might you benefit from sharing time with your spouse in the Word of God and in prayer?

Sharing Is Hard for Grown-Ups, Too

My husband was always needed. Hardly a Sunday went by when I wasn't asked, at some point, where my husband was. To which I'd reply, "I'm not sure. He dropped me off at the door hours ago, and I haven't seen him since. But if you could do me a favour, when you find him, please let him know I'm here."

I related to the woman in the Song of Songs when she was asked, *"Where has your beloved gone, most beautiful of women? Which way did your beloved turn, that we may look for him with you?"* (Song of Solomon 6:1)

Sharing my husband has never been easy. Others have vied for his time and attention for as long as I can remember. It was extremely challenging when the kids were young.

On a typical Sunday morning, my husband went to the church hours ahead of us to get a head start on the day. That left me alone to get four children up, dressed, and fed before venturing into our weekly daytrip to church. And I mean daytrip! Our mantra was "First to arrive, last to leave."

He'd eventually come back to retrieve us, and we'd make the trek back to church together. He'd head one way, and I the opposite way, and we'd hope that our children found their way to their respective places as responsibilities awaited both of us upon our arrival. It always helped when we were welcomed inside by a triage of willing teenagers to help me unload and place my kids at their designated destinations.

Into the service, we'd go. In the early days, the pastoral staff sat on the platform. That left me to fend for myself alone in the pew with four children. I dubbed myself "the pastor's widow." However, I eventually used this to my advantage, or at least the advantage of others. For instance, I could choose to sit wherever. I used this freedom to minister to others as I sat with whomever I wanted to. I was able to worship in solitude and silence if I chose.

As I was called to engage in my own ministry outside the church, my husband had to learn to share me as well. He even joined me in my venture the odd time and manned my book table.

Thankfully, we both grew more accustomed to sharing each other. There is beauty in seeing the Lord use our spouse to reach out to the needy, comfort those who need comforting, lead us in worship, speak truth into those who need wisdom, and shepherd the flock under their charge. When we can find that proper perspective, being married to someone in ministry is a privilege—and it's a privilege to share them.

Survival Tip ────────────────────────────────

Use your loneliness to keep someone else company. It's hard to share our spouse with those who constantly beg for their time and attention. Rather than being resentful, why not consider an outward focus that prevents pity parties? Describe one of the poor-me moments you've had and all the feelings that went with it. Here are a few suggestions to turn your self-focus into others-focus. Take a moment as you enter the sanctuary to scope the territory. Ask the Lord to help you find someone who could use some company. Turn your focus from your lonely self to those who may be lonely. Or choose to simply sit alone. This enables you to have your own moments of prayer, quiet, and contemplation. It allows you to be ministered to by the Word of God or quietly pray for your spouse as they perform their pastoral duties. Remember what Philippians 2:3–4 tells us: *"Do nothing out of selfish ambition or vain conceit. Rather, in humility value others above yourselves, not looking to your own interests but each of you to the interests of the others."* Who is someone you could encourage with your company?

What About Me?

My husband encouraged me to stay home from church one Sunday evening, something that was unheard of. Two of my kids were still deep into their afternoon nap and I desperately needed a nap for myself. I knew that the moment my newborn's eyes opened, her stomach would be awaiting her dinner.

I was just closing my eyes when I heard a knock at the door.

There stood a gentleman from our church on my doorstep. I can't say that my first impression was to tell him how glad I was to see him.

"You need to be at church," he implored.

Thinking this had to be something important for him to come and be our chauffeur, I hurriedly woke my two groggy, unimpressed children and scrunched my hungry, screaming baby into her car seat with my five-and-a-half-year-old oldest daughter in tow, carrying the diaper bag.

Upon our arrival at the church, ready and waiting friends whisked my four children away. I was escorted to the front row of the church to sit at my surprised husband's side. What was going on?

I didn't have to wonder for too long before we were welcomed into a surprise tenth ministry anniversary celebration!

Over the next two hours, I watched my husband's ministry life unfold before my eyes, pictures telling his story. Words of thanks were given and testimonies rang out, singing his endless praises. All the while I sat quietly, keeping my restless pride at bay.

What about *me*?

Eventually, my husband leaned close and tenderly put into words what I'd been thinking. This was all that was needed to release the tears I'd been holding captive. His acknowledgement let me know that my part in his ministry was vital, even if there were no pictures to show for it.

Thankfully, he always affirmed me in the part I played to enhance his ministry. He often gifted me with comments like "I couldn't do what I do apart from what you do."

In this humbling moment, he made the partnership we shared evident to me. I believed him with all my prideful heart.

Survival Tip

> **Recognize the vital role you play.** There's nothing better than knowing that your spouse is on your team. Partnership is vital to ministry success. In too many instances, a minister's spouse is their demise. Resentment, jealousy, and pride are game-changers. A partnership doesn't have to take place exclusively in the spotlight of ministry, either. In fact, a lot of that partnership takes place right at home—supporting, encouraging, listening, and loving in ways nobody else can. Use the gifts God's given you to serve the Lord as you minister alongside one another. You play a vital role in the success of your spouse's ministry, whether or not anyone else acknowledges it. What is the role you feel called to play? Ask your spouse what you can be doing to support them in their ministry. As 1 Thessalonians 5:11 says, *"Therefore encourage one another and build each other up, just as in fact you are doing."*

Like a Bridge Over Troubled Waters

We were in trouble. Ministry life had whisked us away and sent us into a frantic state of affairs in our all-consuming lifestyle. Both of us had been lured away by a mistress called Ministry. We knew we needed help.

So we scoped out the internet until we found a retreat for pastors and wives that operated out of British Columbia. The retreat consisted of a week of intense coaching, counselling, and healing. Our goal was to obtain a Get Out of Ministry Free card.

As part of our week, we were entitled to two counselling sessions. We were assigned a psychologist from South Africa. After identifying my husband's depression and fear of failure, mixed with my fear of rejection, our counsellor assigned us a simple piece of homework.

"Go for a long walk today and forgive each other," he strongly advised.

Forgive each other? What was he talking about? What did we have to forgive each other for? What kind of place was this? What were we doing here anyway? He had no idea what we were really up against. This wasn't about our marriage. This was about a church that had wounded us deeply. It was their fault we were in shambles.

However, to appease our counsellor and have something to report on the next day, walk we did—for hours. We apparently had a few things to discuss. We walked so far that we had to stop along the way to purchase my husband another pair of walking shoes.

For the first half of our adventure, we spent most of our conversation talking about how ludicrous the homework assignment was. We finally stopped and sat on a dock, gazing out onto a beautiful lake with scenic mountains in the distance.

As we sat there, something began to happen. Our reflection on the water brought clarity to our clouded hearts. As we lifted our eyes and gazed toward the mountaintops, our help came straight from the Lord (Psalm 121:1).

There, we spoke honest words to each other. We cried with each other, confessed to each other, prayed with each other. And we forgave each other.

Survival Tip

> **Seek counsel when you need it.** We're all human. Each of us is working through our own problems, even those in ministry. Professionals need help, too. There's no shame in asking for help when you need it. You just have to select it wisely. It will take humility and honesty with someone you can trust. Don't avoid discussing things that could easily get between the two of you. As we read in Ephesians 4:15, *"Instead, speaking the truth in love, we will grow to become in every respect the mature body of him who is the head, that is, Christ."* Love each other well. Keep short accounts. Don't sweat the small stuff. By the way, most of it is small stuff. Forgive each other—over and over again (Matthew 18:21–22, Ephesians 4:32). Is there an area of your marriage you need to work on or seek counsel about? Why not go for a long walk with your spouse today and have an honest, possibly long overdue conversation?

Consecration

Our denomination's annual national convention was something we always looked forward to, partly to reconnect with other ministry couples we only got to see once a year due to our inhibiting Sunday schedules. It also gave us time away to reconnect with one another as a couple. We got to stay in a hotel without our kids for two to three nights and dine at restaurants where I could eat using either of my hands—while my meal was still hot.

The keynote speaker was another highlight. It was a blessing to be ministered to rather than doing the ministering. This particular year was an even more special treat, since Dr. Tony Evans would be speaking.

We entered the large conference room at the hotel. After a time of worship, Dr. Evans took the platform. In his larger than life frame, he masterfully commanded his audience from behind the podium, the banner behind him boldly splaying a paraphrase of Joshua 7:13: "Consecrate yourselves. For tomorrow I will do great things!"

That's what initially captured my attention. But it was the words Dr. Evans spoke that held me captive. He told us how he and his family took family trips together. Being the man on a mission that he was, he aimed to see how far he could manage to drive before he had to stop for gas or restroom breaks. He'd make sure the gas tank was full and bladders were empty at the start of their trip. He hoped he could make significant headway before everyone's bladders were full and the gas tank empty.

Then he segued into the co-relation between car trips and ministry. He explained that in ministry we often go as hard, fast, and long as we can without taking a break. Some do it with pride. "I'd rather burn out than rust out," they say.

The problem is, either way, you're out!

"There's a good reason for rest stops on the side of the highway," he said emphatically. "They are for rest and refreshment. We as ministry couples have to take advantage of them."

If there had been an invitation at that point in his message, I would have accepted it. Instead I sat in my seat, waiting patiently, my heart beating rapidly, hands sweating profusely, until he finished.

Thankfully, he did extend an invitation at the end of his message. I would have responded to him even without one, but I was thankful for the excuse.

I looked at my husband, who sat at my side, and he looked back at me with a knowing expression. We both realized this was an invitation we needed to respond to together. Then we held hands and made a bolt for the front of the room, where we knelt and wept together at a makeshift altar.

Right there, at the base of the banner, we recommitted our lives, our marriage, and our ministry to the Lord. We consecrated ourselves, for the Lord still had some great things in store!

> **Recommit yourselves to each other daily.** You need to remember that your spouse didn't marry the church; he/she married you. Therefore, commit to making your marriage the best it can be. Every. Single. Day. You can expect your wedding vows to be tested. So do your best to make investments in each other. Date your mate. Commitment is hard work, but it's worth it. Ephesians 5:21–22, 25, 33 says, *"Submit to one another out of reverence for Christ. Wives, submit yourselves to your own husbands as you do to the Lord… Husbands, love your wives, just as Christ loved the church and gave himself up for her… each one of you also must love his wife as he loves himself, and the wife must respect her husband."* How can you enhance your marriage? What can you do this week to renew your commitment to your spouse?

Un-Birthday Celebrations

"What are you doing for the long weekend?" parishioners commonly ask.

Did we have plans? Often not, due to the weekend that came with ministry, but there was no use moping about it—even though I did from time to time. And why did family birthdays and anniversaries always seem to land on board meeting nights or special events on the church calendar?

All I knew was that I needed to get over these disappointments. Living our life in ministry required it. So through the years we learned to celebrate the un-birthdays, all the days between special occasions.

Thankfully, I married a man who has led the way. Even in our dating days, he was prone to write me love notes "just because." It's still not unusual for him to come home with a beautiful bouquet in the middle of the week, or take me out for dinner to give me a break and simply celebrate life.

I know—I'm spoiled.

We've learned that whining about what we don't have only serves to deprive us of enjoying what we do have. And in turn we can miss out on celebrating life as God intended it.

Perhaps we learned this most profoundly the year our son battled leukemia. Birthdays were postponed. Special occasions had to be adapted. Plans had to be cancelled. We even celebrated Jesus's birth weeks after His birthday.

Every day gave us cause to celebrate and live fully in every moment we had to live it together. Each day was a gift.

Ecclesiastes 11:8 says, *"However many years anyone may live, let them enjoy them all."* Tomorrow is never promised. It's as unpredictable as the weather. Therefore, we need to learn to rejoice in the gift of each new day, making sure we stop to smell the roses while they're in bloom.

Survival Tip

> **Celebrate the process.** What a shame it is to wait until it's too late to celebrate something or someone. Life is too short not to live each day to the fullest, savouring, celebrating, and embracing each day as a gift from God. As we read in Ecclesiastes 9:7–9, *"Go, eat your food with gladness, and drink your wine with a joyful heart, for God has already approved what you do. Always be clothed in white, and always anoint your head with oil. Enjoy life with your wife, whom you love, all the days of this meaningless life that God has given you under the sun—all your meaningless days. For this is your lot in life and in your toilsome labor under the sun."* What is something you can do to celebrate your marriage today?

Remember that you didn't marry the church; you married your spouse. And vice versa! Therefore, build your marriage strategically. Invest in it richly. Guard it tenaciously. Enjoy it thoroughly. Love each other wholeheartedly.

Commit yourself to each other for the rest of your lives and you'll discover that two really can become one. A good thing always has room for improvement when it's built and grounded upon the firm foundation called Jesus.

Straight from the Father's Heart

Love is patient, love is kind. It does not envy, it does not boast, it is not proud. It does not dishonor others, it is not self-seeking, it is not easily angered, it keeps no record of wrongs. Love does not delight in evil but rejoices with the truth. It always protects, always trusts, always hopes, always perseveres. Love never fails.
—1 Corinthians 13:4–8

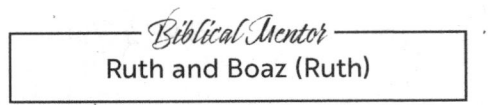

Biblical Mentor
Ruth and Boaz (Ruth)

While the ministry doesn't require a marriage partnership, it can be helpful. It was God's idea from the very beginning, after all.

There's one couple I respect for several reasons: Ruth and Boaz. Their love story impacts all our lives through the bloodline of Jesus, our Redeemer. Their relationship is full of grief and loss, devotion and loyalty, love and redemption. Everything they experienced together was used to fortify their marriage. Therefore, I believe it's noteworthy.

Let's look at what made their marriage work.

Partnership begins with "Til death do us part." If there's one word to describe Ruth, it's devoted. For starters, Ruth was devoted to her mother-in-law. When offered the choice to stay in her homeland, she followed Naomi to hers.

They both knew what it was like to lose someone they loved. In the heart-warming exchange that takes place between Naomi and Ruth, we read,

> But Ruth replied, "Don't urge me to leave you or to turn back from you. Where you go I will go, and where you stay I will stay. Your people will be my people and your God my God. Where you die I will die, and there I will be buried. May the Lord deal with me, be it ever so severely, if even death separates you and me."
>
> —Ruth 1:16–17

It's no wonder these powerful words of Ruth from long ago are often used in wedding ceremonies today. They are powerful words that need to be applied to our marriages: "Til death do us part."

Ruth's loyalty and devotion to Naomi are commendable. As a result, Boaz, too, reaped the benefit of that devotion. Not only for their marriage, but for generations to come. Commitment doesn't come easily in this day and age. Therefore, we can learn a great deal from Ruth's example.

Love is worth the extra labour. At the encouragement of her mother-in-law, Ruth humbly and bravely went to work. Naomi pointed her in the right direction.

Then Ruth took the initiative to follow workers in a field to provide for their household. As a result of her hard-working attitude, she didn't merely glean grain; she gleaned a future.

Ruth's hard work paid off. It put her on the path of meeting her future husband, Boaz.

Our human nature tells us to throw in the towel when the going gets tough. Divorce, prenuptial agreements, and separation are rampant in our society. Sadly, even within ministry couples.

The story of Ruth reminds us that there's good to be found when we stick it out. Marriage is hard work, but it's worth the effort!

A little humility goes a long way. Naomi recognized that Ruth couldn't sit around the house with her all day, so she encouraged Ruth to get herself dressed and put on a dab of perfume to make herself known to Boaz.

Ruth risked her life and her honour by putting herself at the feet of Boaz, literally. What she did on the threshing floor wasn't a seductive act so much as a custom. However, what happened at those feet led to a beautiful, romantic, and God-honouring relationship.

Through this quiet scene, we learn the importance of humility, patience, and honour when we lay at our Master's feet out of respect for our spouse.

There is hope, even when hope seems lost. Just when we believe all is well and we breathe a sigh of relief, things take a turn. Just when we think that Ruth and Boaz will live happily ever after, we discover there's a closer relative who would be Ruth's kinsman redeemer.

We come to find out that Boaz isn't only a kind man but also a wise man. This comes through in shining colour as he presents his case in the court of the elders.

Ruth and Boaz were able to join in holy matrimony because of their love for one another and because of God, who had a greater love story unfolding—a love story that produced Jesus, our ultimate redemption and only true hope.

Ministry can add stress to marriage and create tension between married couples. Don't lose hope. Our Redeemer lives!

God's grace is enough. Every marriage needs a hefty dose of grace—grace extended toward each other. But more importantly, God's grace. God blessed Naomi and Ruth through Boaz in terms of protection, provision, and prosperity—and also He provided Himself. They discovered that His grace was enough.

Ruth conceived and gave birth to a son. When the baby was finally placed in Naomi's arms, it must've been a profound moment. Redemption in fullness. Life after death. Hope after loss.

This is a beautiful picture of the sustaining power of God's grace. Day by day, our lives can be restored, our marriages sustained and fortified. Put your relationship in the hands of a life-giving God—and you, too, will discover that His grace is enough.

Chapter Three
MAKING *Family* A PRIORITY WHEN MINISTRY CALLS

INSCRIBED ON MY HEART AND ECHOING THROUGHOUT EVERY CHAMBER ARE these words:

> *The Lord our God, the Lord is one. Love the Lord your God with all your heart and with all your soul and with all your strength. These commandments that I give you today are to be on your hearts. Impress them on your children. Talk about them when you sit at home and when you walk along the road, when you lie down and when you get up. Tie them as symbols on your hands and bind them on your foreheads. Write them on the doorframes of your houses and on your gates.*
>
> —Deuteronomy 6:4–9

It has always been the prayer of this mother's heart of mine to both impress God's Word on the impressionable hearts right in my home and keep them at the forefront of my heart and mind. It became apparent that my children needed to know they were my priority while ministry begged for my attention. Over time, I learned that everything I did weighed in the balance. They had to become my focal point if my investments were going to have an eternal impact.

The Reverend Mother

At the same time that my husband was ordained into the ministry, I was expecting our first child. Several delegates from surrounding churches in our denomination were invited to attend the church's initiative. Each delegate came presenting a list of theological questions to drill and grill my husband with.

After hours' worth of question-and-answer, my husband was ordained as Reverend David Elliott. It only made sense to me that as I was carrying this reverend's first child, I ordain myself the Reverend Mother. And at that, with all the reverence we could muster, we put into action the Lord's command to be fruitful and multiply.

Natalie, our child of Christmas, was born via unplanned Caesarean section a week before Christmas. I was discharged a week later, on Christmas Eve. She came just in time for us to put her under the Christmas tree and stick a bow on her head to pose for her first picture.

Nine months later, I became pregnant again. As the pregnancy progressed, I could tell by the baby's deliberate movement and the fact that my ribs were nearly broken on a couple of occasions that this child would be an athlete with a strong will.

I was right. When Benjamin was born, I had to learn to stand firm in the battle—often in the church lobby!

Two years after Benjamin came Jacob, the Lord's vehicle to help me to stop and smell the roses. He came along at a time in ministry when things were a bit out of control and we had little time to spare, or so it seemed.

Two years later, on a rainy day, Erin was born like a ray of sunshine. I've called her my sunshine girl ever since.

Thus completed my family, and thus commenced my education. I had no idea how much my children would teach me about love, life, the ministry, and especially about myself. So you can bet that I took good notes!

Survival Tip

> **Learn your children's language of love.** No two human beings are the same, by God's design, including our children. Our children have been uniquely designed by the Creator in all of His creativity. Embrace their differences while loving them all the same—in unique and different ways. Each one needs to know how God uniquely created them. Gary Chapman wrote a series of books entitled *The Five Love Languages*. Consider reading it to help you learn your children's love language. Make a list of your kids' differences, then list some of the unique ways you can love them based upon these differences. Take regular time alone with each child doing the things they want to do. No doubt each one's personal taste and varying interests will give you a wide variety of options to choose from!

Smiles Everyone!

The kids were never more unruly than on a Sunday morning. It made sense, seeing as it was their weekly share-your-parents day. It made for a wild ride to church. Just to add to the excitement, some of our best fights took place in the car. For those of you who have never contended with four children, or possibly even a husband, that's tricky to navigate, especially on a Sunday when you're the pastoral family on display.

One Sunday morning stands out among the rest. We'd had our typical wild ride across town to get to church. All ten minutes of it, but believe me when I say we made all ten minutes count!

David and I were at each other. The kids were on top of each other. We pulled into the church parking lot, filed out of the vehicle, and were about to flee for shelter—as far away from each other as possible—when the church door swung open. One of the deacons smiled as he held the door open wide for us all.

"Good morning, Elliott family!" he exuberantly greeted us.

One by one, he welcomed us in, smiling and asking each of us, by name, how we were doing.

"Good morning, Pastor Dave. How are you, Natalie? It's nice to see you, Benjamin. High-five, Jacob. Hello there, Erin."

Then he saw me—the only one apparently who couldn't hold a poker face. One look and his smile disappeared.

He held his head down and quietly murmured, "Hi Lisa."

Some days it was harder to put on a smile than others.

Survival Tip

> **Let your family be human.** People, including your children, need to see that life isn't always rosy for someone in leadership. We all have bad days. Those under your leadership will appreciate your realness and vulnerability. It may even enhance your ministry. Suddenly, you'll be more relatable and approachable. Can you think of a time when you had to put on a smiling face in order to minister? Can you think of another time when you weren't able to? How did you handle that? How did people respond?

Leaping Tall Buildings in a Single Bound

The joy of the Lord was my strength as a young mom and pastor's wife. I donned my superwoman cape and leapt tall buildings in a single bound. Truth be told, there were no bounds! I gave new meaning to doing all things through Christ who strengthens me as I sought to be all things to all people, all the time!

You name it, I did it. Not only did I populate the nursery, but I also served in and eventually oversaw the nursery. I coordinated children's ministries in a wide variety of ways. I led and hosted small group ministries as the church grew large. I provided initiative and leadership for adult ministries. I taught the ladies' Bible study. I headed up several women's retreats, promoting, directing, and leading every aspect. So good was I in my leadership abilities that I even inspired a men's retreat.

On Sundays, I entertained the crowds with song and dance, leading children's worship, and providing special music in the form of being part of the choir, trios, duets, or solos. I also participated in drama productions. Weekly women's Bible studies opened up speaking opportunities. On one occasion, I even jumped in to save the day and lead a prayer meeting when my husband got sick.

No feat was too great!

To make life even more interesting, we bought our first home. That enabled me to host meetings and small groups several evenings a week, becoming the neighbourhood hospitality house. I valiantly provided new neighbours with meals. I served Kool-Aid and cookies to all the children who happened to drop by. It was nothing for me to entertain up to two to three ladies and their children twice a day, four to five days a week.

One by one, the Lord gave me opportunities to share my faith and introduce many of my neighbours to Christ, four giving their hearts to Him. Could life get any greater?

Add in having to work around my husband's demanding schedule as the senior pastor of a rapidly growing church and it was a busy time, to say the least.

I thanked God for Kraft Dinner and microwaves!

These aren't things worth boasting about. They were my reality and also my means of ministry and household survival. Please, hold your applause. I had enough of it. Throngs cheered me on with questions like "How do you do all you do with four children?" My simple answer was "I don't stop to think about it." And that, right there, was my problem.

Let your kids know they're important to you. It's not harmful to allow our kids to learn the importance of commitment firsthand. They need to know that there's joy in serving Jesus. However, it's equally important for them to know we're committed to them. For starters, love the one you're with. In this day of modern communication, iPads, Snapchat, Twitter, and cell phones, nobody knows how to talk face to face anymore. How have you seen the effects of modern technology on your kids, your family, and your relationships? Seize moments to dream with them about plans for the future, who they want to marry, and what they want to do when they grow up. Stop and think about all the things into which you pour your time, energy, and attention. How can you pour that time, energy, and attention into your kids?

Enjoy, Don't Endure

Frustrated, resentful, and restless are just a few of the words that described my honest attitude as a young mom. If you're a young mom functioning with a minimum of sleep with a maximum of daylight activity, wishing for life beyond your four walls, you know what I mean.

My long days typically started with my four-year-old son Benjamin standing beside my bed at eye level with me. I could always sense his presence before my eyes opened. Once I made eye contact, he'd ask, "Dad at a meeting?"

"Yes," I'd groggily respond.

Then he'd march out of my bedroom and find something to occupy himself until the rest of the household woke up.

I often felt trapped in my home with four young ankle-biters while my husband got to go out and "play" at church. What about me? When would it be my turn?

With four young children occupying my time and attention day in and day out, I needed an escape. As much out of survival as preoccupation, I started claiming the life I needed. The life I felt I deserved. After all, I'd been called to ministry, too! It was just on hold while I was bound to my household.

I was being deprived! My children were in the way of me fulfilling my *true* calling—or so I thought. The church provided no shortage of opportunities to fulfill it.

Resentment kicked in big-time—that is, until Jesus met me in the church foyer one Sunday morning. He came in the form of a godly man my children affectionately called Papa Murray.

Papa Murray was a man whose loving and gentle spirit shone through his eyes. You could hear his heart beating from across the room. He spoke with a smile, no matter what trials of his own he faced, or what age or stage he was. When you asked him how he was, he'd say, "I'm at the peak of life!"

Even at a ripe old age, with great-grandchildren of his own, he weekly volunteered to watch the children in the nursery. He wanted to give us young moms a break so we could enjoy our Ladies Coffee Hour.

Talk about being a blessing for the generations to come! He was one of those people who I wanted to be when I grew up.

Our conversation in the church foyer went like this.

"Lisa, I don't know how you young moms do all you do to keep up with all the activities that have you running hither and yon."

"Well, Papa Murray, you raised six kids of your own. How did *you* do it?"

"Ah, things was different back then," he refuted in his farmer's twang. "The wife was in the kitchen. And me, I was on the tractor." His expression shifted as if transported to another place in time. "All I know is that God gave us our children to enjoy, not endure!"

It seemed there was much I was enduring as a young mom of four kids under five and a half. Most days I just barely got through.

One thing I knew: I didn't want to live with any regrets.

Papa Murray's words struck my heart acutely. Not only did they change my attitude toward parenting, they changed my perspective on life!

On the heels of his penetrating words came the still, small voice of my Saviour, echoing the words of Luke 9:25: "What does it profit you, Lisa, if you gain the whole world but lose your own family?"

Through Papa Murray, the Lord showed me that my kids weren't a barrier to my ministry. They *were* my ministry!

Survival Tip

> **Find creative ways to enjoy your kids.** Here are a few ideas to help you enjoy your kids, rather than endure them. Set aside a weekly family night evening. We installed pizza night once a week. Serve a candlelight dinner with your good dishes to celebrate your family. Take them to a special event or an outing as a reward for their sacrifices for ministry. Pull them out of school for a day to give them priority time and attention. Initiate and set apart special times for one on one interaction where casual conversation can happen. It might take the shape of shopping days, beach days, lunch dates, breakfast dates, dinner dates, or a special event. In her book *Welcome Home*, author Emily Barnes speaks to treating guests like family, and family like royalty. It's a principle we could all take to heart and implement in our homes.[2] Remember, *"Children are a gift from the Lord; they are a reward from him"* (Psalm 127:3, NLT). What are some of the ways you've sought to enjoy your kids? What has made enjoyment challenging for you? What can you do to turn your enduring into enjoying?

Shining a Light on the Path Where My Children Walked

As each of my children entered school, new aspects of our lives were revealed to the unsuspecting world around us. Now it was time for those in the education system to be enlightened.

Benjamin was going to Kindergarten—finally! His teacher arranged a home visit. It was her way of getting to know her students and put the student and their parents at ease before classes started. She scheduled such a visit with each student, and soon our long-awaited day came.

Benjamin was so excited. He couldn't wait to meet her. He had, after all, been waiting to go to school ever since the time he'd found out it existed! He set out a few of his favourite toys for her to see and mapped out a guided tour of the house.

Then the interview began.

"Benjamin, do you have a favourite song?" she asked.

---

2   Emily Barnes, *Welcome Home* (Eugene, OR: Harvest House Publishers, 1997).

Without hesitation, he handed her one of the children's books from a nearby bookshelf. Then he took his stance behind the wooden children's table and chairs set. Being the pastor's son he was, he proceeded to lead us all in his favourite song. It just so happened to be a hymn.

With a reverent quiver in his voice, he said, "Turn to hymn number 429."

Then he waved his conducting hand in a horizontal figure eight, toe-tapping in cadence, and shamelessly belted out, "Holy, Holy, Holy, Lord God on my team!"

I wanted to crawl underneath a chair.

"Benjamin," the teacher announced, "thank you for leading us in what is also my favourite hymn! You see, I'm a church organist's daughter."

Phew! What an unexpected revelation!

And then there was poor Jacob. He was required to write a biography for a first-grade assignment. In it, he wrote, "My dad could have been a pro-football player." And while inaudible, with an obvious disgruntled deep sigh, he added: "But instead he became a pastor!"

On another occasion, we went for our annual parent-teacher interview. As the conversation unfolded, the teacher was surprised to find out that my husband, the father of her student, was a pastor.

"I thought you were a church janitor!" she chuckled embarrassedly by her mis-construed perception. She went on to say that when it came up in discussion one day in class, our child had shared that their dad spent all day at church moving papers around.

Thankfully, I was fortunate to be able to help in each of my children's school classrooms. I got to know the teachers and took every opportunity to get involved. I led music in circle time. I took teachers out for appreciation lunches. I even hosted them at our home. In one school, I discovered a few teachers who were interested in spiritual matters, so I created a small group Bible study for them. I even had the opportunity to sing at one of my kids' teacher's wedding.

What a privilege to shine the light of Jesus on the ground my children walked every day.

Get involved in your kids' lives. One of the best ways to be part of our children's lives is to get involved in their world. A big part of our children's lives is lived when they're outside the home. Consider volunteering at the public school to help out with their classes: reading, singing, day-tripping, or baking cupcakes and bringing them in to celebrate the life of your very special kids. Host your kids' teachers for lunches. Welcome your kids' friends into your home. What better way to know where they are and what they're up to? Go and cheer for them on the sidelines of their sports teams. At a minimum, express interest in their interests to become part of their world. Think of some way you can get involved this week.

Out of the Mouths of Babes

It had been a long stretch of nightly meetings. My husband came home to a note placed carefully on his pillow. It was from our daughter, Natalie. She had pasted together multiple coloured strips of construction paper in a series of arches to form a rainbow. The note read, "Daddy, I wish you were home more often."

"Dad, why is it that nobody ever calls you just to ask how you are?" asked another one of our children one night at dinnertime. "Why do they only call when they want you to do something for them?"

One of our favourite games around the dinner table was High-Low. Everyone took a turn telling the rest of the family about the best part of their day and the worst part of their day. It was our way to inconspicuously check in on our kids. I was struck by Proverbs 27:23, which says, "Be sure you know the condition of your flocks, give careful attention to your herds."

During one particularly challenging time in our ministry life, demands and stressors were running high and energy and relief were at an all-time low. I knew I had to seize the moment to rein things in before they got any lower.

One night when my husband was at yet another meeting, the kids began to revolt.

"Why is Dad always at a meeting?"

"Why can't he play with us?"

"When will he be home?"

"Why does he have to be a pastor anyway?"

I decided to play High-Low alone with the four kids, and I was amazed at their response.

I got out a pen and paper and recorded them as they shared, so they knew I was taking their concerns seriously. Together we came up with some constructive ways of handling some of their frustrations. It was better to deal with them than simply remain frustrated by them.

My husband and I implemented a question on our dates from time to time with our kids: "On a scale from one to ten, how am I doing as a parent and what can I do to bring it closer to a ten?" We took turns answering this question.

I learned a lot through my children. I was given profound insights out of the mouths of babes.

Survival Tip

> **Keep lines of communication open.** Seize every opportunity to engage in meaningful conversation with your kids. It's important that we create a safe space for them to share what's on their hearts and minds. Ask open-ended questions rather than ones that prompt yes or no answers. For example, ask them about their hopes, fears, and feelings about certain subjects. Ask them what they need/want/expect of you. Play a game of High-Low. Together, discuss ways to turn lows into highs. What are some of the most successful and unsuccessful ways you've used to keep lines of communication open? How do they vary from child to child? What can you do to make yourself more available?

Carrying Those with Young

Every time I was invited to my friend's home, I admired a beautiful sketch of Jesus on her wall. In it, He embraced a lamb and held it close to His heart with His nail-scarred hands. The Lamb's satisfied expression is what caught my attention most. It was a look of sheer peace, comfort, and security. I could almost perceive a subtle smile on its face as it nuzzled up to Jesus.

When we left that church, my friend gifted me with a copy of that portrait as a goodbye gift. I couldn't have predicted at the time that I would draw from this picture to gain a sense of peace, comfort, and security in the years ahead, especially where my children were concerned.

One night over dinner, my husband was pulled away from the table to take an important call. After the conversation was through and my husband rejoined us, one of our kids asked, "What's suicide?" The unspeakable conversations we shared as a family! We would have no choice but to address such questions when we were drawn into them.

Our daughter was still a toddler when my husband brought her to church to take care of some business for an upcoming funeral. Unthinkingly, he carried her into the sanctuary where the deceased lay peacefully in a coffin. What followed was a tough conversation for our confused and frightened three-year-old.

And of course there were the hushed late-night discussions between David and me that our children were sometimes privy to from behind their closed bedroom doors. Whether they were aware of it or not, the difficult situations we navigated loomed ominously over our household and permeated our walls.

How do you shelter your kids from the frontline of ministry when the spiritual battle rages on your doorstep? Where do you go to speak as parents when the pressures build? How do you keep your children from absorbing all the tension and heartache and conflict a ministry couple faces?

I'm not sure how, apart from being on our knees in prayer.

I am grateful that *"He tends his flock like a shepherd: He gathers the lambs in his arms and carries them close to his heart; he gently leads those that have young"* (Isaiah 40:11).

Survival Tip

> **Discover the power of being a praying parent.** Prayer is possibly the most underestimated yet powerful gift we can offer our children. Claim a verse for each of your children and pray it over them at every opportunity. Don't stop at praying for them; pray with them. Ask them how you can be praying for them at school, with their friends, at church, and at work. Then commit to it. Check in on them from time to time and check off the answers God has given. Pray for godly influencers in their lives. Pray bad influencers out of their lives. Pray for them as they come and go. Pray through their bedroom as you tidy and clean. Sit on their bed and pray... pray protection over their lives, pray for God's work in their lives. What specific ways can you pray for your kids today? If you don't know, ask them. Take some time to pray right now.

The Altar of Sacrifice

It seemed like our kids were always on the altar of sacrifice while their dad and I took care of ministry-related events. It weighed heavily on my heart constantly. To think of the price we paid for babysitting so we could go and freely serve God's people. It took its toll, not to mention the price our kids paid.

Church social events were always the first to be slotted into our calendar. It was hard to decipher whether our exhaustion was from the perpetual activity or the guilt we experienced from having to leave our kids in the care of someone one more time, all in the name of the ministry.

Amid crazy days and church-related evenings, nap time became my time with the Lord.

Inevitably, two-year-old Benjamin would creep down the stairs with a *thud-thump, thud-thump*. Through the banister rungs, he'd watch me sitting in the chair where I spent my time with the Lord. He'd come up and ask me what I was reading, hoping to strike up a conversation to skirt around his nap. Most times I would cart him back to his bedroom. But one afternoon he persisted in coming down the stairs.

Rather than put up a fight that would leave us both more exasperated and frustrated than before, I relented. Setting aside my Bible, I asked if he'd like to help me build a fire in our fireplace. He loved doing that kind of "manly" activity. So he nodded his head in hearty agreement.

As we gathered the wood and laid it one stick at a time, Ben lambasted me with a barrage of questions.

"Abraham built a fire too, didn't he, Mom?"

"Yes, he did, Benjamin."

"And he built an altar out of wood too, didn't he?

"Mmmhmm."

"And then he laid his son, Isaac, on it, right?"

"That's right, he did."

"Mom, that's kind of like what God did when He sent Jesus to die on the cross for us, isn't it?"

I was speechless. When had he taken that in? Insights gained from a two-year-old, not easily forgotten. Even so, who knew that, years later, I'd be offering that same son and laying him on the altar of sacrifice to the Lord?

Seize teachable moments. There is a lot to be said about Deuteronomy 6:4–9. It's important that we seize moments of meaningful conversation with our children as we walk, eat, rise, and go to bed. Otherwise we may miss some valuable teachable moments with them. It's important to seize moments to teach them about life's hard stuff, valuable stuff, and the stuff of life. Use things they're familiar with as object lessons, just like Jesus taught by using parables. Consider ways you can teach simple truths to your kids from what you're learning, what you're reading in God's Word, and maybe even some of the questions you're exploring. Record some of these lessons for future reference. Be watching this week for a teachable moment. Then record the lessons that come out of it for both you and the one you shared it with.

No Regrets

Two weeks after the birth of my fourth and final baby, Erin, I was readmitted to the hospital due to complications. Two weeks later, our four-year-old son Benjamin was diagnosed with pneumonia and admitted onto the same floor where I'd been. Nurses welcomed me with, "And which room would you like to occupy this week, Mrs. Elliott?"

Regardless, the ministry had to go on! So there we sat at a fundraising banquet, trying desperately to engage in what felt like meaningless conversation while I struggled to eat my meal. All the while, our son was sick in the hospital.

Later that evening, we received a phone call from the hospital. The nurse had dialled our number and a little voice on the other end of the phone asked, "Mom, can you come?"

What were we thinking? I can still hear his voice, and sadly I regret that moment. Why did church always have to come first?

Fast-forward fourteen years and that same son was diagnosed with leukemia. One thing was sure: Ben wasn't going to spend one night alone in that hospital room. We lived that entire year not wanting to live with any regret for serving the church at the expense of our kids.

Of course, that didn't stop ministry from beckoning us. The church begged for our attention: staff management, preaching, meetings, expansion plans, plans to host visiting missionaries, welcoming newcomers, and ministering to the masses.

Finding the balance between family needs and church responsibilities wasn't easy, but never more so than the year our son was sick. Even more challenging was trying not to hold the church's relentless demands against them.

One night in the hospital, as my husband and Ben lay awake in their beds, he asked Ben if he had any regrets.

"Nope," Ben replied. Then without missing a beat, he asked, "How about you?"

David expressed his regrets over having been so caught up in church ministry when Ben and his siblings were little.

After a minute or two, Ben said, "Well, at least you learned from it, Dad."

Take it from me: life is too short to miss today! So live it as best you can, with no regrets.

Survival Tip ———————————————

Stop and smell the roses while they're in bloom. Tomorrow is never promised, so seize opportunities when they arise. Enjoy simple pleasures. Live life fully in every moment you have. "If only" will only cause you pain and regret. Today is a new day. It's an opportunity for a fresh start. So instead of regretting all the things you haven't done, consider all the things you can do—starting today! What are some specific investments you can make today in the lives of your children? What are some of the great memories you've made? Perhaps set aside a special evening this week when you and your family can stroll down memory lane together. Make a list of the memories you share.

Dear Younger Me

It struck me as I watched my daughter, suddenly a mother herself of four children under five and a half, just how much history was being repeated. It was like watching my life unfold before my eyes.

Some days when we spoke, I felt like I was talking to myself! I often found it challenging to think outside my head to nurture and guide and coach and speak encouragement into her life. If I'm completely honest, in some cases I hadn't a clue what to say or what advice to give or what counsel to offer due to my subjectivity.

I was her age when I felt I was finally getting a grip on my life as a mom and wife. It took years to master the art of balancing family and ministry. That's when I began prayer-journaling to stay focused. It's also when I felt convicted to get my priorities straight. Out of this conviction, I created a Proverbs 31 cross-stitch sampler that still hangs in my home as a reminder of all the lessons God taught me, and continues to teach me, through my children.

One day I asked myself, *What would I have wanted someone to speak into my life?* So, with my daughter in view and my heart in reflective mode, I wrote a few notes to self.

Dear Younger Me,

You are special. Know and believe that you are worthy of this high calling as a mother. Just think: of all the women in the world God could have chosen to be the mother of your children, He chose you! You are a beautiful, unique creation of His (Psalm 139). He rejoices over you with singing (Zephaniah 3:17).

Be good to yourself. Do things for yourself that will keep resentment at bay. Life as a mom is exhausting. Sleepless nights and long days under constant demand require rest. It can be hard to catch a break. Therefore, give yourself a timeout every day—not for bad behaviour, but to enable you to be the best you can be and offer the best you have.

Do your best to enjoy rather than endure your kids. I know that's harder than it sounds. You're going to have moments where you feel overwhelmed, but that's to be expected. It certainly doesn't mean you're a bad mommy. It's a challenging job you've been given as you raise a family. But it's also a high calling. Try and find something enjoyable to do with your kids as often as you're able. These days are fleeting! They'll be gone before you know it.

You'll need to surround yourself with others who will support, encourage, pray, validate, and offer perspective. Don't be afraid to ask for help when you need it. You'll need all the help you can get.

Love, honour, and respect your spouse. Loving your husband is the best gift you can ever give to your kids.

Finally, above your love for your husband and kids, love the Lord your God with all your heart, soul, mind, and strength.

Remember that the joy of the Lord is your strength! Tap into that joy every day. It's important to intentionally carve out time with the Lord. Depending on the season of life you're in, you may not be able to feast at God's table. So "snack" on God's Word. Know that one day (which is coming sooner than you think) you'll have time to yourself again. Continue to put the Lord first in your life. Give Him the best of your time, and He will make the best of your time.

Deuteronomy 30:19–20 tells us, *"Now choose life, so that you and your children may live and that you may love the Lord your God, listen to his voice, and hold fast to him. For the Lord is your life…"*

You can do it! I know you can. Love,

Your Biggest Cheerleader

Survival Tip

> **Share your life's lessons.** Take some time to reflect and record your life. Think of all the lessons you've learned. How would you have lived differently if you could live it all over again? What words of encouragement would you offer yourself? What would you warn yourself against? What counsel or advice would you give? Now, take your thoughts and write a Dear Younger Me letter. Think of what you'd like to pass on to your kids once they're grown. You may want to keep a journal to give them one day down the road. They'll be able to read, perhaps learn from your struggles and joys, as well as see the thread of God's faithfulness. As we read in Psalm 145:4, *"One generation commends your works to another; they tell of your mighty acts."*

Our children were never meant to be a deterrent from ministry. They *are* our ministry. Therefore, rather than making them compete with the church, it's important to let them know just how important they are. We must show them that they can find joy in serving Jesus by demonstrating our faith in action, not only practicing what we preach but also preaching what we practice.

Encourage them to be all God intended them to be and to use the gifts and talents He's given them as a part of His body, the church. Make sure you thank them for sharing you with the church. Let them see the need to take time alone to spend with the Lord, investing in and living out your relationship with the Lord right before their eyes.

Pray for them. Pray with them. Share God's Word with them. Live it out with them.

Straight from the Father's Heart

*By wisdom a house is built, and through understanding it is
established; through knowledge its rooms are filled
with rare and beautiful treasures.*
—Proverbs 24:3–4

> *Biblical Mentor*
> ## The Virtuous Woman (Proverbs 31)

Some say that the virtuous woman in Proverbs 31 was a real woman, possibly Solomon's own mother. Others hold that she was wisdom personified. Still others portray her as the ideal woman.

In any case, we can learn a lot of wisdom through her example. Treat her as an inspiration rather than a threat. Rather than esteeming her as unattainable, take note of her noble character. Consider how you can apply the following principles to your life where prioritizing your family is concerned.

Recognize that parenthood is a high calling. Know and believe that you are worthy of this high calling as a parent. Just think: of all the people in the world God could have chosen to be the parent of your children, He chose you! You are in the process of fulfilling a vital ministry right within your home to your spouse and children. Influence begins at home.

> *A wife of noble character who can find? She is worth far more than rubies…*
> *Many women do noble things, but you surpass them all.*
> —Proverbs 31:10, 29

Opening your door can open hearts. How great it is that our kids can see a hospitable home modelled for them. Through example, they learn how to welcome others into their homes and hearts. They see needs beyond their front door. They learn the value of treating others like themselves. Furthermore, when you involve them in hospitality they feel part of the experience rather than threatened by it.

> *She opens her arms to the poor and extends her hands to the needy… She watches over the affairs of her household and does not eat the bread of idleness.*
> —Proverbs 31:20, 27

Preparation minimizes chaos and confusion. A lot of things happen at the last minute, and nothing teaches us that more than when we have young children. All the more reason to plan and prepare in advance.

Our kids need to see the benefit that comes when we take the time to invest in our future: there's less stress, less confusion, and fewer hasty decisions. The more prepared we are on the front end, the more easily executed our plans will be on the back end. Plan the work, then work the plan.

When it snows, she has no fear for her household; for all of them are clothed in scarlet. She makes coverings for her bed; she is clothed in fine linen and purple... She is clothed with strength and dignity; she can laugh at the days to come.

—Proverbs 31:21–22, 25

Loving your spouse is the best gift you can give your children. Children learn through example. They're always watching. They especially take close note of the relationship between their parents. Therefore, love, honour, pray for, encourage, support, and respect your spouse. It will be a gift to your children and your children's children.

Her husband has full confidence in her and lacks nothing of value... Her husband is respected at the city gate, where he takes his seat among the elders of the land... Her children arise and call her blessed; her husband also, and he praises her...

—Proverbs 31:11, 12, 28

Investments you make today pay off tomorrow. Motherhood is a relentless and often thankless job. One day your children will appreciate all your investments. Therefore, use every opportunity to plant seeds of life, hope, and truth into their hearts and minds. That will flow out of your personal spiritual investment, which can't be underestimated.

Time spent nurturing your relationship with the Lord in front of your kids every day offers eternal dividends.

She speaks with wisdom, and faithful instruction is on her tongue... Charm is deceptive, and beauty is fleeting; but a woman who fears the Lord is to be praised.

—Proverbs 31:26, 30

Chapter Four

FULFILLING YOUR CALLING WITHOUT *Burning Out*

IF YOU'VE EVER FLOWN ON A PLANE, YOU'LL KNOW THE SAFETY DRILL EXERCISE. Included in this onboard presentation is the importance of placing the oxygen mask on yourself before you ensure the safety of a fellow traveller.

"Why?" you ask?

Because you can't assist someone else with breathing if you can't breathe yourself!

I learned the hard way that in order to care for others, you must first care for yourself. It's absolutely essential to fuel your emotional, mental, and physical tank, filling your lungs with oxygen rather than pumping your veins with the adrenalin that's so easy to rely on in an emergency.

Proper time management, self-awareness, and personal investment are key factors in leading a healthy ministry. It's necessary to set a steady pace for a successful flight and consistent altitude. Ultimately, one must learn the importance of breathing deeply the Spirit of the living God. Acts 17:28 tells us, *"For in him we live and move and have our being."*

Welcome to the fuel tank of my heart.

Statistics

At a crisis point in our ministry, my husband and I came across some shocking statistics in an article entitled "Unfair Expectations on the Pastor's Wife."[3] The article

---

3   Kristi Gaultiere, "Unfair Expectations on the Pastor's Wife," *Soul Shepherding*. Date of access: August 8, 2021 (https://www.soulshepherding.org/the-pastors-wife/).

expresses the devastating effects of stress and burnout in the lives of pastors and their families. These statistics have likely changed since that article was published, perhaps even worsening, but they are still worthy of note:

- Hundreds of pastors leave the ministry each month due to moral failure, spiritual burnout, or contention in their church.
- Seventy percent of pastors constantly fight depression.
- Eighty percent of adult children of pastors have had to seek professional help for depression.
- Eighty percent of pastors and eighty-four percent of their wives feel unqualified and discouraged in their role in ministry.
- Eighty percent of pastors' wives feel left out and unappreciated by the church members.
- Eighty percent of pastors' wives wish their spouse would choose another profession.
- The majority of pastors' wives say that the most destructive event that has occurred in their marriage and family was the day they entered the ministry.

One thing was certain: I didn't want to become another statistic!

Survival Tip

> **Take inventory.** Ministry life is exhausting—and when we're exhausted, we become vulnerable. In our vulnerable state, we can do some pretty stupid things and make unwise decisions. It's easy to listen to lies about ourselves. In those moments, we don't feel adequate or equipped to be in ministry, let alone be any good to anyone. We're the worst spouse, parent, and friend—says no one but ourselves. Spending time in God's Word allows the Lord to speak into your heart to remind you of the truth. Ultimately it's the truth that will set you free (John 8:32). How's your fuel tank? Are you running on empty? What's consuming your energy? Can you recall some vulnerable moments in your ministry life when you wanted to pack it all in? What made you feel defeated? Perhaps it's time to take inventory. Ask the Holy Spirit to help you sift through your commitments.

He Makes Me to Lie Down in Green Pastures

I'd just had my second Caesarean section. After a week's stay in the hospital, I was released. Good thing! I had a wedding to attend. My husband was officiating. And, of my own accord, I needed to be there!

I said goodbye and thank you to all the helpful hospital staff. My husband helped me to the elevator, carrying our new precious bundle in his car seat. He then patiently walked alongside me as I precariously made my way to the car. He had pulled up to the front doors of the hospital to make it easier on me.

I had packed one of my fancier maternity dresses in my hospital bag. It would work beautifully for me as a wedding guest. Within a half-hour, we were at the church. Again, my husband opened the car door and assisted me as I slowly unfolded from my freshly stapled abdomen in hopes that I didn't split open. Then he led me into the church, where I took a seat in the back pew.

My next C-section wasn't much different. Especially in terms of my incessant need to somehow prove myself and rise to any challenge that came my way.

By my fourth and final C-section, I ran into a few complications that required me to take sedatives and take things easier than I'd been accustomed to. Thankfully, a group of ladies from my small group volunteered to take turns coming to my house to clean and provide meals and childcare, allowing me the rest I needed to make a full recovery.

Why hadn't I asked for this help before now? Was it pride? Was it self-sufficiency? Was it sheer stupidity?

A year later, as I sat in the doctor's office sobbing, I described some of my symptoms: lethargy, memory loss, and the feeling that I was chasing a truck I couldn't catch up with. She ordered bloodwork and promptly diagnosed me with low thyroid.

She might as well have told me I had cancer. It hit me hard. Not nearly as hard, however, as realizing that perhaps the Lord had been trying to get my attention all these years.

It was a humbling experience as He pulled out my battery and *made* me lie down in green pastures. But in the long run, I was happy that I consented. I was tired and in need of refreshing.

Why did I always have to be emotionally and physically laid out flat on my back before I paid attention to the Good Shepherd's invitation to rest?

Survival Tip

> **Listen to your body.** We all have a limit and it's important to know what those limits are. Recognize when your physical resources are running low, and bunker down when your emotional reserve is bottoming out. Headaches, muscle pain, ulcers, lethargy, irritability, lack of motivation, and bad attitudes are all warning lights on the dashboard of our lives. Which ones have you experienced or are you experiencing? Have you ever paid for it by exceeding your limitations and not listening to your body? What was that experience like? Listen to your body, or your body will make you listen to it.

So Many Good Things

I loved Martha from the first time I read about her in Luke 10. She shot from the hip. She didn't mince words. She got things done. She was ambitious. Perhaps she was a little too impulsive, but that's who she was, who God made her to be. She was task-oriented, mission-minded, generous, efficient, and a practical need-meeter. Martha wanted what was best for Jesus and she used her God-given gifts and resources to serve Him.

However, as I read into the passage about Martha, a few things indicated that something wasn't right. Martha was distracted by preparations, envying Mary's listening luxury.

There was a clearer indicator that something was off-kilter: she demanded that Jesus do something about it. That alone got my attention. It sounded all too familiar!

I'd always been active, working best under pressure, high energy, multi-focused, and with multi-interests. A do-it-all type of person. Do it all myself, do it all at once, and do it all as fast as I can. Translated into the ministry, I was a little imbalanced in an all-or-nothing kind of way.

But I loved it. I thrived on it! I was addicted to ministry and the adrenalin rush and fulfilment it gave me. I rose to the applause of others as they watched in awe.

For as long as I could remember, I'd functioned as an extrovert. I filled my days with people and more people, thinking it was people who energized me when in reality people fed my adrenalin. Unfortunately, I didn't learn this about myself until it was almost too late. That's when I learned that there's a vast difference between the two. My real strength came from times of stillness and solitude. I was just too afraid to be left alone to understand my real needs.

Meanwhile, a few things began to occur to me in my increasingly flustered and frustrated state. I became worried and upset by *so many things*. I was driven by my people-pleasing tendencies and my fear of failure and rejection. Guilt propelled me. I was pressured by expectations, my own included, which were often higher than anyone else's.

No matter how I sliced it, life's demands had gotten out of balance and become overwhelming. My priorities were out of whack. Gone was my perspective, joy, and hope.

That's when it occurred to me that the problem had never been with what Martha was doing, but rather what she was forfeiting in order to do it. Mary had chosen the more important thing, having invited Jesus in! Martha was too busy serving Him to spend time with Him, more concerned with the task than the person. Performance substituted intimacy.

In the midst of her *doing*, Martha lost perspective of spiritual matters and exchanged them for secondary matters. Her greatest strength became her greatest weakness. If only she'd realized that all Jesus required of her was her company. He hadn't asked for a five-course meal. He would have likely been satisfied with a glass of milk and a peanut butter pita!

Jesus said that only one thing was needed, and Mary had chosen it. I needed to do the same.

Survival Tip

> **Put the big stones in first.** There's an expression that says, "God loves you and everyone else has a wonderful plan for your life." It's easy in ministry to put everyone else's needs first. It's easy to allow the urgent needs of others to take over the important people right under your roof. When we put God first, He'll instruct us in how to put everything else in the proper order. Read through *Tyranny of the Urgent* by Charles E. Hummel for some insightful advice.[4] Take undisturbed time alone, as Mary did, to invest in the important thing. Time alone with Jesus offers encouragement, hope, wisdom, strength, validation, and renewed perspective. As Matthew 6:33 says, *"But seek first his kingdom and his righteousness, and all these things will be given to you as well."*

---

4   Charles E. Hummel, *Tyranny of the Urgent* (Downers Grove, IL: InterVarsity, 1967).

We the Willing

For years, my husband and I lived by a motto by Mother Teresa that we found quoted in Phil Callaway's book, *Who Put the Skunk in the Trunk*: "We the willing, led by the unknowing, have been doing the impossible for the ungrateful. We have been doing so much for so long with so little that we are now qualified to do anything with nothing!"[5]

Someone once said, "The biggest trouble with success is that its formula is just about the same as that for a nervous breakdown."[6] And apparently that's where I was heading. I just didn't realize it until one morning when I woke up with a headache and feeling a little shaky on my feet. Not to mention my emotions were a tad unstable.

I called my neighbour.

"What's wrong with you?" she asked before I'd hardly had a chance to say hello. "Send your kids over right now."

I got off the phone and did as I was told. I struggled to tie my son's shoes, then just gave up and sent him and his siblings on their way next door barefoot, shoes in hand. I couldn't shake the feeling of being caught up in a slow-motion picture.

Scared, I called my husband.

"Is everything okay?" he asked.

"I feel like a bomb is ticking in my head and is ready to go off any second."

"I'm coming home."

And for the first time in our ministry history, he dropped everything at church and walked through the door of our home five minutes later. When he approached me, I fell into his arms and sobbed uncontrollably for the next number of hours.

What was wrong with me? Was the church crisis we were facing finally taking effect? It had been an intense time and emotions were running high. I was so thankful that my kids were safe and my husband had thought to come home. I didn't trust myself to be left alone.

That night, I lay in bed beside my husband, shaking, stuttering, and sobbing as the wheels began falling off my wagon. Together we got out a piece of paper and began listing all the ministries at church that I not only attended but was

---

5   Phil Callaway, *Who Put the Skunk in the Trunk: Learning to Laugh When Life Stinks* by (Multnomah, ON: The Crown Publishing Group, 1999). Quoting Mother Teresa.

6   John Holmes, "The biggest trouble with success…" *AZ Quotes*. Date of access: February 9, 2021 (https://www.azquotes.com/quote/956013).

responsible for. We came up with seventeen things! Could it be that I was slightly imbalanced?

I wrote in my prayer journal: "Lord, I feel weak, tired, out of control, behind, disorganized, needing space, and desiring to quit everything. Total defeat in every aspect of my life might well define my feelings these days." I was overwhelmed, overworked, overstressed, overscheduled, overtired, and just about over the edge. I spent so much time doing what I *had* to do that there was no time to do what I *wanted* to do. So what was I to do? What would you do?

The first thing I knew I had to do was opt out of some of the ministries I was so heavily involved in. It couldn't matter what others thought about it.

However, laying aside the opinions and perceptions of others ended up being the most challenging part of it all.

Next, I needed to take some strategic time off to rest and focus on my health and home. Miraculously, the phone didn't ring for an entire month. Supernaturally, any meetings there had been scheduled got cancelled. The Lord knew my body was willing but my flesh was weak.

I therefore needed this timeout to rest and recalibrate. I also knew I had to find a way to make this a regular part of my life.

Survival Tip

Give yourself permission. Guilt isn't a healthy motivator. It can add to the weight of an already overloaded, overwrought state. While it's important to engage in recharging activities, it's of equal importance that we disengage from those that drain our emotional, mental, and spiritual battery. Set aside times of solitude to recharge. It could be as simple as taking an hour with no schedule or to-do list. Make a to-not-do list instead. Make yourself a cup of tea. Take a breather at intervals throughout the day. Jesus often slipped away by Himself to a quiet place for rest, and He gives you permission to do the same: *"Come with me by yourselves to a quiet place and get some rest"* (Mark 6:31). What will you free yourself from today?

We Can Please Some of the People Some of the Time

I stood over the children's section of the book table display at our denomination's national conference. The bold title on the front cover of one book stood out amongst all the others: *You Are Special*, by Max Lucado.[7]

Most everyone else was sitting in on one of the many meetings to vote on some important issue, as most of those meetings went. But I had issues of my own to contend with. I could only hope no one discovered me in my moment of contention. I needed some time alone.

That's when the Lord stepped in and used this children's book to communicate a profound message to my heart. As I opened the book and turned the pages, He opened up my childlike faith.

It was like Max Lucado had written that children's book with me in mind, knowing that one day I'd be in this place of defeat. How had I gotten here? Somehow I'd grown to rely on the stars of approval that people were sticking on me. But who doesn't like to be liked?

Peer pressure isn't just for school-age kids. Keeping up with the Joneses is real. I knew I spent too much time wondering what others thought of me. Much of my behaviour was based on those opinions—too much. I compared myself with them and felt like I could never measure up.

When would I learn that I never would? And really, was it important that I did?

God's Word warns us about people-pleasing: *"Am I now trying to win the approval of human beings, or of God? Or am I trying to please people?"* (Galatians 1:10)

It had always been too easy for me to respond to people's applause. I took it in whatever form I could: verbal affirmation, agreeing to requests for my leadership or involvement, and approval based upon my performance. It's what gave me a sense of acceptance.

The thought of disapproval or disappointing anyone was too much to bear. I was the perpetual peacekeeper. I carried a hot iron everywhere I went to make sure everyone was happy. Their happiness was up to me, after all. So how could I minister without bearing the responsibility of pleasing people, as if their life depended upon me?

I knew I *had* to purchase this book. Not only because it had already impacted my heart, but because of the tear stains that now deemed it mine.

---

7   Max Lucado, *You Are Special* (Wheaton, IL: Crossway Books, 1997).

Check your motive. People-pleasing is an easy trap to fall into. Who doesn't want to be liked? Who doesn't love approval or applause? Who wouldn't want to at least be thanked or acknowledged for their hard work, even if it's behind the scenes? It's important that we check our motives for doing what we do. Besides, people are fickle. Remember, the same crowd that cheered Jesus on one week crucified Him the next. Consider Paul's words: *"Am I now trying to win the approval of human beings, or of God? Or am I trying to please people? If I were still trying to please people, I would not be a servant of Christ"* (Galatians 1:10). There are many things that motivate us to do what we do. Guilt, fear, expectations, messed-up priorities, and peer pressure, to name a few. What's typically your motive?

K.I.S.S. (Keep It Simple, Sister)

I took Matthew 6:33 quite literally. If I simply sought first the Lord's kingdom and His righteousness, I expected everything in my life to fall naturally into place. Wrong. It took a lot of soul-searching to revamp my priorities, a lot of sifting and sorting to simplify all the clutter that had overtaken the sacred space.

To begin with, I dumped the closet of my life onto my bedroom floor. And then I asked the Lord to search my heart (Psalm 139:23–24). Thankfully, I came across a book by Patricia Sprinkle called *Women Who Do Too Much*, and it helped me sort things out.[8]

I began digging through the clutter of my life and asked myself questions. For example, I listed things that were very important, less important, and not so important for me to do. I examined which ones were stealing my joy. I set some goals based on perhaps the most intense questions of all: "If I only had six months to live, how would I spend them? Who would I spend them with? How would that determine my priorities?" I listed all my involvements, responsibilities, and ministries, as well as everything else that filled my time. Then I asked myself what I wanted to do but couldn't find time for.

Based on a decluttering magazine article I'd found—in a doctor's office, no less, while I awaited the arrival of another child I hoped to squeeze into my life somewhere—the process of elimination began. Starting with the front hallway of

---

8   Patricia Sprinkle, *Women Who Do Too Much* (New York, NY: Harper Paperbacks, 1992).

my life, I emptied out every closet, nook, and cranny. I divided everything into three piles: throw away, give away, and put away.

The throw-away pile was full of non-essentials. This pile needed some good weeding through. I couldn't allow others' opinions to affect my decisions. Besides, I knew that not everyone would understand or agree with me.

The give-away pile consisted of those things that could be delegated. I had to realize that my do-it-all instincts were potentially depriving other people of using their own gifts and abilities. I needed to learn to share the load rather than bear the load.

Finally, the put-away pile included things I chose to keep. I understood, however, that even these items were up for grabs depending on the season.

It was a big task to sort through everything in my life. I had to learn how to use the two middle letters of the alphabet—N.O.—to my advantage. A word that, it would seem, some used far too readily! No matter. It didn't mean I had to compensate. All the more reason for this decluttering process to be done and maintained on a regular basis.

One day I came across a timely note that said, "Do not feel totally, personally, irrevocably responsible for everyone… That's my job. Love, God."

As Solomon once wisely said, *"There is a time for everything, and a season for every activity under the heavens… a time to keep and a time to throw away"* (Ecclesiastes 3:1, 6). Ultimately, simple and pure devotion to Christ is the prescription for a life in balance.

So keep it simple, sister!

Survival Tip

Get back to the basics. Before we can find balance in our lives, we must understand what caused us to be imbalanced to begin with. We need to first simplify our focus. As Hebrews 12:2 says that we should *"[fix] our eyes on Jesus, the pioneer and perfecter of faith."* Revisit the day you met Jesus. Perhaps revisit the physical place you were when you committed your life or your ministry to Him. Ask the Holy Spirit to help you get back to the basics of your faith and relationship with Him. Time spent with the Lord needs to be our top priority. The restorative power of God's Word speaks into our hearts and provides us with wisdom, strength, and peace. When you give God the *best* of your time, He'll make the best *of* your time. Now, picture being given six months to live. What will you do with the time you have left?

Emergency vs. Urgency

When we were first married, I worked in a pharmacy. Right beside the cash register, there was a sign posted for employees that said "An emergency on your part does not constitute urgency on mine!" I eventually took it as my slogan to help me weigh the tyranny of the urgent.

It used to be every time a crisis was laid on our doorstep, my husband and I would drop everything to attend to that need. It took us a while to catch on, but we learned that if we waited for even an hour before responding to the situation or call for help, it would, in most cases, resolve on its own. We learned to be responsive rather than reactive.

Phone calls, emails, drop-ins, drop-offs, demands, expectations, unforeseen needs and crises, tasks, meetings, more meetings, favours… they all pile up, don't they? Add the weight of personal pressures, needs, and self-imposed expectations and it gets heavy. The demands don't ever go away. Therefore, *we* need to.

Jesus did. To beat the crowds, He got up early before the line-ups began to form. Even then, he was sought out and demanded of.

"Where have you been, Jesus? Didn't you know the people are asking for you?"

"Jesus, your mother and brothers are outside begging for your attention."

"You've run out of wine? No problem. My son's here to help."

"Jesus, all these people have been here a long time and they're getting hungry. Where are *you* going to find food to feed them all?"

"Why is Jesus paying so much attention to those people? Doesn't He know we need Him at the synagogue?"

"Where have you been, Jesus? Didn't you know our brother was sick and needed your touch?"

It's no wonder He literally headed for the hills regularly, both to get away from the crowds and to be alone with His Father. This can be seen again and again in the Gospels.[9] He set personal boundaries. He permitted Himself to sleep and invited others to rest.

If Jesus was really the Saviour, I figured there was no need for two of us!

---

9 See Luke 22:39, John 6:15, and John 8:1.

Survival Tip ────────────────────────────

Let your yes be yes and your no be no. The way to feel like a failure is to try to make things happen in people's lives that you aren't responsible for. Even Jesus didn't physically place hands on everyone who crossed His path. Whenever He turned to say yes to someone, He turned His back on many others. He knew when to act immediately and when to delay, as in the death of Lazarus in John 11. He knew when His time had not yet come (John 7:8) and when the right time had (John 16:32). Think of a time when you said yes to something you regretted. What were the consequences of your decision? The next time you're tempted to say a hasty yes, pause and consider the cost of that decision for you, your spouse, and your family. That way, you reserve your yes for the Lord's will to be done over someone else's. Ask the Lord to help you know when to say yes and when to say a God-pleasing no.

Massage Therapy

I'd never had a massage before. But if there was ever a time to experience one, it was now. A fellow pastor's wife had encouraged me to do it and even gave me the name of her registered massage therapist.

So there I was. As we stood in the dimly lit room with spa music playing softly in the background, I explained to her that I'd never had a massage before. She must've picked up on my awkwardness, because she put me right at ease and explained the professional approach she'd be taking. She told me that she'd leave the room and allow me to lay face down on the massage table. She assured me that she'd knock before she entered to make sure I was ready.

As she moved her hands over my back, I could feel the pressure being relieved. I held my breath in an attempt to stuff down unexpected emotions I hadn't allowed myself to experience in a very long time. They were rising to the surface of my skin. I had gotten good at holding back tears, practicing during emotional movies.

"How do you feel now?" she asked as she wrapped things up.

"Is it normal to feel like crying?"

"Yes. People respond in a lot of different ways as tension is released. Some sleep through the entire time. Others talk the time away. And yes, tears are more than normal."

"Good to know," I said. "The next time, I think I might just sob through the entire experience."

She smiled and assured me that would be just fine with her.

Massage became a regular part of my therapy. At times I've sobbed my way through an entire hour. Other times I have meditated on scripture. Then I apply it to every ache and pain in my life, every spiritual muscle that needs to be worked out, and every stress or tension that needs to be released. That way, I can better run the race with health and endurance.

My body, mind, and soul have been affected not only by simple human touch but the touch of the Master's hands. While I lay prostrate, I commit every part of my life to the Lord, from the top of my head to the bottom of my feet. I become mindful of His presence working out my salvation, letting the weight of the world rest upon His shoulders, and casting all of my cares upon Him. There on the massage table I lay my life before my *"Wonderful Counselor, Mighty God, Everlasting Father, Prince of Peace"* (Isaiah 9:6).

Survival Tip

Make personal investments. In a society prone to make withdrawals, it's important to make healthy and wise investments that will recharge, energize, and replenish us—not to mention, bring us joy! Mini-vacations, massage therapy, coffee with a friend, physical exercise, a healthy diet, hobbies, activities, and creative outlets all can give you joy and fulfillment. It's amazing how much therapy a little creativity will provide. For some it may be drawing, writing, carpentry, handiwork, gardening, house decorating, cooking, flower arranging, or puzzle assembling. Ecclesiastes 8:15 says, *"So I commend the enjoyment of life, because there is nothing better for a person under the sun than to eat and drink and be glad. Then joy will accompany them in their toil all the days of the life God has given them under the sun."* How will you invest in yourself today?

Broom Tree

It had been an incredibly long run of ministry—and if we weren't careful, we'd be burning out again. So we booked a pastors-and-wives Sabbath retreat for ourselves.

Unfortunately, I was too exhausted to be excited about it. In all honesty, I hadn't even had time to think about it. I was thankful for the six-hour drive to get there. Even so, I had too much adrenalin pumping to sleep on the way.

We drove the winding country roads to get to the rustic retreat grounds. Upon arrival, we signed into the registration office. Then we made our way to our room in a ranch-style lodge. There, we unlocked the door to our private quarters.

The quaint, log-cabin room was furnished with two cushioned rocking chairs situated in front of a gas fireplace. Also in our self-contained getaway was a table for two, a kitchenette, a two-piece en suite, a heart-shaped bathtub, and a king-sized bed. At that moment, the bed called my name.

An envelope lay on the table which contained a welcome and introduction to Broom Tree Ministries, named after the place of rest where the Lord instructed His faithful but exhausted servant Elijah to go and find shelter. There, under the broom tree, the Lord allowed him to rest and rise to eat, then go back to sleep. Every morning ravens faithfully delivered his breakfast to him.

Broom Tree offered much the same. Their vision statement: "Strengthening the church one pastor at a time."[10]

Someone from the ministry's prayer team had also written a lovely personal note of encouragement, letting us know how they'd be praying for us throughout the week. Propped on our pillow was a little sign that said, "Dear Lord, the church is yours. I'm going to bed. Amen."

I immediately accepted the invitation. I'd barely got my shoes kicked off before I collapsed on the bed and fell fast asleep. That's where I remained for the better part of the week, rising from time to time to eat or go for a walk with my husband or feast on the nourishment of God's Word.

My husband and I determined that we needed to attend more of these kinds of strategic retreats—not only to keep burnout at bay, but also to strengthen our marriage, our ministry, and our very souls.

---

10 You can learn more about Broom Tree Ministries at their website: http://broomtreeministries.org.

Take strategic retreats. Plan regular retreat times to get away as a couple. If at all possible, set apart an hour a day—or perhaps a weekend, week, or month every year—to rest, restore, rejuvenate, and refresh your body, mind, and soul. What could you do that would make your day off more restful and enjoyable? What does a restful holiday look like to you both? Take your dayplanner with you to set some goals together. Most importantly, schedule some strategic retreats—days off, holidays, and time within each day to recharge. Highlight them in green to signify green space or green pastures. Prayerfully respond to the Lord's invitation in Matthew 11:28 – 30, which says, *"Come to me, all you who are weary and burdened, and I will give you rest. Take my yoke upon you and learn from me, for I am gentle and humble in heart, and you will find rest for your souls. For my yoke is easy and my burden is light."*

The Well That Never Runs Dry

You'd think I would've learned by now. My emotional, mental, and spiritual tank was feeling a little depleted for lots of reasons.

After sharing my heart with a good friend, and being encouraged to rest and take some time out to refuel my tank, I did just that. I put the phone down and went for a walk.

While I walked, I simply allowed the Lord's Spirit to speak to mine. I let the sunshine flood my soul and took in the beautiful scenery surrounding me. I took deep breaths to fill my lungs with fresh air. In with the good and out with the bad.

When I got home, I picked up my Bible and was encouraged as I read Psalm 107. The Lord reminded me that I wasn't alone in how I felt. The portion of the psalm that caught my depleted heart's attention and ministered as deep calls to deep says,

Some went out on the sea in ships; they were merchants on the mighty waters. They saw the works of the Lord, his wonderful deeds in the deep. For he spoke and stirred up a tempest that lifted high the waves. They mounted up to the heavens and went down to the depths; in their peril their courage melted away. They reeled and staggered like drunkards; they were at their wits' end. Then they cried out to the Lord in their trouble, and he brought them out of their distress. He stilled the storm to a whisper; the waves of the sea were hushed. They were glad when it grew calm, and he guided them to their desired haven. Let them give thanks to the Lord for his unfailing love and his wonderful deeds for mankind.

—Psalm 107:23–31

I was reminded that when I'm at my wits' end, Jesus's mercies are just beginning. He meets me right where I'm at. He hears me out, lifts me up, and sets me on the right track again. When the tempests blow, His whisper calms the storm and hushes the roaring waves that threaten to pull me under. My Saviour guides me to my desired haven. He gives me permission to set aside the world's troubles and worries, exchanging them for His peace. He promises to not only provide for all my needs but be all I need Him to be.

The Lord has performed too many wonderful deeds, and has allowed me to witness too many of His incredible works, to fail me now. He gives me enough hope and strength to keep pressing on when my courage melts away. Ultimately, He *is* my hope and source of strength.

This is exactly the truth I need to fill up my depleted self.

Survival Tip ———

> **Recognize your need to fill your spiritual, emotional, mental, and relational gas tank.** Our heavenly Father knows our needs (Matthew 6:25–32). He gives us our daily bread (Matthew 6:11). He breathes life into our dry bones (Ezekiel 37). He offers rest to the weary (Matthew 11:28). He leads us beside quiet waters to restore our souls (Psalm 23:2–3). He is the all-knowing, all-powerful, all-gracious, ever-faithful God! Let Him fill you with His love and fuel you with His power. Are you weary? Are you running on empty? What do you need from Jesus to fill you up? When was the last time you sat by the living water? Why not take some time today to allow God to restore your soul?

The empowerment of rest and refreshment cannot be underestimated. It gives us joy, peace, and a renewed perspective.

Take the time to be holy. Take the time to be still and know that He is God (Psalm 46:10). Take the time to sit at the feet of Jesus (Luke 10:39). Take the time to learn of Him. Exchange your burden for His, for His yoke is easy and His burden is light. When you do, you will find not only physical rest but rest for your soul (Matthew 11:28–29).

Straight from the Father's Heart

Do you not know? Have you not heard? The Lord is the everlasting God, the Creator of the ends of the earth. He will not grow tired or weary, and his understanding no one can fathom. He gives strength to the weary and increases the power of the weak. Even youths grow tired and weary, and young men stumble and fall; but those who hope in the Lord will renew their strength. They will soar on wings like eagles; they will run and not grow weary, they will walk and not be faint.
—Isaiah 40:28–31

```
┌─────── 𝓑𝒾𝒷𝓁𝒾𝒸𝒶𝓁 𝓜𝑒𝓃𝓉𝑜𝓇 ───────┐
│         Elijah (1 Kings 17–19)         │
└────────────────────────────────────────┘
```

Elijah was a human being, even as we are. He prayed earnestly that it would not rain, and it did not rain on the land for three and a half years. Again he prayed, and the heavens gave rain, and the earth produced its crops.

—James 5:17–18

Elijah's fervent prayers lit a fire only God could have lit. The prophets of Baal could only stand in awe of the one true God. Elijah's efforts left him high and dry and running for his life.

However, Elijah's encounter with God, even in his state of exhaustion, gives us an example of someone who demonstrates how to keep the fire in our hearts burning, even when our wood is wet.

Expect to feel defeated after a victory. We read in 1 Kings 19:3–5:

Elijah was afraid and ran for his life. When he came to Beersheba in Judah, he left his servant there, while he himself went a day's journey into the wilderness. He came to a broom bush, sat down under it and prayed that he might die. "I have had enough, Lord," he said. "Take my life; I am no better than my ancestors." Then he lay down under the bush and fell asleep.

Elijah had just celebrated a tremendous victory, but here we find him fearful for his life. Why? He was exhausted. He had put everything into doing what God asked him to do. He was vulnerable, exhausted, depressed, and burnt out.

We, too, can expect to be vulnerable after spiritual victories, but don't let it quench the fire of your heart. Instead let the Lord's Spirit minister to you through His Word, His people, and the resources He provides to encourage your heart and feed your soul.

A little rest strengthens us for the road ahead. We read in 1 Kings 19:5–8:

All at once an angel touched him and said, "Get up and eat." He looked around, and there by his head was some bread baked over hot coals, and a jar of water. He ate and drank and then lay down again.

The angel of the Lord came back a second time and touched him and said, "Get up and eat, for the journey is too much for you." So he got up and ate and drank. Strengthened by that food, he traveled forty days and forty nights until he reached Horeb, the mountain of God.

We, too, grow weary in doing well—meeting demands, ministering to people, advising, counselling, listening, and serving. It can all take its toll. Sometimes all we need after a time of intense ministry is a little sleep and nutrition. Allow God to provide that for you.

Honesty is the best policy. The story continues in 1 Kings 19:9–10, which says,

And the word of the Lord came to him: "What are you doing here, Elijah?"

He replied, "I have been very zealous for the Lord God Almighty. The Israelites have rejected your covenant, torn down your altars, and put your prophets to death with the sword. I am the only one left, and now they are trying to kill me too."

Elijah knew that he could be honest with the Lord, and his honesty allowed the Lord to speak back into His life.

The Lord knows what we're thinking even before a word escapes our mouths (Psalm 139:4). He understands what we can't quite put into words and intercedes for us at those times through wordless groans (Romans 8:26). Therefore, we need not be afraid to tell the Lord exactly how we're feeling. When we admit our limited resources and put them into the Lord's hands, He refuels us so we can carry on in His strength.

As Romans 12:11 tells us, *"Never be lacking in zeal, but keep your spiritual fervor, serving the Lord."*

Standing in the Lord's presence gives us a fresh vision. Next, we read in 1 Kings 19:11, *"The Lord said, 'Go out and stand on the mountain in the presence of the Lord, for the Lord is about to pass by.'"* When we're tired, our perspective is skewed. The Lord invites us into His presence so we can experience His power and see things from His perspective. In His presence, we can find all the renewal we need.

The Lord empowers us by His Holy Spirit. He strengthens us with His Word. He answers when we call out to Him in earnest prayer. He restores and assures us as we remain still in His presence. When we are still, we will know that He is God (Psalm 46:10).

Isaiah 30:15 tells us, *"This is what the Sovereign Lord, the Holy One of Israel, says: 'In repentance and rest is your salvation, in quietness and trust is your strength…'"* Often it's once He refreshes us that He gives us further instruction to continue to serve Him with a new vision for His work.

Knowing when to pass the baton gives opportunity to others. The story goes on:

> *The Lord said to him, "Go back the way you came, and go to the Desert of Damascus. When you get there, anoint Hazael king over Aram. Also, anoint Jehu son of Nimshi king over Israel, and anoint Elisha son of Shaphat from Abel Meholah to succeed you as prophet.*
>
> —1 Kings 19:15–16

Because Elijah was in tune with the voice of the Lord, he was able to receive further instruction. He was able to discern when his responsibility would be done and his mission accomplished.

Due to his humble sensitivity to the Spirit of God, he also knew when to pass the mantle of leadership. He was given the opportunity to bring Elisha under his wing and give him the training he needed through his godly example. Not doing so would have deprived Elisha of fulfilling his own calling.

As a result of Elijah's wise delegation, Elisha went on to do even greater things than Elijah for the work of God's kingdom.

Even as we actively serve the Lord, it's not a bad idea to pray concerning who we can pass the baton to. That's not only a way to prevent burnout, that's discipleship, Jesus-style.

Chapter Five

FINDING JOY IN THE JOURNEY WHEN *Transitions* ARE TOUGH

Don't get too comfortable as we explore this particular territory of my heart; it's always in transition. Therefore, we'll be quickly passing through. As we do, you'll want to take note of a few things I've gathered along the way.

If your journey is anything like mine, you've got some changes ahead. As the dust settles, you'll wonder if you'll fit in. Will you be able to relate to those you've been called to minister to? Will you be accepted? Will you be understood?

You'll have to recognize so many new faces and be required to memorize so many names. You'll be expected to get to know so many people by heart. You'll have to somehow keep track of them, lead them, and hope they follow you. It all goes with the territory.

Living Things Grow

Our house backed onto a cemetery and I'd already picked out my burial plot. This was the only place I'd ever known as a ministry wife. I was loved, safe, and secure. This is where we'd live and serve until the Lord called us home.

Or not.

We'd always wondered how we would know it was time to leave one church for another. If and when that time did come, I wanted my husband and me to be the first to know. I dreaded the thought of overstaying our welcome and being forced to walk the gangplank.

The children of Israel always knew when it was time to pack up their tents: *"Whether the cloud stayed over the tabernacle for two days or a month or a year, the Israelites would remain in camp and not set out; but when it lifted, they would set out"* (Numbers 9:22). God gave the Israelites a cloud by day and fire by night as their guide.

I can't say that we saw a cloud or a fire, but I was thankful we'd pitched our tents close to the sanctuary of the Lord so we'd know when it was time to pack up and move.

Over time we'd learn that it usually began as a stirring in either my heart or my husband's. The winds would blow subtly, rustling in our minds and stirring our souls. The sand would shift beneath our feet. Relationships would seem off-kilter. Conversations in the church foyer would leave us feeling as though we were on the outside looking in. It would seem like the train we were on was taking another track.

I should have seen the change coming as the leaves began turning colour. But why at that moment when the church was bursting at the seams? We had just completed a building program and were ready and raring to go. It seemed like the timing couldn't be worse.

I knew my tendency to make myself comfortable and settle into the familiar. It's not that God didn't want me to be uncomfortable, but He didn't want my comfort to turn into complacency or for me to take comfort in things and places and people outside of Him.

My husband had developed a vision statement for our first church ministry: "Living things grow. Growing things change. And there is no growth without change." This statement impacted that church and influenced our entire approach to ministry from then on.

However, it didn't make change any easier.

Change is good for us, they say. A change is as good as a rest, they suggest. I agree. I love change—as long as it doesn't affect me! It's for certain that living things grow and growing things change. I just didn't expect the growth that came with those changes to produce so many growing pains.

Accept change as a part of healthy growth. It may seem odd that our unchanging God is a God of change. However, when you consider that His ultimate purpose is to transform us into His image (Romans 8:29), well… that changes everything! The Lord uses change around us to produce change within us. It's all part of the growing process. Think about the changes you're experiencing or have experienced. What makes the process so painful? How has the Lord used change to produce growth in you? How have you known when it's time to make a transition? Often He confirms His will through others, through circumstances, and through His Word. When have you experienced one or all the above? How have you recognized His voice? Remember what we read in John 10:3–4: *"He calls his own sheep by name and leads them out. When he has brought out all his own, he goes on ahead of them, and his sheep follow him because they know his voice."*

Sad, Glad, Mad, and Bad

Having never transitioned before, we opted to seek the counsel of a wiser couple who had more ministry experience. We wanted to use wisdom and be careful about whom we confided in since we were still prayerfully working through what we sensed the Lord laying on our hearts. We certainly didn't want to stir anything up in people's minds prematurely and unnecessarily.

We mainly needed someone who could also help us discern the Lord's leading and whether we were hearing Him right.

The couple we found seemed to be exactly what we needed. Not only did they know us personally, but they had preceded us in the church we ministered in and knew some of the players involved. Additionally, this pastor was a mentor to my husband, a wise man of God, and someone whose opinion we respected.

He and his wife were helpful, insightful, and supportive. They listened to our hearts and were careful not to feed us speculation that didn't apply to our unique situation. They recognized that each person's experience is different. No two journeys are the same.

They offered a few words of counsel, including to listen very carefully to what people said about us as we said our goodbyes. The words people said about us would confirm our calling and affirm us in our gifting, and we'd apparently need all the encouragement and affirmation we could get.

Another mentor friend offered a word of caution: "If you resign, you can count on four types of responses. Some will be sad. Some will be glad. Some will be mad. And some will be bad."

And he was right!

In each of our transitions, people wanted to know why we were leaving and what had prompted us to go. Was there something wrong? There were always those who begged us to reconsider. Some took it personally. Others tried hard to understand. Still others questioned our motives. How did we know it was God leading us on?

How do you explain the unexplainable? It's like declaring that you're building an Ark to people who haven't experienced rain. All we knew was that God's plan, ways, and timing are always perfect. We had to trust His heart and not lean on our own understanding. As we acknowledged Him, He'd direct our path (Proverbs 3:5–6).

Survival Tip

> **Seek advice from those who have gone before you.** According to Proverbs 11:14, *"For lack of guidance a nation falls, but victory is won through many advisors."* Who have you sought out for advice during times of transition? Why? What kind of advice have you received from others who have gone before you? What advice would you give someone following after you? When we've ministered in one place, especially for an extended time, we can expect people to react when we feel it's time to move on to something new. We must allow for a grieving period, and it can be manifest in different ways. How have people responded or reacted to you during times of transition? How have you been encouraged by those who understand your call to a new post?

Firmly Planted in Mid-Air

We gave our resignation and sold our house, but we had no idea where we were going. This became a trend for us. Nonetheless, the Lord gave us clear indicators, both through His Word and happenings in our ministry, to help navigate the stirrings and restlessness in our hearts.

The last days spent in any church are always exhausting days.

On one of those days, I arrived home from my grocery shopping and had barely dropped my bags on the countertop when I noticed my husband on the phone, listening to a voice on the other end. He excitedly gestured for me to get on the other phone and listen in.

"You're going for an all-expenses-paid trip to the Holy Land," said the person on the other end.

What kind of phone prank was this?

But it was no joke! Before we knew it, we were booking flights and packing suitcases to head to Israel.

For two whole weeks, we ran where Jesus walked. We spent precious time in the Garden of the Tomb, where it's believed Jesus was buried. We sat in the designated area, straining to hear our tour guide through the noise and honks of horns in the congested bus terminal beneath us, taking note that, much like in Jesus's day, life went on while He hung on the cross.

I wept on the Mount of Olives while sitting in the groves of the Garden of Gethsemane. I felt a sliver of the anguish and loneliness Jesus must have felt that night before His betrayal and death. I sang at the well where it's believed Mary, the mother of Jesus, went when the angel of the Lord appeared to her and disclosed His plan and the significant part she'd play.

Part of our tour also landed us on a boat in the middle of the Sea of Galilee. Encircled by the surrounding hillside, it occurred to me that this was a full-blown representation of my life. We were caught between two ministries, torn between two church families, firmly planted in mid-air.

Or perhaps more appropriately, we were floating in the middle of the sea. At any moment we could be capsized if the wind stirred up.

There, being tossed to and fro, I learned the value of holding on to the Anchor of my soul.

Survival Tip

> **Trust God in the "in-between."** God doesn't lead His children along only to leave them stranded. There are things to learn in the process of time, and much of life is lived "in the meantime." What are some of the lessons you've learned during your in-between times? What areas of your life and ministry have you explored during times of transition? Why not take some time to consider some of those lessons right now? You may need them for the next time you find yourself caught in between. As we trust in His perfect timing and wait upon His leading, *"Let us hold unswervingly to the hope we profess, for he who promised is faithful"* (Hebrews 10:23).

Happiness Is...

"Are you happy in your new church?" a man asked me in the church foyer.

We had been called back to a former church to perform a wedding. No doubt my reply wasn't what he had expected.

"Happy?" I asked. The first few months in our new place of ministry had been a nightmare. I mustered enough courage and went on. "It's been the most challenging time in my entire life. However, if being in the centre of God's will is happy, then I'm ecstatic!"

You see, I had already learned that being in the centre of God's will isn't necessarily a happy place. But it's the right place.

"You'll be blessed for your obedience," many told us. "God will honour you for your decision to follow Him."

Blessing? Honour? Neither of these words is one I would have used for our current circumstances.

Thankfully, good friends of ours had shared from their own experience an invaluable secret to obedience success. They suggested we keep a record of all of the ways we saw God working.

In 1 Samuel 7:12, this is called Ebenezer: *"Then Samuel took a stone and set it up between Mizpah and Shen. He named it Ebenezer, saying, 'Thus far the Lord has helped us.'"*

The reason our friends recommended this strategic recordkeeping is that they knew we would eventually question whether we'd made the right decision. If things went south, we would still be able to navigate according to our True North and thus be assured that we were right where He wanted us, in the very centre of His divine will—even if it wasn't a happy place.

They were right, and here we were. We had landed in what felt like a warzone in the middle of Satan's playground. And we had every right to question our move. Things were not as they seemed and it seemed as though we had heard God wrong.

But we were wrong.

As it turned out, the lessons we learned during this period became markers we revisited every time we made a transition or wondered what we were doing. We had to trust the process. We learned the value of seeking God's guidance through Scripture. We learned to trust in each other's sense of God's leading, making sure to openly discuss our hearts' wrestling and stirrings.

I learned that while living in the centre of God's will may not be a happy place, I wouldn't want to be anywhere else.

Survival Tip

> **Establish spiritual markers.** In the Bible, God's people set up spiritual markers to commemorate and remember points in time when God appeared. Abraham built several altars and returned to them. In 1 Samuel 7:12, the term Ebenezer is used, which refers to a time when God helps. The children of Israel were encouraged not to forget (Deuteronomy 8). Joshua gathered stones (Joshua 4:9). Take some time to record your ministry journey. List some of your greatest joys and challenges amid transitions. Record the times when the Lord showed up in a significant way to guide you on your journey.

Lord, What About Her?

This was *my* church, *my* community, *my* life. I knew the Lord was calling us to a new place of ministry, but I liked *this* one. I was comfortable and happy here. I had invested much here. I had loved much here. And I felt I still had much to give.

Regardless of how I felt, the Lord had made it clear that it was time to move on.

In contrast, *she* hadn't been here long enough to call it hers, and *she* didn't even seem to desire to. *She* had nothing but bad things to say about the people I loved. So why did *I* have to leave and *she* get to stay?

I took my complaint to the Lord and arm-wrestled Him over it. As always, He let me vent it all—good, bad, and ugly.

"Lord, what about *her*?" I quipped.

The ensuing conversation was much like one I'd read before:

When Peter saw him, he asked, "Lord, what about him?"

Jesus answered, "If I want him to remain alive until I return, what is that to you? You must follow me."

—John 21:21–22

With a gentle chiding, He drew me close to His heart. And true to form, He answered a question with a question: "What *about* her? Don't you think I've got *her* covered? Don't you think I have a bigger picture at work that isn't just about *you*? What does it matter to you what I do with *her*? *You* follow me."

I guess He had a point there. I needed to fix my eyes on Him and mind my *own* business so He could accomplish His perfect will—for *both* of us.

Survival Tip

> **Fix your eyes on Jesus.** It's challenging enough to leave a ministry or people you've grown to love, much less when you get distracted by others who get to stay and claim the territory that used to be yours. That's why it's important to believe in God's greater plan. As Isaiah 55:9 tells us, *"As the heavens are higher than the earth, so are my ways higher than your ways and my thoughts than your thoughts."* Think of a time when you didn't want to leave yet God was calling you to go. How did you process your emotions and thoughts?

A Birthday Wish from Heaven

I was having a nasty-attitude day. It was my birthday. But that didn't matter. I was in the middle of packing up my house, one more time, and my attitude reeked to high heaven. I just wasn't aware of how heaven would respond—until it did.

As in every move we'd made, it was time to begin the process of downsizing, decluttering, and dumping… weeding through and ridding myself of all the non-essentials. This time around, I also decided to go through all the cards I'd collected through the years. I had an entire hope chest full of them! Each card held a different sentiment, representing a special relationship and significant time on my ministry journey.

I sat on the floor, moping. On one side I had a big green garbage bag ready to catch all the memories my hope chest contained. On the other side sat a big box of Kleenex, ready to collect all my tears. It's ironic how hopeless I felt as my hope chest was emptied of its contents. Was there still hope for me?

I decided to give all these cards one final glance. I would treasure the memories one last time before tossing them in the open bag. Then I determined to bring them immediately to the curb so I wouldn't be tempted to retrieve them.

As I sorted through the pile, one card caught my eye. It somehow stood out from the rest. For whatever reason, I chose to pause, lean back against the couch, and read it.

It just so happened to be a birthday card.

"Happy birthday to me," I sarcastically wished myself.

The card had a large picture of Garfield on it, grinning from one cat-ear to the other. He sported a pair of metallic shades. The card said "Lookin' Good."

If the front of the card had caught my attention, the inscription on the inside caught me completely off-guard. It was from my son, Ben, who had passed away years earlier. It was the only card I could remember ever having received from him.

He'd given it to me after I'd had a car accident and the inscription was in his writing. Using his own uniquely created language, using nicknames he'd given me, it read,

> Hava Dzumas (Dzum, Dzump, mom etc.) Happy Hava B-Day… As the card says 'Lookin' Good'. So it's true, your back situation isn't lookin' good but we're going to focus on happy stuff not depressing. So your situation isn't lookin' good but you are. So as Garfield once said … … .. Happy Birthday, Dzu.

At a time when I needed it most, God used Ben's words. Not only did he wish me a happy birthday from heaven but he helped me adjust my earthly attitude. There, in my heap of cards and a Kleenex full of my tears, a Bible verse came to life: *"And by faith [he] still speaks, even though he is dead"* (Hebrews 11:4).

Survival Tip

> **Grieve your losses.** To move is to experience loss and grief. Therefore, allow yourself the necessary time to grieve those things and people you have left behind. Be honest about the things you don't like about your transition. Then ask God to help you accept the things you cannot change. Discuss the wrestling of your heart with someone who knows you well and with whom you can entrust your thoughts and feelings as you adjust to your new environment and ministry. Grieving the things you've lost, or left behind, will allow you to make room for all that God has waiting for you to embrace.

The Perpetual Newbie

I could pick them out blindfolded. It was like I had an inbred newbie-detector that kicked into high gear in every church foyer I walked through. I didn't even have to scout them out. I'd welcome them as they walked in, asking a series of get-to-know-you questions. I put them at ease by openly admitting my poor memory at recalling names, taking it upon myself to show them around, pointing them in the direction of restrooms, the nursery, and children's program areas.

I suppose it shouldn't have surprised me. I had always been the student recruited to welcome new kids into the classroom, share my textbooks until theirs were ordered, and introduce them to other students.

It's not hard to find the newbies in a crowd. They're typically the ones standing alone or wandering aimlessly. My heart always went out to them, likely because I knew the feeling.

It can be wearisome to be the one expected to initiate relationships and spearhead ministries. It was unnerving to make my way as the perpetual newbie into circles of lifelong friends. It's hard not knowing the jargon, not remembering names, not knowing quite what's being talked about. All the while, you never know how much you'll have to invest until you have to start all over again with a whole new group of people.

Let's just say, I've long since stopped asking, "Are you visiting with us today?"

You have to be bold, unafraid, and determined to take the initiative. Perhaps that's what really spurred my husband and me on to start up a newcomers group in every church we pastored. It gave us such a sense of belonging as we intentionally sought to create an environment where others could feel they belonged. Who doesn't need that?

Survival Tip

Take the initiative. Don't wait for life to happen. Make it happen. If not for you, do it for someone else. Try to put yourself in a new person's shoes. Take the initiative. Don't be afraid to approach people you don't know. Find out a bit about them. Ask engaging questions that won't be too imposing. For instance, "Are you new to the area? Do you know anyone else here? How did you find us? Would you like me to show you around?" If they're interested, give a guided tour. Introduce them to a few people. Start a newcomers ministry at your church. Colossians 4:5 tells us, *"Be wise in the way you act toward outsiders; make the most of every opportunity."* What has your experience as a newbie been like? List some of the ways in which you could use your own experience to welcome someone new.

Land Mines

Here I was, finding my place—again. It was orientation all over. I bravely walked toward the front pew of our new church where a woman sat laughing, chatting, and carrying on with a few others who were rehearsing a skit for the children's program. I'd heard she headed up the program.

With my home daycare upbringing and extensive training in children's ministry, it only made sense that offering to volunteer in this program was the place to start. It would allow me to meet and interact with some of our new parishioners in a familiar and comfortable role.

So I humbly approached this woman, presenting myself as personably and pleasant as I could.

I smiled. "Hi! I'm Lisa."

"Yes. I know."

"I thought I'd let you know that if you're looking for workers, I'm willing to volunteer to lead the children's worship."

I was naively unaware that my willingness to help would be anything but welcomed. I knew just how difficult it typically was to recruit volunteers.

As if to brush a mosquito off her face, she told me that *she* already had that area covered. *She* led the children's worship and had been in charge of it for several years.

It quickly became apparent that I was a threat to her sense of control and well-being.

I'd never experienced the likes of it. So I quickly retreated. The last thing I needed to be was a threat. I'd find another place to serve.

It's always tricky making yourself at home—on someone else's turf.

Survival Tip _____

> **Find your place.** It's important to know where you fit into a congregation of God's people. You're as much a part of the body as anyone. Therefore, you can be assured that there's a place for you. It's simply a matter of finding it. You'll know in a hurry if you're stepping on someone else's territory, but that doesn't mean you should throw in the towel. Rather, prayerfully consider another area of ministry where you can serve the Lord with gladness. Sometimes it's the Lord's way of helping us move beyond our comfort zone. Other times we're being used to move someone out of theirs. Either way, we need to be open to explore and find the place where God wants us. Can you think of a time when you trespassed on someone else's ministry? How did that situation unfold? What did you learn from the experience? How might you approach it differently going forward? As Colossians 3:12, 14–15 reminds us, "*Therefore, as God's chosen people, holy and dearly loved, clothe yourselves with compassion, kindness, humility, gentleness and patience… And over all these virtues put on love, which binds them all together in perfect unity. Let the peace of Christ rule in your hearts, since as members of one body you were called to peace.*"

A Cry for Help

One morning, I was reading and wrestling about yet another move. I turned my Bible open to Acts 16 and read about Paul's vision from Macedonia of a man calling for help (Acts 16:9–10). The Lord impressed upon my heart that there was some church out there that was calling for our help. We were to discern which church it was and leave immediately to help them.

I remember sitting beside my husband, across the table from one particular search committee, and sharing this passage from Acts with them. Then I looked up and stared each person in the face and asked, "Is it you?"

They were convinced it was. But something, or Someone, told us they were not. And we were determined to find where we were supposed to go.

Here we now sat in front of yet another search committee. I shared the same passage of scripture with them, and this time there was no denying that it was their cry for help. I heard it loud and clear: *"It seemed good to the Holy Spirit and to us…"* (Acts 15:28)

Interestingly, once we'd settled into our new place of ministry, rarely a Sunday went by without someone saying, "Thanks for responding to our cry for help. The Lord knew we needed you here." I was glad I had paid attention to my Good Shepherd's voice.

Survival Tip

> **Pay attention to the Lord's prompting.** When we're making transitions, it's important that we not only sense a push but a pull. It's not good enough to want to leave some place because you're having a bad hair day or sensing God moving you *from* somewhere. It's equally important to sense His calling you *to* someplace else. Make a list of reasons you believe it's time to make a transition. Write a list of questions to ask a search committee. You're not the only one being interviewed! Why not make your transition a scriptural journey? Note any significant scripture as it speaks to you. What scripture(s) has the Lord used to direct your path? Let God's Word guide you. God's Word is a lamp to our feet and a light to our path (Psalm 119:105).

Relax and Release

"Don't you trust me?" the Lord asked. The words echoed in the chambers of my heart. It wasn't the first time I had heard Him ask.

"Of course, I trust You!" my heart retorted.

And I had. I'd trusted Him as my Saviour at the altar when I was fifteen. I'd trusted Him when He had redirected my path from community college to Bible college. I had trusted Him to provide when I ran out of finances in my final semester. I had trusted Him as I became a pastor's wife. I had trusted Him in ministry when I felt out of my comfort. I had trusted Him in every transition we'd made, not knowing where exactly He was leading me and my family.

As recently as months before, I had responded to an altar call. There, I had lain prostrate before the Lord, pouring my heart to Him, giving my all to Him as if for the first time. This is how I had learned to trust Him throughout my life—one altar at a time.

"What more do I need to entrust to You?" I asked. "I've given You everything. I've given You my life. I've given You my ministry. I've given You my marriage and I've given You my children!"

"Really?"

"Well yes, Lord! I completely gave You my son Ben just after his nineteenth birthday. He's in Your presence and under Your care now, until I see him again in heaven. I've given You my daughter Natalie, miles and miles away in another part of the country. I've given You my youngest son, Jacob, so he can serve You in full-time ministry wherever you need and lead him. And then there's my youngest daughter, Erin…"

"Yes?" He implored, sensing my apprehension.

"Lord, my youngest daughter is my only hope of having one of my children living close to me. You wouldn't ask me to give her up, too. Would you?"

"Why not? Don't you trust me?"

There were those words again. In all honesty, I wasn't sure if I did. While I wanted to trust Him, I wasn't sure I could. That was a hard confession to make. It was especially hard because His faithfulness had been proven to me many times over throughout my life. Regardless, trusting again didn't come easily. It never does. It often comes at a price. And I just wasn't sure I was ready to pay that price again.

There have been times in my life when all the Lord required of me was my willingness to surrender. However, I knew in my heart that this likely wasn't one of those times. I knew that full-out surrender was the only way to alleviate the pain I was experiencing.

After days of wrestling through tears and heaving sobs, I finally put my heart into the hands of the One who had created it. Holding my heart in His hands, He assured me with His Word: *"And everyone who has left houses or brothers or sisters or father or mother or children or lands, for my name's sake, will receive a hundredfold and will inherit eternal life"* (Matthew 19:29, ESV). He reminded me that His intentions are always good, that He always has a plan and hope and a future for those whose hope is in Him (Jeremiah 29:11).

He wasn't out to get me or take something from me, like I'm prone to think with my limited faith and earthly perspective. I just needed to trust and entrust— one more time.

Survival Tip ――――――――――――――――――――――――

Let go and let God. It's hard to embrace what God is giving you when you're holding on too tightly to something else. God is a God of fresh starts and new beginnings and new lessons to be learned. What are some of the things you're holding onto that prevent you from taking hold of all that God has waiting for you? What's making it so hard for you to let go? Make a list of these things you're holding dear. Then, one by one, entrust them to God in prayer. Philippians 3:13 says, *"Brothers and sisters, I do not consider myself yet to have taken hold of it. But one thing I do: Forgetting what is behind and straining toward what is ahead…"*

Bloom Where You're Planted

"Bloom where you're planted." I learned the importance of this principle in our first church pastorate, and it came through the testimony of a young girl.

I distinctly remember the impression the Lord left on my heart through her testimony after a year-long excursion overseas as a part of her education. She had shared with our congregation that, sadly, she'd spent the first half of her year homesick, complaining, moping, and missing everyone and everything from back home. However, halfway through the year, the Lord had gotten a hold of her heart and she'd realized that if she didn't gather herself and make the best of the rest of her time, she'd completely miss out on this once in a lifetime experience.

At that time, my husband and I were seeking God's will and trying to discern whether it was time to leave our first place of ministry to explore another part of God's vineyard. It was as exciting as it was petrifying! Thankfully, I duly noted the words of my young friend. I knew that wherever the Lord led us, I'd better make the best of it if I wanted to experience all He had in store for me.

When I enter new territory, my tendency is to cling to the past. Everything in me wants to fall back into old patterns, crave the familiar and everything that my sense of security and well-being relies upon, much like the children of Israel as they considered the daunting Promised Land ahead of them. Although they were told that it was flowing with milk and honey, all they could see were the giants in the land. Instead of taking the risk toward new and different, fear kept them captive, craving those good old leaks and onions. Did they realize they were yearning to go back to slavery?

Several years and a few more ministry moves later, I found myself in the same place, listening to the wise advice of that young teenager to bloom wherever I'm planted.

Providentially, our new community just so happened to be called Blossom Park.

Therefore, I made it my prayer to be a pleasing aroma of Christ (2 Corinthians 2:15). To be identified by the fruit of the Spirit I bore (Galatians 2:20). To produce fruit that will last into eternity (John 15:1–20). To extend the hope of new life that comes with spring in a world that lives in hopeless and perpetual winter. To make the most of every opportunity (Colossians 4:5).

The only way to ensure all of that happened was to choose to bloom and grow in His vineyard, wherever He planted, or transplanted, me.

Survival Tip

> **Make yourself at home.** God leads us to new places in our lives to teach us things about ourselves and new qualities about Him. Don't be afraid to claim your new territory and make yourself at home. Treat your new place as if it was permanent. Who knows? It might be. So live in it as if it was your own. Walk and pray through your new neighbourhood and community. Ask the Lord to open doors of opportunity right outside your front door. Join a group, a Bible study, a walking club, etc. Host a party, a neighbourhood barbecue, a community garage sale, or an open house. Instead of turning to an old friend, seek out a new one. As Isaiah 43:19 says, *"See, I am doing a new thing! Now it springs up; do you not perceive it?"* What is something new you could attempt, even if you've been where you are for a while?

Things Have Changed

I'll never forget one morning a few months into our marriage. I woke up and entered the living area of our humble two-bedroom apartment, furnished with our grandparents' hand-me-downs.

There, sitting at our recycled kitchen table, I found my husband, staring into his coffee cup.

"Is something wrong?" I asked.

"Things have changed" was his sullen reply.

They most certainly had. The reality was sinking in for both of us. We weren't just a newlywed couple responsible for getting to know one another. Rather, we were a ministry couple already deeply invested and overwhelmed with responsibilities to an entire church family.

With no family around and ground root relationships at the church, our only option was to get to know each other. We had to cling to each other. We had to learn to love, support, and most importantly trust each other and the One who had led us to this point in our journey.

That was then, and this was now—several moves, four children, several grandchildren, and as many pastorates later. We had a much better understanding of what change really looked like. We'd well learned that ministry transitions affect every single aspect of our lives. It's not merely an address change.

Throughout the years, we've often looked back and reflected on our early ministry and marriage. We talk about the days of hard work, overexertion, mental exhaustion, and emotional imbalance. It all mingled with a deep sense of fulfillment and purpose, days filled with memories and relationships and heartache.

We take time to consider all that the Lord has faithfully brought us through. We remember all the sights we've seen, all the places we've been, all the lives we've invested in, and all the people we've met on an ever-changing landscape.

While God calls some to stay put, He called us to venture out. And most of the time, I'm glad He has. Otherwise we would have missed out on a wealth of valuable lessons, a treasury of wonderful people, an abundance of blessings, and a heart full of impressionable life experiences.

There's no question that transitions are unsettling. Transitions aren't simply a change; they are life-changing.

Yes, things certainly had changed. But looking back now, change hasn't been all that bad.

Survival Tip _____

> **Enjoy the changing scenery.** God's plan is full of twists and turns. While the scenery changes, our God is unchanging. He is faithful. He is good and everything He does is good—even if it doesn't feel comfortable. Here's the thing: He is more concerned with our character than our comfort. He's more interested in our holiness than our happiness. That said, He wants us to enjoy all He's given us to enjoy with all the variety He provides for our enjoyment. How have you given evidence to God's unfolding will in your life? How does this give you hope for the future? How can you determine to live out your today, right where you're planted?

We are in a constant state of transition. So when you think of it, a change is simply a time of transition between two transitions. Life on this earth is just that—a transition. We're all pilgrims searching for a place where we can settle. We're looking for a place that will satisfy the longing of our souls, much like those we read about in Hebrews 11:13–16.

To me, that place is free from burdens, criticism, expectations, sin, shame, pain, sickness, sadness, depression, misunderstandings, miscommunications, harm, responsibility, brokenness, death, danger, tears, and heartache. It's a place free from making any more moves or transitions.

It sounds like heaven to me!

Meanwhile we groan, longing to be clothed instead with our heavenly dwelling, because when we are clothed, we will not be found naked. For while we are in this tent, we groan and are burdened, because we do not wish to be unclothed but to be clothed instead with our heavenly dwelling, so that what is mortal may be swallowed up by life.

—2 Corinthians 5:2–4

Change is what life on this earth is all about, until we make our final transition to our heavenly home. On that day, we'll be like Him, for we shall see Him as He is (1 John 3:2). In the meantime, we must build our foundation on the One who is sure. Jesus Christ is the same yesterday, today, and forever (Hebrews 13:8).

Straight from the Father's Heart

Lord, you have been our dwelling place throughout all generations.
—Psalm 90:1

Biblical Mentor
Abraham (Genesis 12–25)

By faith Abraham, when called to go to a place he would later receive as his inheritance, obeyed and went, even though he did not know where he was going. By faith he made his home in the promised land like a stranger in a foreign country; he lived in tents, as did Isaac and Jacob, who were heirs with him of the same promise. For he was looking forward to the city with foundations, whose architect and builder is God.

—Hebrews 11:8–10

When Abraham left his country, his people, and his father's household to go to a land the Lord would show him, I'm not sure he had any idea what he was in for. Regardless, in obedience to the Lord's call on his life and in hopes of the promise to come, He set out. What an incredible journey of faith he and the Lord took together.

Here are a few principles we can learn from him, especially where navigating transitions is concerned.

There is a blessing that comes with obedience. We read in Genesis 12:1, *"The Lord had said to Abram, 'Go from your country, your people and your father's household to the land I will show you.'"* Like Abraham, we, too, must be willing to pack up all our earthly belongings, gather those we love, and leave the familiar and comfortable to pursue God's plan and purpose for our life. He blesses us for our obedience, even when it doesn't always look the way we thought it might.

When you build an altar, God will meet you there. The story goes on to say,

The Lord appeared to Abram and said, "To your offspring I will give this land." So he built an altar there to the Lord, who had appeared to him.

From there he went on toward the hills east of Bethel and pitched his tent, with Bethel on the west and Ai on the east. There he built an altar to the Lord and called on the name of the Lord.

—Genesis 12:7–8

Several times on his journey of faith, Abraham built an altar where he met God—sometimes to discuss matters of the heart, other times to seek His direction and next steps, and often to be reminded of all He'd promised. When was the last time you met God at the altar?

You can trust God's plan, even when it doesn't make sense. God's promise to Abraham to make him into a great nation was beyond his wildest imagination. His wife was infertile and it didn't even make sense. That presented a problem. The next thing he and his wife did was devise their own plan to help God along.

The good news is that God worked it all together for their good, because they loved Him and knew they were called according to His purpose (Romans 8:28). Through it all, they learned to trust Him. And we need to, too, even when it doesn't make sense.

Anticipate a test when you choose to follow the Lord. Inevitably after a step of obedience, there is a test—and the first test Abraham faced was a famine in the land. It was so severe, in fact, that he had to make a detour.

While Abraham didn't handle these tests perfectly, He grew in His faith as a result of them. Just because we pass one test doesn't mean there won't be others. It's all part of the growing process.

Abraham's faith was tested many times on his journey. He faced many temptations and opportunities to walk away from the promise God had made to him. He faced deadly detours such as disappointment, deception, dispute, disillusionment, and even points of despair. And with each one, he continued to believe that God would remain faithful to His promise (Hebrews 11:8–12). We must stay the course, trusting the Lord's leading and fixing our eyes on Him (Hebrews 12:2) so we don't get distracted and lose our way.

Standing on God's promises gives you a sure foundation. Abraham was put to the ultimate test when the Lord asked him to offer his son Isaac as a sacrifice. And then He blessed him as a result of his obedience. He learned that obeying is better than sacrifice.

From Abraham, we can learn that we need to obey God's requests, even when we don't understand His reasons. His plan is greater, and it's always for our good.

> *Now faith is confidence in what we hope for and assurance about what we do not see…*
>
> *By faith Abraham, when God tested him, offered Isaac as a sacrifice. He who had embraced the promises was about to sacrifice his one and only son, even though God had said to him, "It is through Isaac that your offspring will be reckoned." Abraham reasoned that God could even raise the dead, and so in a manner of speaking he did receive Isaac back from death.*
>
> —Hebrews 11:1, 17–19

Chapter Six

MOVING THROUGH *Hurt* TO BECOME A WOUNDED HEALER

PLEASE, BE CAREFUL AS YOU TREAD THROUGH THIS PIECE OF MY HEART. THERE is brokenness here. Beneath your feet, you'll find fragments of friendships, broken promises, shards of betrayed confidences, and shattered trust. Don't trip over the cracks and crevices. These are evidence of the scars I bear, and while they've healed they still bear pain from the wounds inflicted.

Thankfully, through the thorough examination of the Great Physician, I've been given a prescription for life (Deuteronomy 30:19–20). I've received the kind of healing and comfort that can only come from the Comforter (2 Corinthians 1:2–4). By the very wounds of my Saviour (Isaiah 53:3), I've learned how to become a wounded healer.

Take my hand and let me lead you to the Healer Himself, for *"the Lord is close to the brokenhearted and saves those who are crushed in spirit"* (Psalm 34:18).

The Unintentional Interim

Deception, unresolved conflict, leadership division, mistrust, and unconfronted sin were all laid out on the welcome mat upon our arrival at our new church. We blindly walked into it, no one having thought to inform us.

No one ever expects to be blindsided. I guess that's why they're called blindsides.

My husband, referred to as Uriah in those days, was put onto the frontlines while his leadership team retreated. He was pushed onto a limb that got cut off behind him, leaving him hung out to dry.

Meetings and beatings became weekly rituals, not to mention the awkwardness of entering the church building. There were angry stares, group huddles, and hushed conversations as we entered the foyer, silence as we approached.

We bore it all. We confronted it all. We mediated what we needed to. We advised where we were invited. We listened as we were able. We ached more than anyone knew. We did all we knew to do. But it never seemed like enough. We were caught in the line of fire, shot at from both sides.

After our departure from that church, my husband was called "the unintentional interim." We came to learn about people who are professionally trained to serve as conflict resolution specialists. They are called "intentional interims." They walk into situations like the one we were in; the difference is that they do it on purpose.

From that time on, you can bet we were very intentional about the future ministries we walked into.

Survival Tip

> **Ask good questions.** When you go into any meeting with a prospective church or ministry, you're not the only one being interviewed. So go into it with a long list of well-thought-through questions. Questions about expectations and responsibilities (of both the employee and spouse), hot spots (areas of contention or mistrust or conflict, past and present), church culture, openness to counsel and change, church finances, salary, holidays, sabbatical policy, funds for ongoing training, etc. Work with your spouse to create the list. While there's never any guarantee that you won't bump into some kind of surprise along the way, it's vital to do your homework ahead of time to find out all you can about the church you're considering. Make sure there is an allotted time during the interview to ask your questions. Most importantly, pray for the Lord's discernment and clear direction. What questions are you asking?

The Christmas Gift Exchange

She and I got along famously. She was a refreshing change from the church friends who gathered in the church foyer talking about what they were serving for Sunday dinner. The two of us enjoyed a lot of the same interests. Her husband had come to the Lord under my husband's teaching, and that sealed the deal.

She and her husband joined our small group and we enjoyed many engaging discussions. We shared openly about the Word of God and what the Lord was doing in each of our lives.

I trusted her implicitly. My kids felt comfortable with her, too, an added bonus. She made meaningful investments in their lives, like offering to hang out with them so my husband and I could go out on a date. One time she had my daughter over to her place for a girls' day out.

Another time, I invited her over for a Christmas bake-off. She was excited to learn some of my recipes and gain some hands-on experience. It was bedlam with four young kids in the mix, but also a lot of fun.

Or so *I* thought.

After that, I noticed that she hadn't called for a few days, which wasn't normal. I called to check in on her, but no answer. I kept trying over the next week or two. It seemed odd that she wouldn't return my calls.

Then one day she called me from her workplace. It was a weird time of day for her to call, but I welcomed it. I mentioned that I had missed her. She was very curt in her response.

When I asked if she was all right, she erupted. "No, I'm not all right!"

Surprised that I didn't have a clue why, she proceeded to unleash some pent-up frustration. No, let's call it what it was—anger. Outright rage. And all directed toward me.

Her rampage caught me completely off-guard. I didn't understand where all of her anger was rooted. So I asked her to give me insight into what I had done or said that had offended her.

She didn't hesitate to inform me.

After she told me the issue, I quickly recalled the offending conversation. My interpretation of the exchange was quite different than hers. The comment I'd made that had offended her so deeply hadn't even been directed at her. In fact, it had been aimed at me!

Regardless of my good intentions, though, she carried on with her rampage, ripping me apart, up one side and down the other.

This unexpected "gift exchange" happened just before Christmas, and I'll never forget it. It was more of a Pandora's box, and I wasn't sure what on earth I had done to deserve it.

Sadly, my friend and I didn't spend much time together after that. Years later, however, we did have the opportunity to revisit that fateful day. She asked for my forgiveness, feeling that she had paid penance for her false accusations, and I forgave her. But our friendship was never the same. Nor was my ability to trust.

Survival Tip

> **Take a risk.** When we're hurt, our tendency is to shut down and avoid danger at all costs. But that's no way to live. There is no freedom in locking ourselves up in a prison of bitterness and resentment. To love is to risk, and to risk is to be wounded again. There's a lot to be learned about ourselves and others through conflict resolution. But that's Jesus's model. And even so, living that way still comes with the risk of being caught in the line of fire. Jesus warned us, *"I am sending you out like sheep among wolves. Therefore be as shrewd as snakes and as innocent as doves"* (Matthew 10:16). People will betray you, hurt you, take advantage of you, and misunderstand you. Even those you minister with and to. We live in a sin-sick world. Expect to be hurt, but don't stay there. Take the risk to love and serve again. It's worth the risk. When is a time when you didn't take a risk and regretted it? When is a time when you took a risk and were thankful you did?

Confidentiality Corner

The confidentiality corners I'd been forced into started to take effect, putting my mental, emotional, and physical health at stake. Headaches were now deemed "Sunday headaches." I'd come home from church, after sensing the friction and conflict through the airwaves, and pop Tylenol for the rest of the day.

These headaches weren't completely foreign to me. They brought me back to the days of my childhood when my parents were separating. My heart picked up on everything that wasn't being said, resulting in tension headaches. One of my spiritual gifts, I suppose?

Who could I turn to who would lend me an ear, give me a shoulder to cry on, and understand some of my pain and frustration and fear without condemning me? All I needed was someone to simply pray for me.

The church is designed to be a safe place. It's where spiritually hungry, emotionally sick, and relationally wounded people come for spiritual food, physical protection, and emotional healing. It's where the broken body of Christ gathers for encouragement, support, prayer, and mutual love and affection.

Those called to minister are supposed to readily offer help, support, wisdom, and biblical counsel whenever called upon. But where do the pastor and his wife find all of that? Who's the pastor's pastor? Where do he and his wife go when they need godly counsel or support? Who do they confide in about matters too personal to share with those to whom they're ministering? Who do they talk to about matters of the heart? Where is it safe to let their guard down? Who would even understand if they did?

When hurting people unleash their frustrations, those who minister can't be reactive. Instead they need to respond in a godly fashion—graciously. They must find the inner strength and self-control not to fight back, retaliate, or get defensive. When spoken to in anger, frustration, or disrespect, they're required to smile and nod. When they're betrayed, hurt, deceived, or wounded, they must humbly minister to the masses regardless.

Despite what's been hurled at them five minutes before the worship service, they must get it together to graciously, tenderly, and effectively provide biblical truth. Somehow they have to manage everybody else's crises and conflicts and confusion with confidence, competence, and compassion, putting aside their own needs.

It sounds a lot like what Jesus had to contend with. It must hurt to be Him.

Survival Tip

Be quick to forgive, slow to trust, and slower to entrust. Are there times when you've learned or had to apply this principle? Forgiveness is key to any healthy relationship. It is the foundation of our relationship with Christ. However, just because you've forgiven someone doesn't mean you have to trust them again. Sadly, not everyone can be trusted. The person who wronged you may be unsafe. Not entrusting yourself to them again isn't unforgiveness; it's wisdom. Jesus used wisdom in all His encounters, especially with those who didn't believe in Him. In John 2:23–24, we read, *"Jesus would not entrust himself to them, for he knew all people."* When was a time when you either had a hard time forgiving or needed someone else's forgiveness? How did that situation unfold? How have you discerned whether a person could be trusted? Remember the words of Proverbs 4:23: *"Above all else, guard your heart, for everything you do flows from it."*

Oasis

To say it had been an incredibly tough run in ministry would be an understatement. We weren't just burnt out; we had been burnt. And I couldn't imagine having to spend eternity with some of the so-called Christians who had caused us such pain.

It wasn't just our ministry that was suffering. Our marriage was in trouble, too. We were ready to pack it all in … for the glory of God, of course. He could have all of it!

We knew we needed serious help, but we didn't know where to safely find it. Then we discovered a ministry online called *Oasis Retreats*. We couldn't get there fast enough. The only problem was that it was across the country in the mountains of British Columbia. A few arrangements had to be made where childcare was concerned if we were going to attend.

The four-and-a-half-hour flight there was used to talk ourselves out of our need for such a retreat. What were we thinking? But oh well, it was too late now.

When we arrived at the retreat centre, the host came to greet us. "Welcome, David and Lisa. We're so glad you're here!"

"Really?" my cynical self asked.

He offered a hug, which I mustered the grace to return—barely.

Then we were directed to our cabin. There, hanging on the doorknob, was a gift bag. I harumphed to myself and tossed it on the bed. I could scavenge through it later. We were going to be here an entire week, after all.

We gathered as a group of six couples that night and discovered that one of the couples wasn't a pastoral team. They'd, in fact, been hurt by a pastor. I knew it happened. I would've been naive to think it didn't.

Our host couple shared their ministry story. But how could it be? They were telling *our* story. The initial excitement, the burnout, the betrayal, the wounding, and the less than stellar grand finale that led to more hurt and betrayal …

I poked my husband's side with my elbow. I knew he was thinking what I was thinking. Even with my calloused heart, I could feel the familiar, penetrating nudge of the Holy Spirit. My heart hurt from all it contained. It hurt even more from the validation we'd just received through someone else's story.

Once we were all dismissed, I went to our host and asked if I could redeem our hug. That's when the tears I'd held back for years began to flow. The love of my heavenly Father flowed through the gentle hug of this stranger. My tear ducts opened and didn't close again the entire time we were there.

Right at the foothills of the mountains, we had an inverted mountaintop experience. I affectionately called it a pastors and wives rehab. The words of Psalm

121:1–2 resonated in my heart: *"I lift up my eyes to the mountains—where does my help come from? My help comes from the Lord, the Maker of heaven and earth."*

People here got it. We had headed for the hills in the hopes of receiving a doctor's note to get us out of pastoral ministry. Instead we were given a prescription for how to stay in it. We learned to know ourselves and our limitations, how to respond to stress, the necessity of biblical conflict resolution, to seek proper affirmation, and to own our part but not be ashamed of ourselves for what we hadn't done.

For five full days of sessions, counselling, and group sharing, we drank deeply from the well that never ran dry. We had, indeed, found an oasis.

Survival Tip _____

> **Acknowledge your need for healing.** If we're not careful, we can get stuck in our pain, much like the paralytic whom Jesus asked, *"Do you want to get well?"* (John 5:6) You see, unless you recognize your need to be healed, you'll continue to be paralyzed. You can find personal, marital, emotional, and relational healing if you first acknowledge your need and choose to get well. Take advantage of resources like asking a trusted friend to pray for you. Be willing to seek professional counsel. Ultimately, with His help, the Comforter and Healer will guide you through your pain. When is a time when you experienced the Lord's healing? What is an area you're stuck in? Acknowledge it before the Lord, then ask Him to give you strength to move ahead in a healthy way: *"Heal me, Lord, and I will be healed"* (Jeremiah 17:14).

Hurting People Hurt People

Our home was all packed up. To protect and preserve our ministry, our marriage, and our children, we needed to get away from that place.

As I took the hands of my family and gathered them up in our minivan, I looked straight ahead. I didn't want to be rendered a pile of salt when this was all said and done. There was no turning back.

Now we were living out of suitcases in a trailer, parked outside my in-laws' cottage, while most of our earthly belongings were crammed into a storage bin. We felt it was worth the inconvenience, and best for everyone, to allow us a few months to regroup before commencing our next ministry.

Our trailer home wasn't the only place we stayed over the course of our time off. In fact, by the end of the summer we'd slept in fifteen different beds. We performed weddings, did camp ministry, and bought a house, making several long trips back and forth over the miles. You know, the typical events one involves themselves in when on a break from ministry.

As the six of us vagabonds piled out of the vehicle to stay with the in-laws, I remember the look of confusion on their faces.

"Don't mention the C-word," I said to them. "That is, church or Christian. I don't want anything to do with either of them!"

They were pretty gracious to accommodate all six of us, not to mention deal with the likes of my disillusioned self. I felt vulnerable and volatile in my wounded state. Questions ravaged my mind like, "What gives people the right to rip into others?" I'd concluded that Christians don't just shoot their own wounded; they leave them to die. "Christian cannibals" is what I called them. I felt like I was that little gopher in a game of Whack-a-Mole, poking my head up and getting clobbered by a mallet. Was there anywhere safe?

I had been hurt, and if I wasn't careful I knew I could cause a lot of hurt as a result. Hurting people hurt people. And if there's one thing I'd learned, it's that there are a lot of hurting people in this world. Broken, hurting, walking-wounded people—God's people. Me included.

Knowing the effects of my toxic heart on those around me, I decided to do some serious business with the Lord—in solitude. Every Sunday morning, as everyone left for church, I'd grab my Bible, pull out a lawn chair, and plunk it on the front lawn. I turned to the book of Acts to be reminded of the early church and how God had originally intended it to behave. The first words of Acts 28:1 jumped off the page at me: *"Once safely on shore… "* Would I ever feel safe again? Sunday after Sunday, the Lord spoke profoundly into me. As He did, I felt the Great Physician's gentle, steady hands weave His healing thread around my heart to bind up my wounds.

Survival Tip ——————————————————————

Take the time to taste the tears. Whatever kind of feelings you're experiencing, it's important to feel them. Let the tears fall, be they angry tears, frustrated tears, lonely tears, fearful tears, anxious tears, or bitter tears. There's healing in them. The psalmist said, *"My tears have been my food day and night"* (Psalm 42:3). There's an entire book of the Bible called Lamentations, written by Jeremiah, the weeping prophet! Jesus is referred to as the *"man of suffering"* (Isaiah 53:3). He's well acquainted with grief. After Lazarus' death, He wept (John 11:35), and as Romans 12:15 tells us, we are to *"mourn with those who mourn"* (Romans 12:15). The Lord catches and collects our tears and records our sorrows (Psalm 56:8). If we don't take the time to feel our pain and taste our tears, we get stuck in our pain rather than making our way through it. God feels your pain. There is healing in our salty tears. Salt is a healing agent. So take the time to taste the tears. When have you experienced the healing of tears?

Damaged Goods

As my husband and I sat before a search committee, we shared our story. We explained that we'd arrived at our previous church with no wind in our sails. We'd no sooner arrived than we'd discovered people underneath our boat drilling holes in the bottom. We were shipwrecked. Disillusioned, cynical, broken, and dishevelled, we lay lifeless on the beach—damaged goods.

"Why do you want to come to minister at our church?" someone asked us.

With all the inner strength I could muster, I answered with a straight face: "I don't."

Truth be told, I knew that any amount of time would be too soon to enter a church building again. No less as a pastor's wife! I had lost all confidence in God's people. If heaven was going to be full of them, I'd find another eternal residence, thank you very much.

They allowed the shock to settle in before asking their next question. "Lisa, how do you nurture your relationship with the Lord?"

Now they had me! I just so happened to have my prayer journal with me. I had been carrying it around with me all weekend, documenting the conversation I'd been carrying on with the Lord over the previous months.

I pulled the journal out and began to read aloud my intimate thoughts, typically reserved for the Lord. When I looked up, there wasn't a dry eye around the table.

Then one of the search committee members said, "Well, we've just done had church!"

Who knew we were just who they were looking for? They explained to us that they weren't in such great shape themselves. They'd come through a mass exodus and needed someone who would understand their aching hearts. A match made in heaven, perhaps?

My husband was hired despite my cynicism and new arm's length approach to ministry.

Surprisingly, when we arrived the people were gracious, loving, kind, and patient with me. They gave me the space I needed to process all the hurt that had obscured my vision of God's people. Much like Paul and his shipwrecked crew, *"the islanders showed us unusual kindness. They built a fire and welcomed us all because it was raining and cold"* (Acts 28:1–2).

We'd landed on safe shores at last, having recognized that safety isn't ultimately the absence of enemies or problems or threats, it's the presence of God.

Survival Tip

Be honest about where you're at. Allowing ourselves to be honest about where we're at is a significant step towards healing. If we deny our feelings, we stuff them down instead. And that's not healthy for anyone. Elijah was found curled up in a cave when the Lord sought him out and asked, *"What are you doing here, Elijah?"* (1 Kings 19:9) Elijah didn't hesitate to tell Him! Then there's David. We read his authentic honesty, pouring out of his heart throughout the psalms, expressing his feelings to the Lord. Fortunately, we benefit from them. Pour out your heart honestly to the Lord about your frustrations, confusion, distress, sorrows, and fears. It will help you release your emotions and gain perspective. The Lord can handle your pain. He can work with your honesty. Write your prayers in a journal. If you can't put words to your prayers, pray God's Word. Pick a psalm that resonates with your situation and let it put words to your feelings: *"Trust in him at all times, you people; pour out your hearts to him, for God is our refuge"* (Psalm 62:8).

Paradise Lost

We'd come through a significant season as a church. Here on the other side, we were on the verge of another church expansion program. The votes were cast and the result was in the affirmative.

That's what made the following day so hard to wrap our minds around.

Our associate pastor handed my husband a resignation letter. Why not the day before the expansion vote? The sting was that he'd made us commit to helping him and his family settle in for the long haul. When we met as couples we'd agreed that we could use a little stability ourselves. I suppose that part of the agreement had no longer mattered to them.

We didn't know which end was up. They had seemed like the perfect match. We'd met. We'd talked. We'd prayed. We'd been honest. And we were ready to embark on many exciting years of ministry ahead together.

Nonetheless, here we were with the wind knocked out of us. It felt like we'd been climbing a steep mountain and gaining momentum. Now we were left standing at the precipice about to be pushed over the edge.

Once upon a time, we all lived in paradise. But sadly, we didn't live happily ever after.

Survival Tip

> **Trust God's greater plan.** Let's face it: it's painful when things don't work out quite as you planned. It's disappointing when someone gives you their word and they let you down. Paul and Luke had to part ways over a disagreement (Acts 15:3–16:10). No doubt it wasn't how either of them thought things would end. We may never understand why things happen the way they do, but one thing can be sure: God's plans always work out according to His ultimate purpose for our lives, no matter how painful it seems. When have God's plans not worked out the way you hoped they would? Let yourself feel the disappointment and betrayal. But don't coddle your self-pity for long. God has greater things in store. In Isaiah 55:8-9, God declares, *"For my thoughts are not your thoughts, neither are your ways my ways… As the heavens are higher than the earth, so are my ways higher than your ways and my thoughts than your thoughts."*

Under the Boardwalk

Ministry wasn't just my husband's job; it was our life! That life could certainly be challenging under the boardwalk—not to mention a little painful at times.

Thankfully, my husband was a team player. He worked hard to maintain a healthy relationship with whatever board he was assigned. Therefore, it only seemed right to include them whenever the Lord stirred in our hearts. Didn't it?

On one such occasion, David and I had worked hard to put into words what we both sensed the Lord saying to us. It wasn't a letter of resignation. It was a letter of invitation, inviting the church leadership board to join us in prayer and fasting for a few months to discern the Lord's leading for the church's future and our part in it.

A leadership retreat was scheduled. As my husband left for the day, I gave him a prayerful send-off—not unlike many others throughout the years, but this one felt different somehow.

During the meeting, my husband walked the board through the document he'd prepared. Then he invited the men to pray for and with us as we discerned God's next steps for us as a couple and for the church family. He shared openly and honestly that he wasn't convinced the Lord was asking us to leave. We hadn't been scouted, nor had we been seeking out other places to minister. We simply needed to earnestly seek the Lord's will.

He'd faced confused expressions before upon sharing thought-provoking news. But never had he been confronted with a long drawn-out silence like the one he received that day. The silence only ended as each man dispersed.

The last man to leave approached him.

"I don't want something like this to be found lying around the house," he said incomprehensibly as he handed the document back to my husband.

Then he left with the others.

If an enemy were insulting me, I could endure it; if a foe were rising against me, I could hide. But it is you, a man like myself, my companion, my close friend, with whom I once enjoyed sweet fellowship at the house of God, as we walked about among the worshipers.

—Psalm 55:12–14

We'd prayed that the Lord's will would be made clear, and it was made *painfully* clear. They say it's not the voice of your enemies but the silence of your friends that hurts the most. I'd have to agree.

Is this how Jesus felt in Gethsemane when His disciples fell asleep? All He'd asked was that they pray with Him for a while. Or as He faced Pilate... only to have him wash his hands clean of the responsibility? What about the lonely hours He spent on the cross, mocked, shamed, betrayed, beaten, battered, and bruised—alone? I could hardly imagine.

While my husband and I committed the next three months to prayer and fasting to discern the Lord's will, those who could have opted to join us had all gone fishing. We were left to fend for ourselves under the boardwalk.

Survival Tip

Pray for your leadership. We can rest assured knowing that Jesus is the head of the church (Colossians 1:18). His reign is *"far above all rule and authority, power and dominion, and every name that is invoked, not only in the present age but also in the one to come. And God placed all things under his feet and appointed him to be head over everything for the church"* (Ephesians 1:21–22). It's therefore important to trust Him to govern our churches. Our part in it is to pray for those in authority, just as 1 Timothy 2:1–2 instructs. Pray as they're put into position. Pray as they make decisions. Pray as they give leadership to you and the rest of the church. Romans 13:1 says, *"Let everyone be subject to the governing authorities, for there is no authority except that which God has established. The authorities that exist have been established by God."* When have you felt the sting of those in authority? List some of the things you appreciate about your current leadership team. Why not consider writing your deacons or board of elders a note of appreciation, letting them know that you're praying for them today?

The Just In Case

I've never been one to carry purses. The closest I came was carrying a diaper bag when my kids were young. There is, however, one tote I've carried around for years. I call it the Just In Case. I hold onto and carry this tote around with me at all times, just in case.

Within my Just In Case I hold things like hurts, disappointments, resentments, grudges, old sinful patterns, negative thoughts, harsh and painful memories, and even old, dying, or unhealthy relationships. Would you believe my case even holds a big picture album to keep the faces of my offenders firmly planted in my mind's eye? To make sure I don't forget any of these things, I keep an up-to-date record of the wrongs done to me, just in case I might need that record of wrongs to prove the offence to the offender.

There's also an old tape recorder stored away in there that at any given moment can replay some of the conversations that have hurt me. Ah yes, the voices of past offences fresh in my mind, just in case I forget about the hurt they've inflicted. And of course I need to keep it on hand when my motives or irate behaviour seep out of my tote and are questioned.

Eventually it got too heavy and I had a difficult time carrying it around. I knew I was holding onto things the Lord wanted me to let go of, but I'd grown so attached to them. I had to ask myself why it was so important to hold onto everything.

The answer came with a rush of emotion one day while I conversed with the Lord in the confines of my prayer closet.

My Just In Case had become so large that it crowded the space, and there was only one thing to do: present my case to Him. Piece by piece, God helped me to unpack it. I emptied all the stuff I'd stored up. I soon found out that these things were invading the sacred and spacious place He longed to create in my heart.

He assured me that one day all wrongs will be made right. Justice will be done. He will rise, every knee will bow, and every tongue will confess that Jesus Christ is Lord. Jesus will have the final word. On that day, I will humbly approach His throne and fall at His feet. Because not only will I see myself as I am, I will see Him for who He is. With Him, I rest my case.

Survival Tip ─────────

Let go of bitterness. If we're not careful, our pain and bitterness can keep us in misery longer than we ever planned to stay. Therefore, it's essential that we choose to forgive, just as Christ forgave us (Ephesians 4:32). As Hebrews 12:14–15 says, *"Make every effort to live in peace with everyone and to be holy; without holiness no one will see the Lord. See to it that no one falls short of the grace of God and that no bitter root grows up to cause trouble and defile many."* Romans 12:18–19 adds, *"If it is possible, as far as it depends on you, live at peace with everyone. Do not take revenge, my dear friends, but leave room for God's wrath, for it is written: 'It is mine to avenge; I will repay,' says the Lord.'"* Simply stated, forgiveness is letting go of your right to hurt the offender back and not being dependent upon the response or reaction of the offender. It also doesn't mean that we forget the past. Rather, it's choosing not to remember it—in other words, not talking about the offence any longer, or reminding yourself or anyone else of the offence. Forgiveness is about letting go of the grip you have on the offence and letting go of the grip it has on you. Who do you need to forgive? Consider writing a letter to that person. Whether you give it to them or not, it will be out of your heart and can be left to rest in God's safekeeping.

Rebuilding the Ancient Ruins

The meeting was scheduled so that both my husband and I could be part of it. I rallied a few prayer partners to stand on guard for our hearts as we met. We had left this church many years ago, but the board had recently called us back.

The chairman of the board began by filling us in on the intent of the meeting. They had been studying the book of Nehemiah together and the Lord had helped them identify some areas of the church where walls had been broken down.

Each board member had gone to their personal prayer closets to seek His face. By the time they met again, the Lord had disclosed some significant issues and damage that had been done. They were impressed to make things right, and we had been found amongst the ruins.

Next, something remarkable happened. One by one, the men took a turn to acknowledge the hurt we'd experienced. They spoke on behalf of those who had been part of the damage but were no longer around, or at least no longer on the board. Each one asked our forgiveness.

David and I were given the opportunity to respond, and we did it prayerfully. We acknowledged that, yes, our ministry, family, and marriage had all been gravely affected. However, we chose not to dig up any unnecessary rubble and were able to extend grace. The men were humbled and astounded. They thanked us with tears in their eyes.

After the meeting, I revisited a promise the Lord had given me during that dark time. It had served to give hope and healing that all of our efforts hadn't been for naught:

> The Lord will guide you always; he will satisfy your needs in a sun-scorched land and will strengthen your frame. You will be like a well-watered garden, like a spring whose waters never fail. Your people will rebuild the ancient ruins and will raise up the age-old foundations; you will be called Repairer of Broken Walls, Restorer of Streets with Dwellings.
>
> —Isaiah 58:11–12

The day had finally come when His promise was fulfilled. My Redeemer had come through again to restore, heal, forgive, and rebuild the ancient ruins.

Survival Tip

> **Remember who the real enemy is.** It's easy to make people who have offended or hurt us the enemy, even God's people. They aren't the enemy. But there is one who is, and we need to be aware of him: *"Be alert and of sober mind. Your enemy the devil prowls around like a roaring lion looking for someone to devour"* (1 Peter 5:8). Ephesians 6:13 then tells us, *"Therefore put on the full armor of God, so that when the day of evil comes, you may be able to stand your ground, and after you have done everything, to stand."* What piece of the armour of God do you need to put on today? Remember what we read in 2 Chronicles 20:17: *"You will not have to fight this battle. Take up your positions; stand firm and see the deliverance the Lord will give you…"* Is there someone you need to reconcile with? Ask God to use your pain for His purposes

We have a Saviour who understands our pain, suffering, and sorrow. His own family rejected Him. His hometown didn't accept Him. Religious leaders were always plotting, accusing, trapping, mocking, criticizing, analyzing, scrutinizing, and eventually abusing Him. He was betrayed by some of His closest friends. Crowds of people who cheered him on one week crucified Him the next.

He's able to relate to us because He was made fully human in every way. He Himself suffered (Hebrews 2:17–18). Isaiah 53 offers a good picture of this "man of sorrows." He was wounded for our transgressions, despised and rejected of men, familiar with pain, oppressed, and afflicted.

But here's the good news: by His stripes, we are healed!

Yes, He understands. He draws close to our broken hearts (Psalm 34:18). In His perfect time and in His perfect way, with careful precision, the Great Physician binds up our wounds (Psalm 147:3).

Straight from the Father's Heart

Therefore, as God's chosen people, holy and dearly loved, clothe yourselves with compassion, kindness, humility, gentleness and patience. Bear with each other and forgive one another if any of you has a grievance against someone. Forgive as the Lord forgave you. And over all these virtues put on love, which binds them all together in perfect unity.
—Colossians 3:12–14

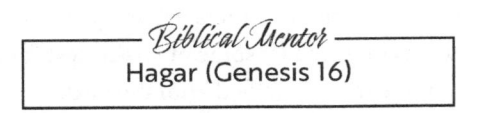

Biblical Mentor
Hagar (Genesis 16)

The first step toward becoming a wounded healer is a personal encounter with the Healer Himself. He's the One who sees us. He understands our pain. He wants us to experience forgiveness and reconciliation, beginning with an authentic relationship with Him.

Consider Hagar, for instance. Here are some simple truths we can learn from her encounter with God. You may want to take note of them the next time you find yourself wounded and wandering in the wilderness. Let the God who sees you open your eyes to a whole new way of looking at your pain and allowing Him to use it for His purposes.

God pursues you relentlessly. After Hagar was hurt by Sarai, she fled. Interestingly, Hagar means "flight." Did her parents know when they named her how she'd respond to life when things got messy? She ran from Sarai, away from her problems, away from her pain.

Imagine Hagar's pain as she fled alone, pregnant, vulnerable, disillusioned, and disappointed in God's people. The good news is that God ran after her and met her right where she was at—in the middle of her pain, smack dab in the middle of the wilderness. Can you imagine her response when the Lord found her and called to her? I'm sure it was a mix of shame and guilt, but also a sense of relief.

I imagine that when Hagar ran away from Sarai, she didn't expect to run straight into the arms of the Lord! You can run from your pain, but you can't hide from the God who pursues you.

God challenges you personally. When the angel of the Lord found Hagar, He called her by name. This matters because it shows us that individuals matter to the Lord. There's a reason for all the genealogies in the Bible! The Lord says in Genesis 16:8, *"Hagar, slave of Sarai, where have you come from, and where are you going?"* These are thought-provoking questions! How easy it is to be blinded by our pain. We lose our way and become self-focused.

Note that Hagar didn't have any problem identifying where she'd come from or why she was in the wilderness. It was all someone else's fault! Isn't it always? The more difficult question she had to contend with was "Where are you going?"

God doesn't want to leave us stranded, wandering, or worse, comfortable, in the wilderness. If we're not careful, we can get comfortable in the desert. Remember, Ishmael took up residence there!

So let me ask you: where have you come from? More importantly, where are you going? Let the Lord's great faithfulness guide you. Let His new mercies follow you all the days of your life (Psalm 23:6).

God confronts you intentionally. Next, He said to her, *"Go back to your mistress and submit to her"* (Genesis 16:9). Go back? Didn't the Lord know all that Hagar had faced? Wasn't He aware of all the hurt that had been inflicted upon her? That didn't seem to matter to Him. Perhaps what mattered more than her past pain was her future healing.

Sarai had called her a slave woman, and even the angel addressed her as the slave of Sarai. Talk about adding insult to injury. But what was she more a slave to, the pain of her past or the pain of her sin? God knew the only way she could be healed was for her to confront her offender.

Let's face it: no one likes confrontation. However, sometimes it's necessary in order to seek reconciliation and, at minimum, find healing. Romans 12:18 says, *"If it is possible, as far as it depends on you, live at peace with everyone."* James 3:18 tells us, *"Peacemakers who sow in peace reap a harvest of righteousness."*

Somewhere along the way back to Abram and Sarai, Hagar came to know the truth, and the truth set her free! (John 8:32).

God invests in you purposefully. In Hagar's darkest hour, the Lord heard the cry of her heart and said to her,

> *I will increase your descendants so much that they will be too numerous to count."*
> *The angel of the Lord also said to her: "You are now pregnant and you will give birth to a son. You shall name him Ishmael, for the Lord has heard of your misery."*
>
> —Genesis 16:10–11

No doubt none of this made any sense to Hagar, especially in the middle of the desert. Think of Hagar's confusion. But the Lord had plans and a purpose. It didn't matter that this wasn't His original plan.

He has plans for you and me, too, even when we find ourselves in the middle of the desert. Jeremiah 29:11 reminds us of this: *"For I know the plans I have for you... plans to prosper you and not to harm you, plans to give you hope and a future."*

God watches you closely. Finally, we get to perhaps the best part of Hagar's story:

> *She gave this name to the Lord who spoke to her: "You are the God who sees me," for she said, "I have now seen the One who sees me." That is why the well was called Beer Lahai Roi; it is still there, between Kadesh and Bered.*
>
> —Genesis 16:13–14

When we've been wounded, especially by God's people, we can be blinded by our tears, as well as blinded by our pain, anger, fear, and the lies we listen to. That's when we become disillusioned. There is much reassurance to be found as we look to Jesus to see Him as He is, and even more so when we sense His loving gaze upon us.

When you're abandoned, God sees. When you struggle to endure, God sees. When you work behind the scenes and nobody seems to notice or appreciate you, God sees. When you're vulnerable, lost, and broken, God sees.

> *He will not let your foot slip—he who watches over you will not slumber... The Lord watches over you—the Lord is your shade at your right hand; the sun will not harm you by day, nor the moon by night. The Lord will keep you from all harm—he will watch over your life; the Lord will watch over your coming and going both now and forevermore.*
>
> —Psalm 121:3, 5–8

Chapter Seven

BUILDING *Relationships*
THAT PROVIDE SUPPORT

LIFE CAN GET LONELY, ESPECIALLY WHEN YOU'RE IN A PLACE OF LEADERSHIP. ALL the more reason to rally the troops and gather the support you'll need for the journey—those who believe in you, stick with you, and pick you up when you fall down.

I've built a support system of these people. They line the hallways here in my heart. Each is a representation of many who have made rich investments in my life at significant times on my ministry journey.

Take note. You're going to need some of these.

Cheerleaders

I was a cross-country runner in junior high and high school. I remember the early morning workouts and after-school practices. I remember the courses we ran through hot sunshine, rain, sleet, and hail. I remember the hills we trudged, and the swamps. I remember the uneven ground and ankle-deep muck. I can still feel the crusty running shoes and sports socks that had to be replaced often. I remember the rib cramps, the physical exertion, and exhaustion. I remember collapsing in my bed at night after long, hot showers.

But as much, if not more, I also remember my running partner. We kept pace with and encouraged one another. And when one of us fell, the other was there to help the other up. The race wouldn't have been nearly as enjoyable without her.

Years later, two of my kids ran on their school's cross-country team. In typical form, the parents all stood at the start of the race cheering for their "Johnny." And on this particular course, they then did an about-face to cheer little "Johnny" across the finish line.

That's when I had a brilliant idea. Rather than conforming to the crowd, I'd plant myself strategically in the middle of the course. Because I also remembered, all too well, how lonely the race got in the middle of it. I remembered the agony of defeat as other runners faster or fitter than I passed me by. I remember wanting to pack it in right then and there.

So I stood at the top of a steep incline, spotting the runners coming towards me. But wait! Was I seeing what I thought I was seeing? A few kids were at the bottom of the hill holding sticks. As the runners approached, they jabbed at them, sometimes tripping them up, and worse, they were taunting and jeering.

My heart could hardly bear it. To counteract the adversaries, I started yelling, shouting, and cheering at the top of my lungs. Above the taunts below, I encouraged the runners as they tackled the incline, stumbling, panting for air, and dusting off their knees.

At first, I know I startled some of the runners. Who was this maniac mama at the top of the hill? But then they responded to my cheers. Most of them smiled at me as they ran by. Some laughed at my comical gestures. Some gave me high-fives on their way by. Amazingly, most of them picked up their pace. Some were even inspired to make a pass of someone who'd already passed them.

I waited at my post until the last runner came by, continuing to cheer, with as much force as I could muster. My heart was full.

And yet it hurt. The whole scene saddened me as much as it inspired me. It made me think of the Christian race. How easy it is to stand at the starting line and cheer on the new believers with all our might. We gather to encourage them across the finish line when Jesus calls them home, but how many of us cheer others on in the middle of the race when they need it the most?

I determined to post myself strategically in the lives of others to encourage them on their journeys. I could only hope to find some who would do the same for me.

Survival Tip

> **Find a walking (or running) partner.** Seek out a godly friend who will walk alongside and encourage you to grow in your walk with the Lord. It could be someone who literally walks with you or someone who helps you keep in step with the Spirit (Galatians 5:25), someone who helps you find strength in the Lord (1 Samuel 23:16). What kinds of people encourage you in your walk with the Lord? How have they encouraged you in the race? We read in 1 Corinthians 9:24, *"Do you not know that in a race all the runners run, but only one gets the prize? Run in such a way as to get the prize."* And Hebrews 12:3 adds, *"Consider Him who endured such opposition from sinners, so that you will not grow weary and lose heart."*

My Bosom Buddy and Lifelong Friend

We were tweenagers, ten and eleven years of age, when we met. We were Ontario's version of Anne and Diana from *Anne of Green Gables*, kindred spirits in every sense of the word.

For years, we spent a week every summer at camp together, where she introduced me to Jesus. Together we fell more deeply in love with Him and grew in our knowledge of Him. We sang songs of praise about Him as we lived the abundance of life.

We couldn't get enough of each other. We'd spend hours on the phone, calling each other as soon as we walked in the door from school. We'd then take a break for dinner and call each other, talking until bedtime. We covered all the territories—school and friends and boys and life as we knew it. That's what made sleepovers a bonus. We could talk and laugh all night long and into the wee hours of the morning.

And that we did—much to our parents' chagrin. To this day, we finish each other's sentences, understand each other's thoughts, and hear each other's hearts, even from across the miles.

She stood at my heart's side through my parents' separation when I was twelve. She coached my heart in all its early days of soul-searching in my early teens. She prayed for me as I sought out God's will for my life at Bible college. She rejoiced with me when I fell in love with the man I'd marry. She stood beside me as the maid of honour at my wedding. I played a supportive role in hers in a nine-month pregnant state. She kept pace with me as we both began having children. She wept with me when I lost one of mine through cancer.

She's supported me throughout my ministry life—not as one who stands off to the side but rather walks alongside me. Oh yes, did I mention that she's also a pastor's wife? Bonus!

How good of God to not only bless me with a lifelong friend who's traced my multiple ministry moves, heartaches, joys, and sorrows for decades, but one who "gets" ministry. Lifers like this are hard to find.

Survival Tip _____

> **Remember where you've been.** Who's that person who knew you back when … ? This is someone with whom you can easily pick up from where you left off, someone who knew you when you first came to know Christ. It's someone who knows you from before you were in ministry. It's important to remember where you came from. It not only keeps the essence of who you are intact, it helps measure how far you've come.

Lessons from the Older and Wiser

I was barely into womanhood before being deemed a pastor's wife. So young and fresh was I that I qualified to attend the college and careers class. There I sat, new diamond ring sparkling on my finger, with a group of young adults, some barely out of high school.

I was quickly promoted to lead a weekly ladies Bible study! Someone from the college and careers group must've reported my good behaviour. It certainly wasn't my astute knowledge of Scripture that qualified me. I barely knew the books of the Bible by heart. I can only suppose the women felt that my Bible college education was enough. Did they know I failed Old Testament?

I wondered what a twenty-three-year-old pastor's wife was doing teaching the Bible to women who could have written it! And with all due respect, I'm sure a few had stood on the mountainside when Moses received the Ten Commandments!

What would I have done without them?

Their insight into God's Word and how it applied to their lives brought it to life for me. I learned lessons from the older and wiser straight from Titus 2:3–5:

> *Likewise, teach the older women to be reverent in the way they live, not to be slanderers or addicted to much wine, but to teach what is good. Then they can urge the younger women to love their husbands and children, to be*

self-controlled and pure, to be busy at home, to be kind, and to be subject to their husbands...

I learned some tricks of the trade where hospitality was concerned. I picked up on homemade baking and gathered a wealth of recipes along with some great cooking tips and kitchen skills, including hands-on tips for gardening, harvesting, and canning.

I watched and took notes as they raised their children. I observed the way they treated their grandchildren. And I hoped that, Lord willing, one day my children would reap the wealth of education I reaped as seeds were sewn into me.

As I fumbled my way along, the grace extended to me over and over again was nothing short of a miracle. Their input, advice, counsel, and godly example were invaluable, especially in those early years of ministry as a new bride and young pastor's wife. Little did I know they were building a safe platform for me, cushioned with grace, to be trained and groomed for future ministry.

I had a lot to learn. I was greener than grass, yet on the observation deck of many who had walked this ministry life a few steps ahead of me. I was in awe of their gracious spirits and smiling faces, curious to learn what it took to be that way when I got to that stage of the game.

As I grew into different ministry roles and entered new seasons of life, I was thankful to have learned the necessity of seeking out others who were older and wiser.

Survival Tip —

> **Be open and willing to learn from the example of others.** Watch and take note of the example of others who know and love the Lord, be they people in ministry or with a bit more seasoned experience in life. A lot can be learned through observation. Take note of others' attitudes, approaches, and ways of doing things. Don't be ashamed to ask for help or advice from those you think could offer you valuable input, practical and spiritual. Ask good questions. Request input on ministry, childrearing, and how to love your spouse well. Then follow their godly example. According to Philippians 4:9, *"Whatever you have learned or received or heard from me, or seen in me—put it into practice. And the God of peace will be with you."* Learning is a lifelong process. Watch and learn. List examples of people you've learned from. How have they taught you or impacted your life? What lessons could you pass on to others?

Weeping Willows

My firstborn, Natalie, was headed off to her first day of Kindergarten and I was an emotional mess. Would she be okay? How would her teacher treat her? Would she make friends? Was she going to be able to open her snack box? What if she couldn't? What if others teased her?

I got her on the school bus, then hopped in my car, buckling my other three toddlers into their respective car seats, and followed. I parked the car once I arrived at the school and entered the classroom. Thankfully, I wasn't the only parent with similar concerns. We all stood and waved at our precious gems.

After a few minutes, the teacher politely asked us all to leave.

"We'll all be waiting here for you in a few short hours," she said with a sweet smile.

I left the school utterly lost, not because I didn't know where I was but because I'd lost my emotional bearings. What was I going to do now? Go home and wait it out? Not this girl!

I knew just where to go. I drove to my friend's home.

She'd become a special friend over the time she had attended our church. I had recognized her by her eyes the first time she walked into the church foyer. Then it had come to me: she was a nurse, having attended the birth of two of my children.

She rejoiced with me in the purchase of our first house and suggested she come and go for a prayer walk around the property with me. She knew in her heart that God had big plans for the neighbourhood where He was about to plant us.

Speaking of planting, she helped me with my very first perennial garden. She was older than me by half a generation and had raised four children of her own. Therefore, she was used to me calling upon her for practical advice, sanity, counsel, and emotional support.

I knew she'd just said goodbye to her oldest daughter that morning as well, giving her a warm send-off to university. Perfect! I knew she'd completely understand—and she didn't disappoint.

There we sat in her lovely garden, right under the weeping willow, and sobbed into the tea she graciously served. Before we knew it, it was time to go and pick up Natalie again!

What a gift she was to me, through both her rejoicing and weeping.

Survival Tip _____

> **Seek out genuine hospitality.** Something special takes place when two people find common ground, not only by the opening of homes but the opening of hearts to allow others in. We see many examples of hospitality throughout the Bible. Think of the times Jesus was welcomed into someone's home and what took place throughout their visit: a meal (Luke 19:1–10), a miracle (Mark 1:29–31), or the simple mutual enjoyment of friends (Luke 10:38–42). His very presence invited others in (John 4). Now *that's* what I call hospitality! We read in Hebrews 13:2, *"Do not forget to show hospitality to strangers, for by so doing some people have shown hospitality to angels without knowing it."* When is a time you've been shown hospitality? How has the Lord used your hospitality or your home (possibly to an angel)?

A Pain-in-the-Neck Friend

"Tell me your life," I invited in my typical get-to-know-you way.

My new friend shared that her father was in the military and she had therefore moved around a lot. She found it challenging to make new friends, or at least was a little tentative due to the nature of her upbringing.

Then she went on to share her newfound love for Jesus. Her marriage had been on the brink of separation, so she'd gone away on a personal retreat to regain some perspective on life. That's when the Lord had stepped into her heart and showed her life from His perspective.

As she spoke, the love of God shone through her sparkling blue eyes. My heart stood in awe at how richly the Spirit of Christ dwelled in her. It was inspiring, invigorating, and inviting. Even though I was the more mature Christian, I knew that when I grew up I wanted to be just like her. I wanted the love of Jesus to shine through me like it did through her.

She went on to share her and her husband's love for travel and authentic food. She also shared of her spiritual burden for her husband's salvation. I told her we'd just have to pray her husband through heaven's gates, and they'd be missionaries.

Amazingly, that's just what happened!

Our friendship began over coffee at my kitchen table. Our divine connection began when she moved halfway around the world. That's when our hearts entwined, much like David and Jonathan (1 Samuel 18:1–4), forming a prayerful heart connection, spiritual accountability, and scriptural encouragement, all wrapped together with mutual love and respect. Whenever we spoke it was like the words of Malachi 3:16: *"Then those who feared the Lord talked with each other, and the Lord listened and heard."*

In the middle of her day, she would find herself washing dishes and crying into her sink as she thought of and prayed for me. Simultaneously, in the middle of my night I would wake up from a dream about her. In my dream, we would embrace and cry together.

What a coincidence, I'd think. But since that time, we've discovered that it's more of a *God*-incident. We've learned that God kept us both attentive to pray for each other through an extremely challenging time in both of our lives in ministry.

The Lord connected us by the heart. However, it's often her neck that feels my pain. She has come to refer to me as her pain-in-the-neck friend, because when the Lord lays me on her heart, I weigh heavily on her neck, to the point that at times she's had to go to the hospital to help control the pain with IV medication!

Afterwards she'll ask me what was going on in my life at that particular time. When I fill her in, she then tells me when her neck began to throb and at what time she felt relieved of her pain. More often than not, these times correspond to the exact points when I've faced some sort of spiritual battle.

We all need someone, like my friend, who we can go to when we need help finding strength in God (1 Samuel 23:16). We need a prayer partner who offers mutual affection, love, encouragement, and godly perspective.

I'm grateful for my sister-by-heart, even if I am her pain-in-the-neck friend. Everyone needs one.

_____

Pray for a prayer partner. Find one or two friends who will provide prayer support, someone you can confidentially share concerns, hopes, joys, and burdens with (Galatians 6:2). As Matthew 18:20 says, *"For where two or three gather in my name, there am I with them."* Gear your conversation toward the things of the Lord. Share together in things He's teaching you, ways He's testing you, questions He's challenging you with, discoveries He's uncovering within you, circumstances He's using to grow you, and truths He's entrusted to you. Proverbs 27:17 tells us, *"As iron sharpens iron, so one person sharpens another."* Allow the Lord to ignite your soul, challenge your mind, and breathe life into your conversation. Finally, pray for one another. There's no deeper connection you can find with someone when the Lord is the one who connects you. List the qualities you'd look for in a prayer partner.

Jesus Loves Me... This I Know?

I was having a hard time loving God's people due to the behaviour of some. Far worse, I was having a hard time loving myself. I was disillusioned, disappointed, and defeated. I didn't feel fit for ministry any longer. I wasn't equipped to face the harsh reality of what it entailed. I struggled with a bad attitude and thought to myself, *If I can't love myself, how can anyone else?*

One Sunday morning, a sweet little old lady met me in the church foyer. Before I could say good morning she took my face firmly between her hands, stared me square in the eyes, and boldly asked, "Do you know Jesus loves you?" I could barely look her in the eye. In those days, I honestly didn't know.

Week after week, she pursued me. And week after week, she offered the same gesture. Taking my face in her hands, she asked me varying versions of the same question.

"Do you know how precious you are to Jesus?"

"Do you know how special you are?"

"You are a treasure! Do you know that?"

She didn't even demand an answer. And that was a relief because I'm not sure I had one.

Her Sunday greetings turned into greeting cards sent to my address with my name squiggled on the envelope. And her messages inside weren't much different than the ones she gave me every Sunday at church.

My tears—lots of tears, necessary tears, healing tears—slowly turned into tears of relief, until I finally believed that, yes, Jesus loves me. Not only did the Bible tell me so, a sweet little old lady in the church foyer did.

Survival Tip

Be alert to where God may show up. God knows just who and what you need, when you need it, and where. Sometimes we just have to be alerted. Keep your eyes wide open as you enter the church. Jesus may greet you as you walk in the door. He may sit beside you when He spots you alone in the pew. He may simply reach out and give you a God-hug. He may kneel at the altar with you and quietly intercede at your side. He might minister to you in a worship song. He might touch your heart in a sermon. He might even join you in conversation as you mingle in a crowd. When is a time the Lord met you right where you were at? Who did He use to reach out to you? Who could you be Jesus to, in order to remind them that He loves them?

Heaven Scent

I was so embarrassed that I couldn't remember her name. I had called her something completely different when I saw her for the first time. I apologized, but her face lit up anyway, her eyes sparkling from the fact I'd remembered meeting her all those months earlier.

I may not have remembered her name, but I couldn't easily forget her heart. She was the head of the evangelism committee at the church where we were being called to. As I grew to know and love her more deeply, I realized that the role suited her perfectly.

No doubt she picked up on my cynicism immediately. Who couldn't have? But then I learned that she had a built-in radar for such things. I just prayed that what I had wasn't contagious. Thankfully, she seemed to be immune.

We were gathered for a committee leadership meeting as part of our interview weekend. She sat to my right at the restaurant where a lovely brunch had been served. We made light conversation throughout the morning.

At the end of the meeting, she stood, wrapped her arms around me and said, "Maybe what you need is simply a time of rest."

I cried. How could she have pegged me so accurately?

Now here we were, standing at the front door of our new house. She stood with the beautiful smile I well remembered, extending an entire meal to me for my family to enjoy.

We met several times for coffee after that. I needed a piece of her spark and spunk. I sopped up all the wisdom and heart I could from her example. Eventually, she shared that she needed to hire a cleaning lady. I told her I'd cleaned houses in other communities we'd lived in. I was hired on the spot as her angel of cleanliness. Heaven scent!

Week by week I went to her house. She'd have the coffee on and two chairs set up at her kitchen table. This was part of the deal; before I could do any cleaning, we needed to catch up. She needed to check in to see how this heart of mine was faring.

As time went on, I did my own checking in on her. Her heart ached for some of her grown children and grandchildren who didn't know the Lord. With tears in her eyes, she'd ask me to please pray for them. And I did. That was also part of our agreement.

She made more investments in my life than I can count—and likely more than she realizes. She had one of the sweetest aromas of Christ I'd ever inhaled. Heaven scent indeed!

Survival Tip

> **Experience the joy of accountability.** There is a great benefit to finding someone who will speak truth into our lives—even if it hurts. Proverbs 27:6 says, *"Wounds from a friend can be trusted, but an enemy multiplies kisses."* We all need someone who will be honest with us, willing to confront us, and lovingly give us a spiritual kick in the pants from time to time. Being accountable to someone causes us to grow, think outside ourselves, and challenges us beyond what we'd expect from ourselves. In what ways could you use some accountability? How could that be a benefit to you?

Boaz

We were packing up and getting ready to leave church after a long weekend of interviews, Q&As, socials, gatherings, and meetings. All this was taking place to help us all determine whether or not the Lord was indeed calling us to this place for our next season of ministry.

As we stood at the front of the church and people said their goodbyes, a new friend pulled me aside and wrapped me in a hug that I still feel to this day.

"If you guys don't end up coming here, you're going to have to explain it to my son," she said through tears.

Her three-year-old boy had been fervently praying for us, thanking God for us as if we were already a part of the church family.

She and her husband had welcomed us into their home at the beginning of the weekend. We'd known it was a friendship made in heaven when we had met each other both sporting jean short overalls. We'd laughed and hugged as our hearts immediately bonded over denim, good food, and fellowship.

She and her husband had also toured us around the city. I fell in love with it through her eyes.

She was eventually hired on staff to lead our children's ministry, and she became my husband's right hand as they worked together in the office. She was an extension of our ministry lives and an extension of my heart. We were blessed.

There's no doubt in my heart or mind that the Lord providentially put her in place. She became the hub of all the activity surrounding our family's crisis years later when our son Ben was diagnosed with leukemia. She became my bodyguard, literally, standing on guard for my vulnerable heart in the speaking engagements following his death. She advocated for us even into our last days with that church family.

When you find one who just loves you for who you are, you've got a keeper.

Much like Boaz was for Ruth, my friend was my Boaz—my guardian-redeemer (Ruth 4:14). I will never forget her and the part she played as the guardian of my heart.

Survival Tip

> **Find a friend who will have your back and hold your heart.** We all need someone who will faithfully defend our cause, pick us up when we fall, and stand with us in our weakness for added support. This was the kind of bond Jonathan and David shared. So great was their love for one another that their souls were knit together. Jonathan loved him as himself (1 Samuel 18:1–4). The true test of their friendship came when Jonathan protected David against his father King Saul's hot pursuit of David's very life (1 Samuel 19–20). It's vital to have a friend who will have your back and hold your heart. Who is that for you? Who's had your back when it seemed that everyone else turned theirs on you? What was the circumstance?

Just Between Us

For years I led a prayer counselling team at a ministry women's conference. We called our team *Safe Place Ministries* and it was intended to provide a soul care sanctuary for pastors' wives where they could find the confidence to entrust, validation of pain, prayer for support, and encouragement to go on.

The year my son battled leukemia, there was the chance that I wouldn't be able to attend the annual conference, and therefore unable to lead the prayer counselling team. I was instead asked to put together a short summary that would inform those at the conference of my situation and allow them to pray for *me*.

I carefully crafted it, wanting to be brief but specific in my prayer request. I also didn't want to provide every single detail. There were far too many. Then I emailed it to the woman in charge of the prayer team to represent me in my absence.

As it turned out, the Lord enabled me to attend at the very last minute, for which I was grateful. However, now I had this writeup with nowhere to put it. As I read it over, I felt that someone out there needed to hear it. So when I got home, I looked up my subscription to a magazine for ministry women, *Just Between Us*. There was a bookmark in the magazine entitled "What's My Story?" And on it, I saw a submission address.

So I emailed it right away. I never thought I'd hear back from anyone—much less within a half-hour of sending it. The response came from the editor of the magazine, who told me that not only did she feel I had a story worth sharing, but that it had touched her life on a level of understanding.

Long story short, we started an online friendship. Our connectivity transcended cyberspace and touched us right where we were at. We began sharing with one another, praying for each other, encouraging one another in the Lord, and helping bear each other's burdens. Eventually we had the privilege of meeting each other face to face, although by then we already knew each other well by heart.

She was a treasure in the darkness. She continues to help me flourish in my ministry, in my walk with God, and in my writing for the very magazine that joined us together. As God opened opportunities for us to collaborate in worldwide ministry, I was grateful for the divine friendship we shared.

Survival Tip

> **Discover a cyberspace heart connection.** Have you ever felt a deep connection with a friend you've never met in person? There can be a unique bond between people, even across cyberspace. I'm not referring to online dating, but rather online friendship. It's amazing how Christians can find a heart-and-soul connection with others who love the Lord far away. Online friendship can be just as rich and invigorating as any friendship can be when He is at the centre of it. Prayer, encouragement, and scripture can all be passed along through the computer. You can even have a ministry partnership if you get creative. Don't stop online. Arrange to have a phone call or a video chat. How has someone encouraged you in the Lord from across the miles?

One Way

I was starved for fellowship, Bible study, confidentiality, and godliness—everything I needed to sustain me—in a place where I could be anonymous. I needed a place where no one knew me, where I didn't have to be the leader or the answer person. I just needed a safe environment where I could be fully me without any expectations.

As I walked into the beautifully set up room, I noticed a dozen or so women standing around chatting and laughing. I was invited to help myself to a beautiful spread of fresh fruit, cheeses, bread, jams, yogurt, chocolate-covered almonds, and dried fruit and nuts. A coffee maker and a kettle were set off to the side along with specially designed mugs and a vast selection of tea.

If the food wasn't enough, the conversation was the icing on the cake. I was immediately immersed in stimulating, meaningful discussion to chew on and digest. It was food for my soul. And I ate it all up.

The two women leading the group were perhaps the most sensitive godly women I'd met in a very long time. It was evident that they were both sensitive to the Holy Spirit and these ministry women around them. The conversation was based on the Word of God and how it applied to our lives. Our identity outside of this circle didn't matter as we all dined together over good food and genuine fellowship.

I'd been invited by a fellow pastor's wife who knew I'd just moved to the city. I was aware of the organization, One Way Ministries, because I'd already been welcomed to the city by them. A week after our arrival, they'd sent my husband and me a beautiful gift basket containing mugs and hot chocolate and nuts and greeting cards, along with all kinds of information about the city.

Extraordinary! As I continued to tap into *One Way Ministries*, I was blessed beyond measure. No two ways about it!

Inevitably, you'll experience times in your ministry and in life when you don't believe in yourself. That's when you need others who believe in you and will encourage you toward what God's called you to do. Moses had Aaron. David had Jonathan. Esther had Mordecai. Ruth had Naomi. Mary had Elizabeth.

There's nothing better than knowing you have a faithful support system—support from those who not only bring out the best in you but encourage you to be the best that God intended for you to be. They lift you up when you fall down and bend down to hear your heart when no one else seems to understand.

God created us for relationship, ultimately with Him. As Proverbs 18:24 says, *"One who has unreliable friends soon comes to ruin, but there is a friend who sticks closer than a brother."*

Straight from the Father's Heart

*May the God who gives endurance and encouragement give you
the same attitude of mind toward each other that Christ Jesus had,
so that with one mind and one voice you may glorify the God and
Father of our Lord Jesus Christ.*
—Romans 15:5–6

Biblical Mentor
Mary and Elizabeth (Luke 1:5–56)

We find a special friendship, sisterhood, and mentorship between Mary and Elizabeth in the Gospel of Luke. As we observe their relationship, we clearly see how they were each other's support during a vulnerable season of their lives. This godly pair shows us what having a supportive community can offer us. Their example inspires us to go out and do likewise. Here are some key ingredients to their mentorship:

Connection. After hearing from the angel of the Lord, Mary knew exactly who she needed to run to for encouragement and support, and she didn't waste any time getting there. Elizabeth and Mary were cousins. However, their connection deepened when they both found themselves pregnant in a miraculous way.

It could be that you're connected to a person because they're a family member. Or perhaps you're at the same age, stage, and season of life. Life's circumstances could connect you to each other. Perhaps your children attend the same school. Or you live in the same neighbourhood, or are on the same committee. Or you could work together. Perhaps you connect at the heart with someone who's been there, done that, someone who understands you and your circumstances. The important thing is to find someone with whom you connect.

Acceptance. Elizabeth greeted Mary with an open door, open arms, and an open heart. That's hospitality.

Elizabeth didn't just whisper a welcome to Mary; she unashamedly belted out her blessing in a loud voice. Can't you just hear her? Can you see the look on Mary's face after having been virtually exiled and outcast due to her predicament? Couldn't you use someone like that in your life?

It's vitally important to provide a non-judgmental, caring environment where inner healing and hope can be experienced in their fullness. Likewise, we need to seek out others who will seek to understand, love, value, and accept us—warts and all.

Mutual vulnerability. To me, there's nothing worse than opening my life up to someone who stares at me through their zipped-up life. I call it the snowsuit effect. Elizabeth was well along in years (Luke 1:7) and Mary looked up to her. Yet Elizabeth esteemed Mary by considering herself favoured. They were both in a miraculously vulnerable condition. What a gift it must have been to enjoy the mutual love and affection that came along with their friendship.

Mary and Elizabeth understood each other on a level not everyone could. We need those who will mourn with us in our mourning and rejoice with us in our rejoicing (Romans 12:15).

Affirmation. In Luke 1:45, Elizabeth proclaims, *"Blessed is she who has believed that the Lord would fulfill his promises to her!"* It's obvious that Elizabeth believed in Mary when there was a chance nobody else did—including her betrothed, Joseph. Likewise, we need those who believe in us because they see God's potential in us. We need those who will affirm us in our calling, as well as those who will support, encourage, pray for, and bless us as we go.

Loyalty. Mary stayed with Elizabeth for three months. Can you imagine the hormones flying around that household or the grocery bill with pregnancy cravings? Three months is a long time and a lot of life to invest in a person living in close quarters. There must have been a lot of confidential moments shared between them. However, while living together under one roof must have created its challenges, they appreciated each other more than ever. They both knew they shared something pretty special. They stuck with each other in the good times and the bad. That's loyalty.

While there's no mention of the relationship between Mary and Elizabeth after their contact in Luke 1, they were equally aware of the high calling God had extended to them. They looked to each other to pray, challenge each other in spiritual things, and keep each other accountable in their walk with Him. Doesn't that sound like the kind of relationship you'd like to share with someone?

Chapter Eight

GROWING THROUGH *Challenges* THAT TEACH LASTING LESSONS

THE HEART IS THE MOST POWERFUL MUSCLE IN OUR BODIES AND IT TAKES A LOT of work to keep it in shape. Believe me when I tell you that my heart has had some good workouts.

However, as challenging as they've been, the lessons I've learned through them have all been worth the pain and effort. Let's call them growing pains. They've stretched my faith, tested my endurance, and strengthened me in areas where I've become weak. Ultimately, they've all worked together for my good (Romans 8:28).

Let me warn you: spiritual training isn't for the fainthearted. It takes a whole lot of discipline, sweat, and a few shed tears in the process. My encouragement is this: to know pain is to know gain.

> *No discipline seems pleasant at the time, but painful. Later on, however, it produces a harvest of righteousness and peace for those who have been trained by it.*
> *Therefore, strengthen your feeble arms and weak knees. "Make level paths for your feet," so that the lame may not be disabled, but rather healed.*
> —Hebrews 12:11–13

Boot Camp

Pastor's wife training began a few years before I became one. What I learned in boot camp was put to good use on the frontlines of pastoral ministry.

I'd been hired as the chaplain at a church children's camp for the summer. That meant I was the spiritual head of both campers and staff. It was a big responsibility that I didn't take lightly. I was required to prepare and teach Bible studies to those who didn't really have any interest in them. Not only was it a hired position but it served as my internship as a camping major at Bible college. I'd therefore be graded on my performance.

I'd only been there for a couple of days when I realized I was the only other Christian on staff—that is, aside from the newly hired camp director and her newly born-again assistant.

It quickly became apparent that I was on Enemy territory—Satan's playground, if you will. Three staff members I had the privilege of leading to a saving knowledge of Jesus Christ were abruptly fired one after another.

Every day I'd take my Bible and head to the beach alone. There, I knelt on the sand and sobbed. Tears stained the pages of my Bible as I poured out my heart to the only One who knew what I was up against. He knew this kind of loneliness. He knew this kind of spiritual attack and oppression. He knew what it was to be mocked and persecuted. Day after day He met me right there at the beach. He collected my tears. He spoke into my pain. He encouraged my heart.

Was it painful? You better believe it! Would I ever want to go through anything like that again? Not a chance! But would I trade the experience I gained? Never! It was invaluable! It may have been the loneliest time I'd ever faced in my life to that point, but it was also the most deeply connected I'd ever felt to the Lord. As He trained me in His righteousness, I tapped into the lessons I learned and accessed them for years to come. They especially came in handy once I stepped onto the frontlines of spiritual warfare in full-time ministry.

The spiritual battle is no joke. Thankfully, I learned early on in ministry the importance of daily putting on the armour of God as I stepped onto the battlefield.

> *Finally, be strong in the Lord and in his mighty power. Put on the full armor of God, so that you can take your stand against the devil's schemes. For our struggle is not against flesh and blood, but against the rulers, against the authorities, against the powers of this dark world and against the spiritual forces of evil in the heavenly realms. Therefore put on the full armor of God, so that when the day of evil comes, you may be able to stand your ground, and after you have done everything, to stand. Stand firm then, with the belt of truth buckled around your waist, with the breastplate of righteousness in place, and with your feet fitted with the readiness that comes from the gospel of peace. In addition to all this, take up the shield of faith, with which you can extinguish*

all the flaming arrows of the evil one. Take the helmet of salvation and the
sword of the Spirit, which is the word of God.

—Ephesians 6:10–17

Survival Tip _____

> **Cry it out.** Tears are God's gift to us. They offer a release of things that
> might prevent healing. Let them fall and see the new life they produce.
> Psalm 42:1–3, 5 tells us, *"As the deer pants for streams of water, so my soul*
> *pants for you, my God. My soul thirsts for God, for the living God. When can*
> *I go and meet with God? My tears have been my food day and night, while*
> *people say to me all day long, 'Where is your God?' … Why, my soul, are you*
> *downcast? Why so disturbed within me? Put your hope in God, for I will yet*
> *praise him, my Savior and my God."* What are some of the lessons you've
> learned through challenging times? What has been produced for your
> good and God's glory through these times?

I Come to the Garden Alone

Our home was a gardener's haven. The property was encased by a ten-foot cedar
hedge. But it quickly became evident that we had purchased a home situated on Enemy territory. The spiritual battle we fought on behalf of our church family fiercely
pervaded our family. The Enemy threatened our ministry, attacked our children, and
attempted to sabotage our marriage. We faced anonymous letters, angry emails, conflict within the leadership, control issues involving founding members of the church,
and blatant sin in the camp, none of which we had been informed about upon our
arrival. Fiery darts from the pit of hell were hurled at us daily.

I stood over my kitchen sink and prayed several times a day. From there, I could
clearly see the hedge. It was a visual reminder of the spiritual hedge of protection
God had placed about me and my family. That's where His angels sat, guarding my
household through the most oppressive time I had ever experienced—guarding,
protecting, defending, upholding, avenging, intercepting, sheltering, preserving,
strengthening, and battling on our behalf.

I met regularly with Jesus in this proverbial Gethsemane. As I meandered along
the pathway strewn with bleeding hearts and wept, something remarkable began to
happen. My tears sowed seeds into the soil, and as they fell a deeper faith was also
planted. A more active prayer life began to take root and new aspects of my relationship with the Lord flourished.

In those dark days, I learned what it was to get on my knees. I experienced the power of fasting and prayer. I learned that quiet and confidence would be my strength (Isaiah 30:15). I learned to be still and know that He is God (Psalm 46:10).

I witnessed firsthand how *"those who sow with tears will reap with songs of joy"* (Psalm 126:5) as I cried and prayed and poured out my heart to my Saviour. I realized the joy I experienced wasn't because my circumstances had changed but because of God's presence with me in my garden.

Every day I would go to the garden alone while the dew was still on the roses. And the Lord walked with me, and He talked with me. He told me I was His own. And the joy the Lord and I shared as we tarried there in my garden, none other has ever known.[11]

A simple truth my husband used in a sermon he once preached says, "It's in the valley that the flowers grow." If that was true, I was becoming a gardener's dream!

Survival Tip

> **Pray it out.** There are no surprises to God where our hearts are concerned. He already knows all about it. Before a word is even on our tongues, He knows it completely (Psalm 139:4). We read in 1 Peter 5:7, *"Cast all your anxiety on him because he cares for you."* And Philippians 4:6–7 adds, *"Do not be anxious about anything, but in every situation, by prayer and petition, with thanksgiving, present your requests to God. And the peace of God, which transcends all understanding, will guard your hearts and your minds in Christ Jesus."* Set up a prayer closet. Make a prayer list. Write out a different list for each day of the week. Pray scripture. How will you choose to pray it out today?

Don't Forget to Remember

I'd invited her over for coffee that afternoon to get to know her and allow her to understand where I'd come from. I wanted to share the journey my husband and I had been on. I felt it was important that she understand what had brought us to this point in our ministry.

I had painstakingly written it all down so I wouldn't forget a single detail. I needed to get it out. I had persevered through much and needed to share it with my

---

11 "I Come to the Garden Alone," C. Austen Miles, 1913.

new friend to take the next step toward healing and continue on in ministry with a healthy attitude.

As we swayed back and forth on my backyard swing, I poured out my heart to her, all while wiping tears and on occasion pausing to blow my nose.

After a while, she put her hand on mine and said, "Lisa, if this is too painful, you don't have to rehearse it with me."

"No. I need to do this."

I knew it was part of my healing to let it out with someone I could trust. I knew that to go forward, I had to visit where I'd been.

When I finished my lament, she lovingly yet more matter-of-factly than I expected said, "Well, now you can put it all behind you and forget about it."

Forget about it? How could she expect me to forget about it? It had become a part of my story. This was the evidence of God's hand of faithfulness in my life and ministry. Valuable lessons I'd learned and spiritual discipline I'd been trained by, with principles that needed to be shared with others. I could only hope that a ministry of healing and hope would be produced from the seeds of sorrow I'd sown with my own tears.

"I don't believe the Lord wants me to forget," I told her with more resolve than I knew I had. "How else will I minister to the broken if I can't remember being broken?"

I hadn't ever more fully understood that God wants us to remember the pain of our past—not to bury us in it or get stuck in it, but to weed through it all and remember His faithfulness and declare it for His glory. Just as Moses recounted the Israelites' journey out of slavery, he reminded them not to forget the Lord their God once they'd settled in the Promised Land (Deuteronomy 8:10–14). That's why we need to remember to not forget, and not forget to remember.

Survival Tip

> **Talk it out.** God has provided us with a built-in outlet. Conversation with a trusted friend, spouse, or professional counsellor allows us to process things that get muddled in our minds. Who is someone safe you can talk to and process with? Who is a good listener? Matthew 18:20 says, *"Again, truly I tell you that if two of you on earth agree about anything they ask for, it will be done for them by my Father in heaven. For where two or three gather in my name, there am I with them."* As you recall your hardships and challenges, don't forget to share of the Lord's faithfulness in the mix. Who is someone you need to talk through some things with? Is there something you need to talk with the Lord about?

Awful Attitudes

Some of the greatest challenges I've ever had to work through didn't come via some outside source. Let's just say they were a little bit more personal. The most humbling part is that I learned it from a group of two- and three-year-olds.

This particular age group was one of my most favourite ministries. Maybe it was because I was able to tap into my home daycare upbringing. Or perhaps it was because I missed my own young children, now grown. Or it could be because they taught me so much about myself, including some of the parts of myself I preferred to keep to myself.

Every Sunday, I arrived early to the brightly coloured room. I'd set up stations for the kids to enjoy. It was always exciting to come up with creative ways to allow them to experience Jesus. To begin with, every week I set the tone with some kids praise music. I played it loud enough that they'd hear it as they came down the hallway and approached the room.

Some weeks they walked in to find bins of instant oatmeal or cornmeal standing in for an indoor sandbox. Other weeks the dry mixture was replaced by water for the kids to float their boats. Often I set up dress-up clothes or playdough with creative equipment like cookie-cutters, rolling pins, and garlic presses—one of their favourite activities.

I created a story corner with colourful spongy mats and allowed the children to take turns as the teacher. Together we shared, laughed, played, danced, and learned about Jesus and how much He loved, welcomed, and esteemed children just like them.

They were the cutest, sweetest, most playful, loveable, and compliant little things—until they weren't.

One Sunday morning, one child came stomping into my joyously resounding room with a dark cloud hanging over her head. Frown upon her brow, she proceeded to grump around the room and grab toys from other children who stood back in her wake—much like the Red Sea stood at attention to allow Moses and his followers to walk on through.

Choosing my timing just right, lest I be caught up in the wake, I asked her, "What on earth did you eat for breakfast this morning?"

"Awfuls," she replied with a pout on her lip. Did she mean waffles?

Playing along with her unintentional slip of the tongue, I said, "Well, please make sure you never eat awfuls again before you come to church!"

Then it occurred to me. How often did I eat awfuls on a Sunday morning? And what was I dishing out every Sunday morning to these young children when I did? Luke 6:45 tells us, *"A good man brings good things out of the good stored up in his heart, and an evil man brings evil things out of the evil stored up in his heart. For the mouth speaks what the heart is full of."* There would be no more awfuls on the menu if I was going to produce lasting fruit amongst this impressionable bunch.

Survival Tip

> **Play it out.** Life in ministry can get serious in a hurry. We can take ourselves too seriously. Therefore, we must learn to work hard, but play even harder. Take time to have fun, let loose, and be a kid again. Phil Callaway's books offer a great source to help you laugh at life—and even laugh at yourself. Look him up online. Tune into his broadcast *Laugh Again*. Release the cares of your day into God's hands. Take every opportunity to seize each day and live it to the fullest. Remember what we read in John 10:10: *"The thief comes only to steal and kill and destroy; I have come that they may have life, and have it to the full."* What are some ways you can have fun? What are things that bring you joy and laughter? What is one thing you can "play" at today?

The Refiner's Fire

It was January and we were beginning our seventh year of ministry in this particular church. I wrote in my prayer journal, "It's our seventh year! The year of perfecting! How will you perfect me this year?"

If the number seven is God's number for perfection, perfect! But then I stopped to think of what it is that allows God's perfecting to be accomplished: refinement. The word swept in and nearly knocked me off my feet. I had already met God as the Refiner, and I was pretty aware of the fact that once we've permitted Him to refine us, we remain in the fire until the Refiner can see in us His pure reflection.

I had relented long ago, so I wasn't expecting Him to crank up the heat.

The Refiner's fire was set ablaze when my nineteen-year-old son Ben was diagnosed with leukemia. The scorching effect continued when he was promoted to his heavenly home, only one year and a week later.

I hadn't gotten to church the entire year, a difficult feat as a pastor's wife. It was even more challenging upon my return. Ministry called. But I wasn't the same person I had been before my son got sick. Life wasn't the same. However, somehow I had to persevere, regroup, and make my way back to what I'd left behind.

Thankfully, the Lord was my portion and the strength of my heart (Psalm 73:26). I sat in Pain's classroom and took thorough notes as God led me through the valley of the shadow of the death of my son. There in the valley, my Good Shepherd assured me that I need not fear evil, for He faithfully walked alongside me. His rod and His staff comforted me. Day by day, step by step, and breath by breath, He led me beside still waters and restored my soul (Psalm 23). My prayer came from Psalm 40:1–3:

> I waited patiently for the Lord; he turned to me and heard my cry. He lifted me out of the slimy pit, out of the mud and mire; he set my feet on a rock and gave me a firm place to stand. He put a new song in my mouth, a hymn of praise to our God. Many will see and fear the Lord and put their trust in him.

The Lord answered my prayer. Many did see and fear and put their trust in Him. He opened up new ministry opportunities, allowed me to take a new approach to my role as a pastor's wife, and gave me a platform to share a new message of hope to the hurting, grieving, and hopeless.

While it didn't alleviate my pain, I was so very thankful that the Lord used my pain for His purposes. This wasn't just fruit. This was abundant fruit, fruit that would ripple and last into eternity by the grace of God.

The Lord did indeed give me a new song to sing. What began as a lament turned into a hymn of praise to my God.

Survival Tip ————

Write it out. There's a certain kind of release that comes with being able to write out our innermost thoughts, struggles, concerns, and joys. Why not consider starting a journal? Record your thoughts, write out scripture, and present your requests before the Lord. Write verses on post-it notes and stick them on your bathroom mirror, fridge door, or car dashboard. Write out a chapter or book of the Bible to allow it to penetrate your heart. Choose one of your favourite verses and write it out in your own words. Take it to heart—literally. As Deuteronomy 11:18 says, *"Fix these words of mine in your hearts and minds; tie them as symbols on your hands and bind them on your foreheads."*

Call Me Mara

I had changed. I was no longer who I used to be, much less the person everybody else remembered me to be. It wasn't all bad behaviour on my part; I was just unpredictable. For the year my son battled leukemia, I didn't attend church. Instead I stayed home or in hospital with him and tuned into Sunday morning services on television.

That year, I experienced the love of our church family from a distance. I saw evidence of their care around my home: a loaded fridge and freezer, a manicured lawn, a clean house, and a stack of gift and greeting cards.

However, when I returned to church two weeks after the funeral, things weren't the same as I'd left them. Not only were there new faces, the faces I recognized looked different. They were sad when they looked at me. I could feel their eyes shift when I entered—some of them questioning, some of them speculating, and none of them knowing quite what to do with me. Unfortunately, their desire to draw near to comfort me or hug me became a threat. I feared their good intentions would provoke the raw emotion that brewed just under the surface.

I could barely breathe as I entered the sanctuary. Even more challenging was the thought of engaging in the ministries I'd previously been involved in. Panic attacks overtook me as I made my way into the church every Sunday.

Initially my grief defined me. Like Ruth's mother-in-law, Naomi, I had a new name. "Call me Mara," I felt like saying to my helpless onlookers. I feared that my grief would become my identity, if I wasn't careful. And that was the last thing I wanted. Nobody wanted things to be the way they used to be more than I did. I didn't want to be a part of this club of grieving parents, and I certainly didn't want to be labelled as a victim.

What's a church family to do? What would you do? Thankfully, I was given the time and space to heal. I walked a lot. I cried a lot. I journaled my thoughts until I had writer's cramps. I gardened. I went for therapeutic massage. Then I cried some more.

Thankfully, friends waited patiently for me to emerge again. And while I knew I would never be the same, I prayed that the transformation God was formulating in me would make me look a little more like Jesus when all was said and done.

Survival Tip

> **Work it out.** When we're wrestling with matters of the heart, sometimes the best thing we can do is physically work it out. Make yourself get out of bed every morning. Don't wait to feel good before you do something; do it and then you'll feel good. Move your body. Clean your house. Work out your grief, pain, and frustration by walking or exercising. James 1:2–4 advises us, *"Consider it pure joy, my brothers and sisters, whenever you face trials of many kinds, because you know that the testing of your faith produces perseverance. Let perseverance finish its work so that you may be mature and complete, not lacking anything."* What is something your heart is wrestling with? What is one thing you can do today to work it out?

Graveyard Church

I couldn't do it again. I couldn't enter that church building one more time to the line-up of people using me to get to my husband. I couldn't be the prey of anyone with a dump truck of troubles or woes or criticisms or concerns, not even one more time.

I had always been accustomed to being the first to arrive with my husband and children, but I was about to break tradition. This girl was going to drop and run, but where would I run to? I didn't feel like sitting in a coffee shop for an hour before the service.

And then I spotted it. A cemetery!

Perfect, I thought. It was just the right location for my pre-church worship service.

I drove along the path around the property. Then I came to a roundabout that seemed like a good place to stop and sit for a while. I parked the car and stared at the headstones surrounding me.

I turned on Steven Curtis Chapman's album, *The Glorious Unfolding*. I cranked up the volume to flush out all the negativity I had been stewing on. In their stead, I prayed and allowed God's presence to fill my vehicle.

My thoughts turned to death, but not in the way one might expect them to. I didn't wish to die, although I wasn't afraid to. Heaven was looking more like home all the time. There had already been so much death—the death of dreams, the death of ministries, the death of our son, and the death of life as we knew it.

So in the deadly silence, I began to pray. Perhaps there were some things God needed to put to death in *me*. Better yet, perhaps there were some things He wanted to resurrect! Maybe there was even new life to be birthed in me?

Week after week, I met with the Lord in the graveyard and prayed that there would be a glorious unfolding in my life. There were lessons I needed to learn from and take note of. There were old habits and attitudes and ways of doing life and ministry that needed to be put to death for the Lord to produce new life.

As I prayed for this new life to spring forth, a resurrection began to occur, reminding me what true life was all about:

- Life is too short to pretend, to simply fake it until we make it. God calls us to be real, authentic, and transparent, especially in our relationship with Him.
- Life is too short to spend on activities that only waste our time. Time is precious to the Lord and we need to use it wisely.
- Life is too short to exist merely for the sake of a paycheck or a pension.
- Life is too short to let the fear of failure, the fear of man, or the fear of the future control us and deprive us of all that God has for us.
- Life is too short to indulge in shallow, idle, and meaningless conversation and miss out on meaningful conversations about life and death and things that matter in eternity.
- Life is too short to hold grudges that in the end will only serve to hold us captive.
- Life is too short to put off investing in and enjoying a personal and intimate relationship with the Lord until a future "there and then" when we could be investing and enjoying it in the "here and now."
- Life is too short to wait for life to happen when we can choose to make it happen.
- Life is too short to allow the boulders in our life to become obstacles rather than opportunities to climb to higher heights.
- Life is too short to waste our time wandering in the wilderness, longing for the life that was seemingly so much better in Egypt—not when God calls us to a Promised Land full of life and growth and fruit in abundance.
- Life is too short to hold onto the past so dearly that we can't grasp and embrace all that God is extending to us through the outstretched arms of Jesus.

Jesus said to her, "I am the resurrection and the life. The one who believes in me will live, even though they die; and whoever lives by believing in me will never die. Do you believe this?"

—John 11:25

Praise it out. There are various forms of praise: prayer, acclamation, celebration, singing, and making a joyful noise (Psalm 150). We can even praise ourselves out of bondage, like Paul and Silas did (Acts 16:25). Colossians 3:1–3 tells us, *"Since, then, you have been raised with Christ, set your hearts on things above, where Christ is, seated at the right hand of God. Set your minds on things above, not on earthly things."* Philippians 4:8 adds, *"Finally, brothers and sisters, whatever is true, whatever is noble, whatever is right, whatever is pure, whatever is lovely, whatever is admirable—if anything is excellent or praiseworthy—think about such things."* What practices can you put into place to maintain a healthy attitude and heart of worship toward the Lord? In Psalm 100:4 we read, *"Enter his gates with thanksgiving and his courts with praise."* Remember: praise is the gateway to the heart of God. Consider writing a daily list of things you're grateful for.

Like all those who have gone before us, fix your eyes on Jesus for all the hope, assurance, peace, joy, stability, and equilibrium you need. Use challenges for your advantage, to develop character and grow you into your Saviour's likeness and produce a harvest of righteousness and peace as you're trained by it (Hebrews 12:11).

We are hard pressed on every side, but not crushed; perplexed, but not in despair; persecuted, but not abandoned; struck down, but not destroyed.

—2 Corinthians 4:8–9

It takes a lot of hard work, training, and discipline, but in the end it's all worth it.

For physical training is of some value, but godliness has value for all things, holding promise for both the present life and the life to come.

—1 Timothy 4:8

Straight from the Father's Heart

*Therefore we do not lose heart. Though outwardly we are wasting
away, yet inwardly we are being renewed day by day. For our light
and momentary troubles are achieving for us an eternal glory that far
outweighs them all. So we fix our eyes not on what is seen, but
on what is unseen, since what is seen is temporary,
but what is unseen is eternal.*
—2 Corinthians 4:16–18

Biblical Mentors
The Hall of Faith (Hebrews 11–12:1–3)

If there's a quality that we need in order to face challenges both within and without the church, it's resilience. We see the kind of resilience it takes displayed in Hebrews 11.

So how did these men and women of old get back up when life threw punches? How did they bounce back? How did they keep on keeping on? How did they maintain momentum and stamina? How did they persevere?

Thankfully, Hebrews 12:1–3 provides a helpful guideline:

> *Therefore, since we are surrounded by such a great cloud of witnesses, let us throw off everything that hinders and the sin that so easily entangles. And let us run with perseverance the race marked out for us, fixing our eyes on Jesus, the pioneer and perfecter of faith. For the joy set before him he endured the cross, scorning its shame, and sat down at the right hand of the throne of God. Consider him who endured such opposition from sinners, so that you will not grow weary and lose heart.*

Fostering meaningful relationships keeps us on track. Hebrews 12:1 begins by saying, *"Therefore, since we are surrounded by such a great cloud of witnesses…"* Although the author of Hebrews is referring to those who have died and gone before us, God has also surrounded us with some great cheerleaders here on earth.

So make sure you surround yourself with people who encourage and energize you. People who inspire you, believe in you, invest in you, and bring out the best in you. People who affirm God's calling in your life, and people you can do the same for.

> *Therefore encourage one another and build each other up, just as in fact you are doing.*
>
> —1 Thessalonians 5:11

Removing distractions prevents dizziness. Hebrews 12:1 goes on to say, *"let us throw off everything that hinders and the sin that so easily entangles."* We read in the book of Ephesians,

> *You were taught, with regard to your former way of life, to put off your old self, which is being corrupted by its deceitful desires; to be made new in the attitude*

of your minds; and to put on the new self, created to be like God in true righteousness and holiness.

—Ephesians 4:22–24

Life is full of all kinds of distractions: deceitful desires, bad attitudes, and a whole list of corrupt thoughts. It doesn't help that we live in a society affected by ADD that keeps us seeking out the next quick fix of adrenalin and excitement. All the more reason for us to cast aside anything that prevents us from successfully running the race. I can feel the dizziness subsiding as we speak.

Perseverance is possible when we pace ourselves. Next, Hebrews 12:1 says, *"And let us run with perseverance the race marked out for us."* Life isn't a sprint; it's a marathon. We're in it for the long haul. The way to persevere is to take it slow, pausing for refreshment when necessary, and then carry on. All the while we follow the path that is marked out for us.

Let's face it: it's hard to keep going when the going gets tough. But it helps when you know what your perseverance will ultimately obtain.

Not only so, but we also glory in our sufferings, because we know that suffering produces perseverance; perseverance, character; and character, hope. And hope does not put us to shame, because God's love has been poured out into our hearts through the Holy Spirit, who has been given to us.

—Romans 5:3–5

Having a focus helps us reach our goal. In the next part of the passage, the writer of Hebrews gives us a focal point: *"fixing our eyes on Jesus, the pioneer and perfecter of faith"* (Hebrews 12:2).

If you aim at nothing, you'll hit it every time. Guaranteed! Therefore, you can't simply choose not to look at or think about something; you have to choose to look at or think about something else!

The people listed in Hebrews 11 were able to endure many hardships because they realized that *"God had planned something better"* (Hebrews 11:40), and they had set their sights on this promise!

Joy helps us look beyond our troubles. Hebrews 12:2–3 says,

For the joy set before him he endured the cross, scorning its shame, and sat down at the right hand of the throne of God. Consider him who endured such opposition from sinners, so that you will not grow weary and lose heart.

Note that Jesus was able to sit down. This tells me that His heart was at rest, even as He endured the cross. How? Because He set joy before Him. That is, He looked beyond the cross to His ultimate purpose—eternity with you and me!

He has also set eternity in our hearts (Ecclesiastes 3:11). The joy of the Lord is our strength (Nehemiah 10:8).

Ultimately, we are given a sense of joy, hope, and purpose by considering the One who has gone before us. Consider His goodness. Consider His strength. Consider His compassions that never fail.

Finally, consider that He patiently and excitedly awaits our arrival through heaven's gates. Our hearts will be able to be resilient and endure any challenge we might face, knowing the best is yet to come!

Chapter Nine

RECOGNIZING GOD'S *Blessings* WHEN YOUR VISION IS OBSTRUCTED

THERE ARE TIMES IN MINISTRY, AND LIFE IN GENERAL, WHEN IT CAN BE HARD to see the blessings. Burdens obstruct our view and warp our perspective. In those moments, we feel sorry for ourselves, feeling forgotten or overlooked.

But God hasn't forgotten us. He's inscribed us on the palm of His hands (Isaiah 49:16). His blessings abound, even though we may not recognize them.

I'd be remiss if I didn't open the door to reveal the place in my heart where some of my personal stock of these blessings is stored. Some are treasures I've found in darkness (Isaiah 45:3). Others have been stored up in heaven, where moths and vermin do not destroy, and where thieves do not break in and steal (Matthew 6:19–21). In every case, my God has supplied my every need according to His riches in glory in Christ Jesus (Philippians 4:19).

Muffin Ministry

We were awakened in the middle of the night by a loud crash. Then we were kept awake for several hours while the yelling, screaming, cursing, and more banging carried on. These were our new neighbours. They had just moved into the apartment below us a month earlier, but we had yet to meet them. What an introduction!

The following morning, after our sleepless night, my husband came up with a brilliant idea. I might add that his notion of brilliance and mine are two very different things.

"Why don't you bake some muffins and take them down to our neighbours today while I'm at the church?" he enthusiastically suggested.

"What?" I impulsively replied.

What if our new neighbours had a gun? What if they hauled me into their apartment and I was never seen again? What if…

I played out several scenarios in my mind.

After giving it some thought, I conceded. Later that morning, giving everyone downstairs some much-needed time to sleep in and me enough time to convince myself that this was a wise thing to do, I made my way down a floor and parked myself in front of their door. What would I find? Would they even answer the door when I knocked?

I took a deep breath and gave a light knock. When the door was gingerly opened, there stood before me a timid woman with dark circles around her eyes and a face that told stories I wasn't sure I was prepared to acknowledge. She had been weathered by the storms of life.

After introducing myself and welcoming her to the neighbourhood, I presented my freshly baked chocolate chip banana muffins. It seemed to be a meagre offering.

She invited me into her apartment and I tentatively accepted.

The air was perfumed with fresh cigarette smoke. The atmosphere was dank and dreary. I could tell by the look of the mess before me that housekeeping wasn't exactly her thing. As she drew me into her living room, I tried not to judge it by appearances. But I wished I could escape the circumstances in which I was now fully immersed.

She said that she wanted to introduce me to her nine-year-old daughter, Jackie. There she lay on the couch, sporting thinning, scraggly, unkempt hair. She displayed a beautiful, bright smile in stark contrast to the dark circles that matched her mother's. She had me with her smile.

"My daughter has a rare form of brain cancer," her mother said.

My heart leapt from my chest cavity and landed squarely onto this feeble child's face. From that day on, she became not just my mission but my sweet little friend.

Not long after our friendship began, I became pregnant with our first child. I'd invite Jackie into my humble apartment to allow her to lie on my couch while I sat beside her. She'd place her small hand on my abdomen and feel the baby move.

Once my baby girl was born, she'd come up and lie on the same couch, cuddling this new distraction from her sad reality.

As she was physically able, Jackie accepted our offer to bring her to our church's children's program. She loved the diversion and enjoyed interacting with other children her age, something she didn't get a lot of due to her condition. She eagerly memorized Bible verses with my coaching.

Then one day, right on the floor beside the changing table in the baby's nursery, Jackie invited Jesus into her barely beating heart.

She met her newfound Saviour face to face by the end of that year. My husband had the painful privilege of performing her funeral. Joy came in knowing we will see her again someday.

Who knew that a muffin mission could have such a powerful earthly impact with everlasting rewards?

Survival Tip

> **Be willing to move beyond your comfort zone.** While it might be unnerving, there's no greater joy than sharing the good news of Jesus Christ. It also holds one of life's richest rewards. Think of ways you can be used by God to shine His light into the darkness of someone's life (Colossians 4:2–7). List five to ten people you know who could use a touch from God. What can you do to bless one of these people this week? It could be sharing the Gospel. What greater blessing is there than to offer a word of hope or truth to a discouraged soul, especially when it's the Living Word? As Matthew 5:16 reminds us, *"In the same way, let your light shine before others, that they may see your good deeds and glorify your Father in heaven."*

We Are Family

In all our years of raising young kids in the fast lane of ministry, we never had the privilege of having family close by. Thankfully we've always been blessed to have those in our congregation take us under their familial wing.

In each church we've served in, our heavenly Father's family has provided us with gifts, celebrations, and bonuses for our service. Food, financial assistance, and practical support have been a few expressions of their love.

I'll never forget when Erin, my fourth baby, was born. I was exhausted most of the time.

One day, I opened my door to find a sweet woman of God standing there with an entire meal.

"I'm exchanging this meal for your kids," she said.

And within the next few minutes, once we'd taken the time to mop up my tears of joy, she had them all suited up and ready for a fun outing so I could rest.

Then there was the time when our firstborn, Natalie, was diagnosed with spinal meningitis at the age of ten months. It turned out that I was already pregnant with Benjamin, which explained the added exhaustion. The visits, prayers, and support our church family provided were invaluable.

Money was tight in our growing household, and as our children grew, so too did their appetites. I remember getting to the till with a cart overflowing with groceries and breaking out in a cold sweat as the cashier rang in the amount. I tried to be as frugal as I could. Most of the time, I was content with the abundance God supplied, but that didn't stop my heart from longing for different frills for my kids.

Speaking of frills, I longed for a pretty little bathing suit for my infant daughter—with frills, if possible. Bathing suits felt like a luxury item, so I hesitated to purchase one.

One day a friend called me, out of the blue, looking for someone she could pass on her little girl's clothes to. She was embarrassed to think she was offering hand-me-downs, but I wasn't too proud to help her out, having been raised by a single mom and well accustomed to being the recipient of such items.

The next day, I opened my front door to find three full garbage bags of freshly cleaned and meticulously folded, seemingly barely worn clothes. I opened the first bag and immediately discovered—you guessed it—not one but four beautiful girls bathing suits. With frills!

Just like our good Father loves to give good gifts to His children, so did I! My heavenly Father heard the cry of this mother's heart. I'm grateful to think that He uses His people to deliver blessings to our front doorstep. He supplies not only everything we need but He gives them with frills on top, even it comes secondhand.

There's nothing like the church when it's doing what God intended it to do and being what God designed it to be. I'm happy to say that we've experienced that kind of church health firsthand. As Galatians 6:10 says, *"Therefore, as we have opportunity, let us do good to all people, especially to those who belong to the family of believers."* I'm so glad I'm a part of the family of God!

Survival Tip ———————————————————

> **Be specific in your prayer requests.** We usually don't have a problem listing our woes, troubles, and concerns. Why not consider listing all the answers to those prayers? Philippians 4:6–7 exhorts us, *"Don't worry about anything; instead, pray about everything; tell God your needs, and don't forget to thank him for his answers"* (TLB). Make a list for every day of the week—one day for family, one day for people in your church family, one day for unsaved loved ones, one day for ministry, etc. Activate your prayer list by letting people know you're praying for them. And make sure you leave some room to record all the answers to your prayers that God provides.

Eggs in a Basket

It started with one woman, then two, and before I knew it a dozen women were sitting in my family room, each married to a husband who didn't know the Lord in a personal way. "Eggs in a Basket," they called themselves.

Every week we'd gather in my home to cry and laugh, studying God's Word and praying for the salvation of their husbands. Most of the women were new believers themselves and each was having a hard time living out her faith in her home. They felt the loneliness of sitting in church alone.

We took on 1 Peter 3:1 as our theme: *"Wives, in the same way submit yourselves to your own husbands so that, if any of them do not believe the word, they may be won over without words by the behavior of their wives…"*

Week by week, we lit my home on fire and set my heart ablaze! The fervent prayers of these women fanned the flame. And as we drew near to the One who ignited our spirits, one by one, after only three months together, their husbands came to the Lord. Twelve eggs in a basket—and the eggs were hatching!

Survival Tip

Be the church. Acts 2:42–47 tells us what the early church was like. When was the last time you were part of a group like the early church? Why not gather a group of people together for a meal, a Bible study, and prayer. Gatherings without the Lord are mere gatherings, but fellowship invites Him into the mix. We read in 1 Thessalonians 5:11, *"Therefore encourage one another and build each other up, just as in fact you are doing."* Hebrews 10:24–25 adds, *"And let us consider how we may spur one another on toward love and good deeds, not giving up meeting together, as some are in the habit of doing, but encouraging one another—and all the more as you see the Day approaching."*

Oak Beams and Sunbeams

For our tenth anniversary of ministry, our church family gifted us with some money. It was intended to contribute toward a trip to Florida to visit Disneyworld. The thought was nice, but the timing was off and a tad unrealistic. I'd just had my fourth baby and now had four children under the age of five and a half. It would take twenty-four hours to drive to Disneyworld, compounded by potty stops and diaper changes and post-partum hormones. It would be a complete disaster. Wishing upon a star to make all our dreams come true would have been more like a nightmare!

So David and I opted to take the money and instead purchase an oak table and chairs for our dining room. Every child's dream! Not. As disappointed as our two eldest children were, we knew they were young and would soon forget about it.

Forget, they did not!

Natalie was prone to bringing friends over many times throughout the week—and each time she welcomed a new friend, she gave a house tour. I'd hear the tour taking place as I prepared snacks in the kitchen.

"This is our living room. This is our kitchen. This is my mom. Up here is my bedroom. And this is our washroom." She'd eventually make her way to our dining room and say with disdain, "And *this* is our trip to Florida!"

Years later, we knew it was time to redeem that trip. We knew, in the words of Ecclesiastes 5:5, that it's *"better not to make a vow than to make one and not fulfill it."*

The church family we were part of at the time rallied their resources to bless us. The kids ministry took up a specially designated offering every week to gift us with. To think, I was part of that ministry team and had no idea that our initiative was to be directed back at my family.

A very generous couple blessed us with their condo for two glorious weeks. To add to the effect, the Lord provided us with beautiful, sunny weather with record-breaking temperatures the entire time we were there.

We laughed. We tanned. We swam. We loved every second of every minute of it. It was the vacation of a lifetime where all our dreams came true!

Survival Tip

> **Make a grateful list.** We are blessed beyond measure! The good news is that we don't have to wait until Thanksgiving to give thanks to the One from whom all blessings flow. List some of the things and people you're grateful for. List some of the ways God has provided for your needs through His body, the church. Write a thank-you note to someone who has blessed you. Take time to list and thank God for all of His goodness to you. According to Ephesians 5:19–20, *"Sing and make music from your heart to the Lord, always giving thanks to God the Father for everything, in the name of our Lord Jesus Christ."*

A Little Bird Told Me So

I sat in my son Jacob's Kindergarten circle listening to all the children share stories and personal items of interest during their show-and-tell time. One little girl captivated my attention with a story of finding an oriole.

An oriole? We had several birdfeeders in our backyard and had attracted cardinals and chickadees, mourning doves, sparrows, and goldfinches. But I had yet to see an Oriole.

Likely catching all the students off-guard, I asked, "How do you attract the orioles?"

"With oranges," she answered matter-of-factly. "We cut an orange in half, and then we set it out in our yard."

It had been a very long, blue winter, and I just needed a bit of added colour. I figured that a brilliant orange oriole might do the trick. So you can bet that the first thing I did when I got home was search for oriole food.

It turned out to be an unsuccessful search for an orange. However, I did find a grapefruit. I promptly cut it in half and set it outside.

Over the next few days, I watched and waited. No oriole. Okay, so the grapefruit wasn't their first preference. I'd pick up some oranges next time I went grocery shopping.

The next day as I stared into our backyard, I whispered a little prayer: "Lord, it's a small, insignificant thing to ask, but my heart would be so encouraged if you would send an oriole my way. Amen."

That afternoon, as I sat reading my Bible in the chair positioned next to the window in our family room, something caught my attention in my peripheral vision. I turned my head toward the window and, perched on the narrowest part of the window ledge, no more than two feet from my face, was the most beautiful orange bird I'd ever seen. It was an oriole!

My heart swelled with joy and tears filled my eyes. Then the bird tilted his head as if to say, "Well, here I am!" I was allowed only a moment to take in this blessed sight, and then the bird flew away.

It wasn't until I'd had the opportunity to absorb this unexpected visit from heaven that it occurred to me that the oriole hadn't even partaken in the citrus treat I'd set out. There was not a doubt in my mind that God had sent the bird on the wings of my childlike prayer. I was reminded of what Matthew 6:26 says: *"Look at the birds of the air; they do not sow or reap or store away in barns, and yet your heavenly Father feeds them. Are you not much more valuable than they?"*

Some days more than others it's easy to become overwhelmed, anxious, and discouraged. Moments like the one with the oriole have proven time and again that I have a God who loves me intimately and cares for the most privately expressed and minuscule longings of my heart.

So I've learned to watch and wait for Him to surprise me with joy as He flies in out of the blue to visit me.

Survival Tip ———————

> **Track your joys.** Keep a journal to record something every day that encourages your heart or brings you joy. It could be a rainbow in the sky, a beautiful sunset, a warm hug, or the smile of a child. These are the simple pleasures that put a smile on your heart, personal messages from the Lord that encourage and boost your spirit. Philippians 4:4–5 tells us, *"Rejoice in the Lord always. I will say it again: Rejoice! Let your gentleness be evident to all. The Lord is near."* We also read, *"Our mouths were filled with laughter, our tongues with songs of joy. Then it was said among the nations, 'The Lord has done great things for them.' The Lord has done great things for us, and we are filled with joy"* (Psalm 126:2–3).

The Great Commission

We had chosen the absolute worst time of the year to move. And if that wasn't bad enough, the house we bought wouldn't be available for another five months.

Thankfully, a married couple we knew from church was moving and offered that we live in their home until we took possession of our own. The board promised that our rent would be covered.

So I was surprised when the owner arrived on our doorstep one day looking for her rent money.

Insult was added to injury when the house was put on the market the day we moved in. What a surprise! This meant enduring several house showings a day as we camped out of boxes.

In the meantime, our two youngest children got chickenpox, and just to add to the excitement, our entire family of six ran two courses of the stomach flu. Unable to attend church for the first two and a half months of us being there, our new church family wondered if their new pastor had a wife.

One day the realtor didn't show up to give the day's showing. Tired of waiting around, I offered to give the tour myself. The next day, these clients made an offer and a Sold sign replaced the For Sale sign.

Jokingly, I told my husband that I deserved the commission. I was the one who sold the house, after all.

A few weeks later, I received a call from friends of ours from a previous church. One of them was our realtor but had needed to pass off our home to a co-worker as he would be away when we were selling. They happened to be visiting the area and wanted to know if they could drop by, so I put on the coffee and welcomed them in.

Before they left, he handed me an envelope. He explained that although he hadn't sold our house, he had received a commission for it. Then he informed me that he felt impressed to bless us with it.

I picked my jaw up off the ground as I thanked them. I got my commission, after all!

Survival Tip

> **Count your blessings.** We aren't entitled to anything, yet God chooses to bless us regardless. Consider and record how the Lord has blessed and encouraged you during times in your life when you needed an extra boost or compensation, even if you didn't deserve it. Find a box, bottle, or decorative bag to collect any encouragement cards, articles, pictures, or encouraging emails you receive for an entire year. At the end of the year, read them. You'll be encouraged all over again! And remember the words of Philippians 1:9–11: *"And this is my prayer: that your love may abound more and more in knowledge and depth of insight, so that you may be able to discern what is best and may be pure and blameless for the day of Christ, filled with the fruit of righteousness that comes through Jesus Christ— to the glory and praise of God."*

You Can Run, but You Can't Hide

I'd spent a couple of hours preparing for and exerting myself in a room full of children. I'd led them in worship, creatively enacted a Bible story, organized the activity, and now it was time to take a bit of a breather before the worship service began.

More than that, I needed a fresh encounter with God. My vision was becoming a little blurred with burdens. All I wanted was some peace and quiet, and a little time to myself.

As soon as my responsibility to the children was finished, I made a beeline to the restroom. I darted through the crowds of children, now mingling with parents. It had been a bad idea to enjoy a second cup of coffee that morning.

Without a lot of time to spare, I dodged into one of the stalls. I had barely locked the door when I heard my name called.

"Lisa."

To say I was a little startled would be an understatement. Then the voice spoke again.

"Lisa! I've been calling your name! Didn't you hear me?"

I was hesitant to respond. My initial thought was to ask, "God? Is that you?"

I opened the stall door, not knowing who was waiting for me on the other side. Before me stood a woman, a dear sister in the Lord whose heart I loved.

From her breathless heaves, it was evident that she hadn't simply sauntered through the foyer to find me; she'd outright ran after me!

She told me that she had wanted to share something she had waited all week to tell me. With tears in her eyes, she described an incredibly powerful encounter she'd had with the Lord earlier that week. It was exactly what I needed to hear that day, especially from someone who was in a hot pursuit to see Jesus, meet with, and hear from Him.

On a day when I didn't have the opportunity to actively pursue Him, He pursued me—and made sure He found me! I knew I could run, but I certainly couldn't hide! As we're told in 1 Chronicles 16:9, *"For the eyes of the Lord range throughout the earth to strengthen those whose hearts are fully committed to him."*

Survival Tip

> **Go on a God Hunt.** When was the last time you intentionally sought the Lord? Sometimes our vision can be clouded by circumstances. We can feel abandoned and alone, even at church. Instead of waiting for God to show up, why not actively pursue Him? This week, make it your goal to seek Him out. Ask Him to reveal Himself in a personal way. Watch and listen for how He's working in the lives of those around you. Who is someone you could share your testimony with, someone you could ask to share their testimony with you? Initiate a conversation with someone and mutually share something recent the Lord's done or is doing in your lives. It will be a blessing to both of you. Deuteronomy 4:29 says, *"But if from there you seek the Lord your God, you will find him if you seek him with all your heart and with all your soul."*

Pennies from Heaven

The significance of pennies takes me back to when I was in Bible college with limited funds—and I mean limited! I was being raised by a single mom, raising three children with no financial support. Therefore, it was up to me to come up with some cash of my own.

So I took on a job as a waitress. It wasn't exactly my dream job or my gifting.

One day, my boss pulled me aside to a table for two tucked away in a cozy corner. He told me that as nice a girl as I was, things just weren't working out. He gave me a choice: he could fire me or I could quit. Quitting would look better on my resume, so I promptly handed in my uniform and began my forty-five-minute trek home.

As I walked along, I began pouring out my financial concerns to the Lord. "God, you led me to Bible college, but my resources have run dry. How do you expect me to graduate without a job?"

My rant went on for blocks.

Then I looked down at the sidewalk and spotted a penny. I stooped down and put it in my pocket before carrying on in conversation with the Lord.

"Where am I going to get the money, Lord?"

I looked down and saw another penny. I put it in my pocket and picked up where I left off.

A few steps further, I looked down and saw another penny. It wasn't until I held all three pennies in my hand that God had my full attention. He finally had a chance to speak, and I will never forget His three words as I stared at the three pennies. "I. Will. Provide."

And. He. Did!

That Christmas, unbeknownst to me, the church we were pastoring took up a love offering while we were away visiting family. On New Year's Eve, I was called to the platform where I was presented with a cheque. When I opened it, I discovered that it covered the rest of my semester—right down to the very last penny!

Since that day of personal provision, I have found hundreds of pennies. And time and time again, God has provided. With each one, I have recited His three words to my heart.

Three pennies was then, but this was now, facing a new challenge in my life, a devastating blow. I went for a walk to pour out my heart to the Lord. And lo and behold, freshly exposed beneath the melting winter snow and ice, right there at my feet, I looked down to find two pennies.

I began to sob. Beyond a shadow of a doubt, I knew that the Lord had placed them there just for me. I'm positive they would have otherwise been overlooked and perhaps remained there indefinitely until a street sweeper swept them up with the winter debris.

Upon picking them up and putting them in my pocket, I knew exactly what they meant.

Just that morning, I had turned to Scripture to allow God's Word to seep into my broken heart. As I opened the Bible to Jeremiah 30–31, I glanced at several highlights. They all started with two simple words that leapt off the page at me: "I will…" Two simple words that represented the two pennies I held in my hand. I didn't take the time to read the words that followed, but you can be sure that they'd be the first thing I looked up when I got home again.

I nearly ran home to see what God was waiting to tell me.

I immediately taped my two pennies to the flimsy page of my Bible in Jeremiah 30–31. Experience assured me that He had been faithful then, so why would He not be faithful now?

Never forget what we read in 1 Thessalonians 5:24: *"The one who calls you is faithful, and he will do it"* (emphasis added).

Survival Tip

> **Reflect on God's faithfulness.** Lamentations 3:21–23 tells us, *"Yet this I call to mind and therefore I have hope: because of the Lord's great love we are not consumed, for his compassions never fail. They are new every morning; great is your faithfulness."* Consider the Lord's faithfulness throughout your life. In what situations has He proven His faithfulness in your past? How have these scenarios given you hope for your tomorrows? Ask Him to keep you alert to His new mercies for today.

The Blessing

I volunteered at my kids' public school often enough to get to know some of the teachers and staff on a personal basis. The school secretary was one of those I grew close with. Every time I entered the school, I'd make sure to drop by the office to say hello and be enveloped in the most welcoming, warm hug. As our friendship grew, we shared more pieces of our personal lives, including our faith.

Over time I learned that, while interested, she didn't have a personal relationship with Jesus.

Eventually, her mother became very sick and was admitted to the hospital. I had noticed that she loved to read, and sometimes she read aloud to her mother as she sat faithfully by her bedside. I took the risk of offering her some good reading from our church's well-stocked supply. Then I asked if she'd like me to pick her up a book or two. She thanked me and freely accepted my offer.

At the time, I was leading a ladies small group in my home every week. We were studying the book *The Blessing* by John Trent. Out of our study, we decided that we, as a group, wanted to put the book's teaching to practice and bless someone. I immediately thought of my school secretary friend. We agreed that a care package would be a fitting way to bless her.

Over the next couple of weeks, we gathered up items. We filled a basket full of books, gift cards, spa treatments, candles, and a wealth of other thoughtful trinkets to encourage and bless her heart.

She was moved to tears upon receiving this gift. Now she wanted to meet these women who had so faithfully prayed for her. She wanted to thank them personally and convey how much the gifts had meant to her.

One blessing led to another, and as a result she eventually received the ultimate blessing: the gift of salvation. What greater blessing is there than that?

Survival Tip —

> **Watch for boomerang blessings.** Acts 20:35 tells us that it's *"more blessed to give than to receive."* I call these boomerang blessings. There are many ways to bless and encourage others: through the spoken and written word, practical deeds, the gift of time, or a listening ear. Think of one way you can bless someone who's lonely, needs help, or could use some encouragement. You'll be blessed if you do it! (John 13:17) There's substance to the fact that a *"generous person will prosper; whoever refreshes others will be refreshed"* (Proverbs 11:25). Paul reminds us, *"A man reaps what he sows… Let us not become weary in doing good, for at the proper time we will reap a harvest if we do not give up"* (Galatians 6:7, 9).

God wants to give us blessings and rewards as we serve Him.

And God is able to bless you abundantly, so that in all things at all times, having all that you need, you will abound in every good work.

—2 Corinthians 9:8

He has so much more for you than you can begin to fathom. And it's paid in full! We just need to get our eyes off ourselves and onto Him.

Let's not miss out on the free gift that cost Him His life! Jesus said, *"I have come that they may have life, and have it to the full"* (John 10:10).

Straight from the Father's Heart

See what great love the Father has lavished on us, that we should be called children of God! And that is what we are!
—1 John 3:1

Biblical Mentor
John the Baptist (John 1:6-35; 3:22-34)[12]

Effective ministry consists of sacrifice and dying to oneself, putting others first and exalting Jesus. John the Baptist offers a godly example of this kind of humility. He said, *"He must become greater; I must become less"* (John 3:30).

I witnessed this same attitude through my son Ben as he battled leukemia at the young age of eighteen. By faith, as Ben's life decreased, God's grace increased. From the heavenly grandstand, he, along with the others listed in the Hebrews Hall of Faith, cheers us on. Like all those who've gone before us, Ben is now living the abundant life in its entirety and experiencing the fullness of God in all His glory.

While he was alive, Ben would always put an extra "ness" at the end of a word, emphasizing the "and-then-some-ness" of something. So with the example of John the Baptist and the inspiration of my son, here are some ways you and I can experience the *much-ness-ness* of God.

Acknowledge His graciousness-ness. God's grace is enough! In fact, it's more than enough!

> *I pray that out of his* glorious riches *he may strengthen you with power through his Spirit in your inner being, so that Christ may dwell in your hearts through faith. And I pray that you, being rooted and established in love, may have power, together with all the Lord's holy people, to grasp how* wide *and* long *and* high *and* deep *is the love of Christ, and to know this love that surpasses* knowledge—*that you may be* filled *to the measure of all the* fullness *of God.*
>
> —Ephesians 3:16–19 (emphasis added)

He's a giving God, a loving God, a grace-extending God, and a life-giving God who can't get enough of us or give enough to us! In fact, He's given it all through the life He died to give us. And we can enter into eternal life with Him as we enter into a personal relationship with Him.

To fully experience the abundance of His graciousness-ness we first have to…

Receive His forgiveness-ness. An unknown author has taken the beauty of John 3:16 and put it this way:

---

12   With the inspiration of Benjamin Elliott.

For God (the greatest Lover) so loved (the greatest degree) the world (the greatest number) that He gave (the greatest act) His only begotten son (the greatest gift) that whosoever (the greatest invitation) believeth (the greatest simplicity) in Him (the greatest person) should not perish (the greatest deliverance) but (the greatest difference) have (the greatest certainty) everlasting life (the greatest possession).

God's gift of eternal life is ours to accept. Therefore, we need to…

Celebrate His goodness-ness. We have so much to be thankful for! Let's make sure we celebrate God's goodness to us!

Enter his gates with thanksgiving and his courts with praise; give thanks to him and praise his name.

—Psalm 100:4

… give thanks in all circumstances; for this is God's will for you in Christ Jesus.

—1 Thessalonians 5:18

All this is for your benefit, so that the grace that is reaching more and more people may cause thanksgiving to overflow to the glory of God.

—2 Corinthians 4:15

We'll experience God's much-ness-ness as we…

Grow in godliness-ness. Take close note of these words of the Apostle Peter:

His divine power has given us everything we need for a godly life through our knowledge of him who called us by his own glory and goodness. Through these he has given us his very great and precious promises, so that through them you may participate in the divine nature, having escaped the corruption in the world caused by evil desires.

For this very reason, make every effort to add to your faith goodness; and to goodness, knowledge; and to knowledge, self-control; and to self-control, perseverance; and to perseverance, godliness; and to godliness, mutual affection; and to mutual affection, love. For if you possess these qualities in increasing measure, they will keep you from being ineffective and unproductive in your knowledge of our Lord Jesus Christ.

—2 Peter 1:3–8

The Lord infuses us with His *goodness-ness* so we can grow in *godliness-ness* and be filled with his *righteousness-ness*, with overflowing *thankfulness-ness*. This is so that we can not only fully experience His *much-ness* but share it with others. Therefore...

Overflow His faithfulness-ness. Our faith was never meant to be kept to ourselves. Therefore, we must fill ourselves to overflow more and more of Him. God has given us more than enough to go around! Great is His faithfulness-ness!

> *And this is my prayer: that your love may* abound more and more *in knowledge and depth of insight, so that you may be able to discern what is best and may be pure and blameless for the day of Christ*, filled *with the fruit of righteousness that comes through Jesus Christ—to the glory and praise of God.*
> —Philippians 1:9–11 (emphasis added)

All this is for your benefit, *so that the grace that is reaching more and more people may cause thanksgiving to overflow to the glory of God* (2 Corinthians 4:15).

Chapter Ten

NURTURING YOUR SOUL TO *Thrive*, NOT JUST SURVIVE

Welcome to the hearth, the most vital room in my heart. This is where my soul is fuelled and fed by the Lord Himself. Here's where the fire burns. Fire is life. For our *"God is a consuming fire"* (Hebrews 12:29).

This sacred place in my heart is the untouchable holy of holies, the inner sanctum of who He created me to be. Every fibre and cell has been intricately knit together in my mother's womb to produce DNA that is solely mine. My strengths and weaknesses, passions and fears, joys and sorrows, all coexist here in the sanctuary of my heart of hearts. Herein lays the essence of who I am. I have been fearfully and wonderfully made (Psalm 139:14). So have you!

As we vulnerably draw close to the warmth the Fire offers, with all that we are, all of our worries and cares are cast into the burning embers. Fear is abolished. Strength is renewed. Hope is restored. Joy is refreshed. Peace is found. And as long as we tend to this Fire and draw near to the eternal flame, we'll not only survive, we'll thrive.

He Who Began a Good Work

I was a honeymoon baby, the firstborn of three. Our family attended a church that was politically correct but spiritually dead. Even at an early age, my heart sensed that something wasn't right. The youth group was more interested in partying than learning about the Bible, so I began helping out in the preschoolers' Sunday school class. I left church each week yearning for something more.

My search for God had begun.

When I was twelve years old, something happened to ignite my heart and whet my spiritual appetite where matters of faith were concerned. It was Christmas. My mom packed up the three of us kids to take a train to visit extended family for the holiday week. It seemed odd that my dad hadn't joined us. When we returned, my dad had moved out.

That same year, my mom took me to an evening service at another church in our neighbourhood. I saw a cute guy there and determined that I'd be back. While nothing ever came of that cute guy, I became the best of friends with his cousin. She invited me to their youth group and I became an active member, attending youth retreats, weekend activities, and summer camp.

I was fifteen when, one evening at camp, an invitation was given to anyone interested in doing business with God. The friend I was with wanted to respond and asked if I'd go up to the altar with her. As my friend and I knelt side by side, she and the camp counsellor spoke. I was minding my own business when the Wonderful Counsellor spoke to me. He leapt from my head into my heart in a single heartbeat.

There at the altar, I realized for the first time that Jesus loved me personally. He had died and rose again for me, and He wanted to have a personal relationship with me. I had encountered the Lover of my soul. I recognized Him immediately. He was the One who had been wooing me for as long as I could remember.

For the next year of my life, I learned that He was able to do immeasurably more than all I could ask or imagine, according to his power that was at work within me (Ephesians 3:20). I couldn't get enough of Him. The more I knew about Him, the more I wanted to know.

It all seemed too good to be true.

To be certain that I wasn't just on an emotional high, I sought out my school friends in the party scene. However, rather than give me fulfilment, it led me to a year of doubting. I no longer heard God's voice. I questioned His existence. My heart was in turmoil.

I knew my Christian friends were all praying for me, and one of my friends advised that I read the Psalms and Proverbs. I was amazed at how the psalmist related to my questions. I highlighted the verses that resonated with me. The writer put words to my searching heart. How could he have known?

By the next summer, the Lord had shown me that nothing compared to what I had found in Him! I realized that Christianity was a lifestyle, not just a decision. I needed to continue to nurture my relationship with Him through time spent in His Word, prayer, fellowship of believers, and a more deeply rooted commitment to Him.

I returned to camp and asked Him to be the Lord of my life.

To this day, my heart skips a beat as I recall that awestruck evening. I'm humbled and overwhelmed by the words of Ephesians 1:4: *"Long before he laid down earth's foundations, he had [me] in mind, had settled on [me] as the focus of his love, to be made whole and holy by his love"* (MSG). I'm assured that He who began a good work in me will be faithful to complete it until the day of Christ Jesus (Philippians 1:6).

Survival Tip

> **Write your salvation testimony.** God is writing your story. Have you put it on paper? Why not take some time to record it for yourself? Consider questions like the following. When did you come to know Jesus as your personal Lord and Saviour? Who was the first person you told? When was the last time you shared your story with someone? Who is someone who might be encouraged to hear your story? What new chapter is the Lord writing on your heart today? As we read in 2 Corinthians 3:3, *"You show that you are a letter from Christ, the result of our ministry, written not with ink but with the Spirit of the living God, not on tablets of stone but on tablets of human hearts."* I also suggest that you take some time to read through *My Heart, Christ's Home* by Robert Boyd Munger.[13]

Four Bibles

The best source of love, encouragement, hope, and direction I own is in the form of four Bibles.

My parents gave me my first Bible when I was eleven years old. It was a paraphrase version that I could understand in my everyday language. It guided me through my early years, especially after I gave my heart to Jesus. It answered my many questions during a year of soul-searching and doubt and spoke living truth into my vulnerable heart.

My second Bible was given to me by my husband during our dating days. That Bible carried me through the formative years of dating, personal spiritual growth, and life as a new pastor's wife and young mom.

I purchased my third Bible when we made our first ministry transition. Its unmarked pages offered me a clean slate. It helped me navigate significant challenges and new ministry experiences, providing the assurance and guidance I needed as I

---

13 Robert Boyd Munger, *My Heart, Christ's Home* (Downers Grove, IL: InterVarsity Press, 1954).

launched into my own personal ministry as a speaker. It also provided all I needed to equip me as a writer.

I eventually purchased my fourth Bible because I recognized it was time to turn a new page in my life—and time to get a Bible with large print to suit the new season of life I was entering into.

Each of my four Bibles continues to help me explore invaluable truth, uncover uncharted territory, and guide me into the heart of God—my True North—as I navigate His unfolding will and purpose for my life.

Open any of my Bibles and you'll find the roadmap of my life. Events, dates, places, and even some names are noted throughout. Multicoloured highlights mark up the pages. You'll see underlines beneath certain words, squiggly lines punctuating principles, and stars and smiley faces emphasizing simple truths. Even the odd sermon outline can be found in the margins.

You're bound to come across simple artwork that includes stick mountain ranges indicating times when Jesus headed for the hills to spend time alone with His Father in the Gospels. Sketches of lips can be discovered, especially throughout the Proverbs, indicating references to godly speech, prompting me to watch my mouth. Hearts remind me of God's rich love toward me and also of the importance of guarding His treasury within my heart.

There is even some evidence of my children's handiwork here and there. Several scribbles appear from times when they got their little hands on it, the odd goopy fingerprint reminding me of my primary ministry—them.

Teardrops have formed wrinkles and reshaped pages, marking significant moments when God probed the inner recesses of my heart. Other pages are so well used that they naturally open to the promises I need to continually claim. Pennies are pasted to remind me of God's faithful provision. A Gospel presentation, which includes a simple diagram and several Bible verses for easy reference, is taped on the inside cover of one, handy for sharing the good news at opportune times. And a few meaningful cards from prayerful friends, those who have come alongside to encourage me in my life and ministry, serve as bookmarks.

Four Bibles trace my spiritual journey. God's Word has been my roadmap and compass, encouraging, validating, assuring, comforting, refreshing, enlightening, sustaining, stimulating, inspiring, chastising, equipping, and guiding me every step of the way. His Word has been a lamp to my feet and a light to my path (Psalm 119:105).

Bring God's Word to life. God's Word is a living document that is intended to be applied to our lives. Here are a few suggestions on how to bring it to life. Read it until something stands out to you. Ask good questions, like the following. What impression did this scripture leave upon my heart? What lesson, insight, or truth did I learn? What command should I take heed of? What is God trying to say to me through this verse or passage? How can I apply this truth to my life? What do I need to change in my life based on what I just read? What new aspect of God's character is He trying to reveal? Make it personal by inserting your name. Psalm 19:7–8, 10–11 says, *"The law of the Lord is perfect, refreshing the soul… making wise the simple… giving joy to the heart… giving light to the eyes… They are more precious than gold, than much pure gold; they are sweeter than honey, than honey from the honeycomb. By them your servant is warned; in keeping them there is great reward."*

Stop, Look, and Listen

Ministry was demanding. Household maintenance was constant. Raising four young children kept me on my toes. I was fully aware that some days I was barely surviving it all. I'd look at my Bible as it sat dusty on its shelf. But who had time to read it, let alone sit and savour time with the Lord?

The Lord, however, felt differently about it. He had a few things to say about my situation; I just wasn't expecting that He'd speak through my two-year-old daughter, Erin.

One busy day in my busy household, while I was in the middle of much busyness, busying myself with very important things—dishwashing and sweeping and tidying—Erin trailed behind me, tugging on my apron strings, begging for my attention.

"Mommy, Mommy! I have something to tell you."

"Okay, Erin, tell me."

"No, Mommy. I want to tell you something."

"Yes, go ahead."

"But, Mommy, you're not listening."

"Yes, I am! Please talk to me. Mommy's listening."

"No, you're not! Sit down and look at me!"

Ouch! At that, I sat down and looked straight into her eyes as she shared what was on her heart. It was like the still, small voice of the Holy Spirit drawing my focus to Him so He could speak directly into the chambers of my heart: *"You see, Lisa, there is really only one important thing. And Erin has directed you to it."*

It's so easy to get caught up in the diapers, demands, and to-do lists. I'm thankful that I learned to stop and sit at the feet of Jesus, fixing my eyes on Him and listening with undivided attention. And to think He used my two-year-old daughter to do it.

Survival Tip

Give the Lord your undivided attention. The Lord extends an invitation to all His children to spend time with Him. His greatest desire is to fellowship with us, speak truth into our hearts, and nourish our souls. *Stop!* We often rush through our time with the Lord to get on with "real life," when in reality He *is* our life (Deuteronomy 30:19–20). Linger in His presence. Take regular, intentional, and unhurried time to sit at the feet of Jesus. Read a passage of Scripture until something strikes you. It could be a word, a verse, or an entire passage. Stop and pay attention to what it's saying to you. *Look!* If you find that your mind wanders easily, make a worry list; write down anything that enters your mind, such as remembering to put the roast in the oven or make that phone call. The Lord deserves your undivided attention. Fix your eyes on Him (Hebrews 12:2). *Listen!* One way to make sure you're listening is to act on what you've heard. How does the passage of Scripture you just read speak to you, personally? What is one thing you sense the Lord telling you from the passage you read? How can you apply it to your life? The Lord has things to say that are meant for you alone: *"Yet the Lord longs to be gracious to you; therefore he will rise up to show you compassion. For the Lord is a God of justice. Blessed are all who wait for him!"* (Isaiah 30:18)

Delighting in the Lord

Psalm 37:4 tells us, *"Take delight in the Lord, and he will give you the desires of your heart."* To delight in someone means to experience great joy and pleasure in their presence… so why was I struggling so much to delight myself in the Lord and experience joy and pleasure in His presence?

It hadn't always been drudgery. Things had begun to shift when I went to Bible college.

It occurred to me that part of the problem was that I'd started to look at my time with the Lover of my soul as an obligation rather than an opportunity. Obligation is, after all, opportunity with the joy sucked out. I'd turned God's love letter into a textbook. More than meeting the Lord as a person and investing in our relationship, I'd turned it into a ritual. So I put a plan into place to enhance my time with Him and make it more like a date than a duty.

To begin with, I chose a time that worked for me. Not being a morning person, I chose the afternoon. When the kids were small, I used naptime to make sure I'd be as uninterrupted as possible. In those days, it was more like snacking on God's Word rather than feasting on it, but I digested whatever I could. It's like Jeremiah wrote: *"When [His] words came, I ate them; they were my joy and my heart's delight"* (Jeremiah 15:16).

As my kids grew, I was able to claim more and more time. Certain seasons of my life allowed me more time than others. Regardless of the quantity of time I had, it was essential that I muster as much quality time as possible.

I claimed a comfortable chair by the window and met Him regularly. I gathered all I needed to enjoy and savour time with Him: my Bible, prayer journal, highlighter, a Bible study, and a few encouragement cards in case He prompted me to pray for someone. Having everything handy saved precious time. Often I lit a candle and made myself my favourite hot beverage as I snuggled under a blanket in the winter, or parked myself on my backyard swing in the summer. These are practices I've carried on through the years.

As I've continued to delight myself in the Lord, He's given me the desires of my heart. Isn't it amazing how that works? I've been enriched, enlightened, and encouraged. I've found contentment, peace, hope, renewed perspective, strength, and joy! Doesn't that sound delightful?

Survival Tip

Make it a date. According to Zephaniah 3:17, *"The Lord your God is with you, the Mighty Warrior who saves. He will take great delight in you; in his love he will no longer rebuke you, but will rejoice over you with singing."* Just think: the Creator of the universe wants to spend time with you. The least you can do is set aside a regular and intentional time to spend with Him. You can be sure that if you don't take the time for Him, something or someone else will take it from you. Give Him the best of your time and He'll make the best of your time. Treat it like a date. Create an inviting atmosphere. Ask yourself, "On a scale from 1–10, how is my relationship with the Lord? What will it take to bring it closer to 10?" Then put a plan in place to make your time with the Lord all it can be. When is your next date?

Timeout

When my four kids were little, I regularly put to good use a "timeout" chair. It was a mommy's helper whenever I needed to put an end to a heated situation, argument, or fight. The chair was used to set them apart, physically and socially, while their emotions simmered.

Timeout typically only lasted for five minutes or so, but it was long enough to give them time to think about their actions, their words, what they'd done, and what they'd do once their timeout was done. It also gave *me* time to think about *my* actions, think about *my* words, and think about what *I'd* do once the timeout was done.

Those five minutes of pause helped prevent a more damaging emotional or verbal reaction and allow for a wiser response. It also allowed for us all to gain a renewed perspective, one that was more objective. It pulled everyone involved out of the chaos and confusion of the situation and enabled them to see the situation more clearly.

A timeout chair wasn't my only sanity saver. I also encouraged my kids to have regular "quiet times." These lulls in activity were strategic, allowing them to regroup and take a rest from stimulating activity or social interaction. Call them intermissions or interludes; they created breathing space and did all of us a whole lot of good.

Fallow time provides us with a change of pace, offering us a new way of looking at things and a new way of approaching things. It changes our perspective, which can otherwise get lost in the hub of busyness and muddle of emotions. I like to consider it as a holy pause.

Fallow time is hallowed time. It's essential for life and health and balance in ministry. It's sacred time that must be kept sacred. As we learn from Mark 2:27, *"The Sabbath was made for man, not man for the Sabbath."*

Survival Tip

> **Remember the Sabbath day and keep it holy.** Taking a day a week for Sabbath rest isn't optional; it's a command. In fact, it's one of the Ten Commandments found in Exodus 20:8–10, which says: *"Remember the Sabbath day by keeping it holy. Six days you shall labor and do all your work, but the seventh day is a sabbath to the Lord your God."* God took one entire day to rest, and so must we. Jesus regularly pulled His disciples aside for rest and refreshment. It needs to be a regular part of our week and implemented into our daily routine. Set apart time in your day to take a deep breath. Step away from your desk. Go outside or go for a walk or drive. Take ten minutes to move your body and clear your head. Take a hiatus from your cell phone or computer. Write down what the Sabbath looks like to you. How do you plan to set that time apart?

Practicing God's Presence

Years into my walk with God, it occurred to me that at Christmas we pause to consider Emmanuel, meaning "God with us." But how intentional was I about considering God within us, within me, all year round?

I was once encouraged to read *The Celebration of Discipline*, by Richard J. Foster.[14] In the book, I was introduced to Brother Lawrence, a monk born in 1614 who lived out and wrote about practicing the presence of God. As I explored the spiritual discipline of practicing God's presence, I was challenged to consider putting it into practice in my own life. I wondered how my life might be transformed if I were to make God part of my every thought, activity, and conversation—to wake up every morning asking, "What do You want to do today? Where do You want to go? Who would You like to see?" Asking these questions then allowed me to watch and engage in His agenda as it unfolded.

Learning to be aware of God's holy presence at every moment of every day has awakened my spiritual senses. Realizing that He's aware of my words, attitudes, and

---

14 Richard J. Foster, *The Celebration of Discipline: The Path to Spiritual Growth* (Grand Rapids, MI: Harper Collins, 1978).

behaviour has brought a new level of accountability into my relationship with Him. With this awareness has come the privilege of unceasing communication.

Just like in any meaningful relationship, there is ebb and flow to the ongoing conversation I share with the Lord. It's ongoing—and that's the point. It's not simply a single timeslot set aside for me to close my eyes and pray, although it can be that.

While I do have some very intentional times of prayer, I'd have to say that most of our conversation is very impromptu and casual. It is more of an "As I was saying…" kind of conversation where we pick up right where we left off.

Practicing God's presence is about taking Him with me throughout the day, like being with a friend for a full day—sometimes sharing in mutual conversation, other times listening intently to what He has to say. Other times it means talking His ear off or enjoying quiet companionship. It's meeting Him over coffee, exploring new territory and pointing out to each other the things we see. There are times when we simply enjoy each other's company in comfortable silence. Other times, one of us will have more to say than the other… although I won't tell you who typically does most of the talking…

As I've learned to practice His presence, the Lord has made known to me the path of life, filling me with joy in His presence (Psalm 16:11).

Survival Tip

> **Choose a day to practice God's presence.** You may want to set aside a day of solitude. Or maybe you'd like to carry on with normal activities. In either case, be intentional about the words you speak, the conversations you share, and the activities you engage in. Be conscious of His presence with you all day long. Read your Bible in snippets throughout the day rather than at one set time. Read a book that challenges your thinking, heightens your awareness of God's presence, and helps you engage in thoughtful, conscientious prayer. Consider reading *The Celebration of Discipline* by Richard J. Foster. This book is a great source to explore spiritual disciplines. What can you do to practice God's presence today? Keep in mind that in His presence is fullness of joy (Psalm 16:11).

Journaling Along

It wasn't until after my youngest daughter was born that I decided to start documenting my spiritual journey. With so many distractions, I found it hard to focus my attention on thoughtful prayer. Who could think of staying awake past 8:00 p.m. with four children under the age of five and a half?

To help me focus, I began recording my prayers in a blank notebook. Daily I laid my four children in bed for their afternoon nap, and daily I laid down my burdens, thoughts, struggles, heartaches, concerns, and requests before the Lord on paper.

Much like the psalmist, David, I began pouring my heart out to the Lord. I was thankful to have such a freeing way to release, process, and express my innermost thoughts and feelings to the Caretaker of my heart. I've often referred to my journals as "Lisa's book of psalms."

Through the years, I've used a wide variety of journals that now make up an entire library. I've kept joy journals where I've recorded the simple pleasures I find in a day. It could be a new bird in the backyard, a rainbow in the sky, a phone call from a friend, a card in the mail, or some other intimate way the Lord has shown me His love.

I've kept a distinct family journal where I've prayed specific things related to my children and marriage. I prayerfully selected Bible verses for each of my children when they were born and have prayed them over again for each one. I also pray for and record a Bible verse for each coming year to keep it at the forefront of my thoughts and prayers as the year unfolds.

When Ben was diagnosed with leukemia, a friend encouraged me to post prayer requests on a Facebook page. This turned into a public journal, serving as an incredible outlet for me to journal my thoughts and keep God's faithfulness front and centre in my mind through that difficult time.

In the aftermath of Ben's death, my family and I began a Grief Journal. In it, each of our family members took turns recording some of our deepest thoughts. Things we couldn't always express verbally. It helped us to process our grief.

In each journal, I record verses that the Lord has drawn to my attention, and I've responded with my thoughts, feelings, and how I intend to put His Word into action. Sometimes I've simply taken dictation from the Lord as He's spoken truth into my heart.

Through the years, prayer journaling has served to clear my mind, helping me to prioritize, focus my thoughts, and find perspective. At times I've written out grocery lists or things that clutter my mind to bring a sense of order and clarity. My theory is: onto paper and out of mind! Through the pages of my journals, I have dreamt and laid out my future before the Lord. I've included book quotes, song lyrics, prayer lists, or cards I've received that inspire and encourage me.

There is something cathartic about recording my innermost thoughts, concerns, joys, and heart impressions with the Lord, especially concerning my relationship with Him, in written form. The bonus is that I'll be able to reread them for years to come. Perhaps I'll gift my children with them one day so they can see the thread of God's faithfulness in my life.

Survival Tip

> **Take good notes.** Consider starting a prayer journal. There are several types that can be easily found at the bookstore. Treat it in whatever way you find most effective. Record scripture, write out entire chapters of the Bible, record prayer requests, record answers to prayer, or simply pour out your heart in conversation with the Lord. Make it a two-way conversation by recording God's Word and responding to it. The options are endless. There are no set rules. From time to time, read back through it to see if there are any common themes.

Fast Forward

I'd read many examples of fasting in the Bible. While I'd never fasted before, it seemed like there was no better time than the present. David and I needed clarity and direction in our ministry, so we invited another couple to join us in a forty-day fast. It seemed drastic, but desperate times called for drastic measures.

I decided to give up sugar for the full forty days. During its course, we set aside a full day a week for a full fast (water only).

I was also impressed to take three days at a strategic point for a water-only fast, like in the book of Esther. In this three-day timeframe, we had back-to-back church board meetings, just as Esther had two banquets. On the night of the first board meeting, after I'd tucked my kids into bed, I crawled into mine. I knew how late these meetings could go.

Soon after, I experienced radiating pain around my lower back and abdomen, like labour pains. The pain worsened to the degree that I did something I'd never done before: I called my husband in the middle of his meeting and begged him to come home.

Within a half-hour, both my husband and the chairman of the board arrived and my husband and I headed for the emergency room. I was diagnosed with a kidney stone, which turned out to be the size of the lead tip of a pencil. It amazed me to think that such a small thing could cause so much pain to the whole body.

There it was! That was the point the Lord had wanted to make. As the body of Christ, all it takes is one kidney stone to cause pain to the whole body.

Since that significant fast, the Lord has called me to other fasts. I've named each one according to the impression the Lord lays upon my heart. For example, Less Is More, which is based on the example of John the Baptist, and Show Me Your Glory, which is based on Moses's experience with the Lord on Mount Sinai. Depending on the nature of what I'm praying toward, it can constitute a single meal, a twenty-four-hour day, or multiple days.

It can be prompted by a situation I'm facing, a spiritual battle I'm fighting, or wisdom and direction I'm seeking. Often there's a prompting of the Holy Spirit in an area of my sinful heart which needs tending. I've fasted in order to allow more of God's control in my life. I've fasted with the sense of needing the Lord's freedom from bondage or oppression. And I've fasted to express my sincere desire to follow His heart and leading in my life.

Typically on my fasting days, I clean my house. This is a tangible reminder of cleaning my spiritual house, the temple of the Holy Spirit (1 Corinthians 6:19–20), to make sure my body is a healthy environment for Him to dwell in. As I wash and vacuum my floors, I remind myself to stand firm on a sure foundation. As I clean bathrooms, I flush out anything in my life that has left an unwelcome residue. I pray through my kitchen with a heightened awareness of what kind of good I'm feeding my family and guests, both physical and spiritual. I pray through each of my children's rooms, cleansing them from all unrighteousness. I dust anything that has settled on the furniture of my heart, perhaps without me even realizing it.

Fasting is a powerful tool the Lord has given us to acknowledge and stand firm in the unseen battles in our lives. It allows us the privilege to see His victory as we stand still on the battlefield: *"Now then, stand still and see this great thing the Lord is about to do before your eyes!"* (1 Samuel 12:16)

Survival Tip

Clean your house. Set aside a full day to prayerfully clean your house. Read and pray through Isaiah 58. Then start cleaning at the heart of your home—typically the kitchen—and as you do, pray through Psalm 139. Ask the Lord to search your heart. Then work from there. All the while, pray concerning the aspects of your life that correlate to the room you're in. Ask the Lord to bring scriptures to mind with each room of the house you clean. Stop to pray in each one. Pray for the person that sleeps in that room, the activities that go on there, or the people who dine with you. You can even pray through your front hallway and all those who you welcome in. Happy cleaning!

Let What You Love, Be What You Do

My husband has always been my number one cheerleader, encouraging me in my victories, consoling me in my failures, helping me overcome my fears and inadequacies, and affirming and releasing me to fulfill my calling. He's watched me from the frontlines as my passion for inspiring women with practical principles from God's Word has grown.

One day he came home with a gift for my home office. It's a plaque that says "Let what you love be what you do." It was his way of applauding me after I'd finally responded to the Lord's call upon my life with a simple yes, after having complicated it for far too long.

My plaque serves as a constant reminder that God created me for His good pleasure (Philippians 2:13). He's given me all things to enjoy (1 Timothy 6:17).

I've learned that it's important to find things that feed and fuel my soul. That includes doing things I love to do apart from the church and my call to ministry. Personally it can be spending time in my kitchen, creating a project, touching base with my children and grandchildren, calling a friend, or having a luxurious bubble bath. It's making time for things that bring me joy, pouring myself into the things I love to do with people I love. The important thing is that I set aside time in my days to do what I love.

It's good for my mental and spiritual health and well-being. When I lose sight of the things I love, I begin to take life too seriously and lose my joy along the way. In whatever shape it takes, I need to give myself permission to have fun in what I do, and let what I love be what I do, all for the glory of God.

Survival Tip

> **Feed your soul with things that bring you joy.** It pleases our heavenly Father when He sees His children enjoying the abundant life He's given us (John 10:10). His desire is that we live life to the fullest in every essence of the word. That's been His plan from the very beginning (Genesis 1). That includes what He's called you to do and who He's called you to be. But it also includes things you simply love. When do you feel like you're doing what God created you to do? What are the ministries, projects, and activities you enjoy? What gives you great joy? What brings your soul to life? What feeds your spirit? Who is someone who makes you laugh? When was the last time you laughed? Remember what Proverbs 17:22 tells us: "A cheerful heart is good medicine…"

Walking with Jesus

I've always loved walking. There's something invigorating about being in the outdoors, breathing in the fresh air, opening my heart and mind up to new sights, allowing my spirit to be set free, and exercising my body—without feeling like it's exercise. It's even better to walk with a friend. I'm grateful to have a friend who isn't just my walking partner, but my partner in life and ministry. There's nothing like walking hand in hand with someone you love.

Better still is walking with Jesus.

I think you'll agree that the most important part of walking with someone is keeping in step, rather than running ahead or lagging behind. The purpose of walking with someone, after all, is to walk *with* them. Such is the case in my walk with Jesus.

For almost as long as I can remember, Jesus and I have been walking together. We often talk as we walk, reflecting on our journey together. There's so much history to reminisce about regarding the things we've experienced together along the way. Excitement causes us to pick up our pace when He introduces a new topic of discussion or leads me on a new path to explore. As scary as it can be, knowing He's leading the way brings me sweet assurance.

"Look over there! Have you ever noticed that?" He says as He shows me sights I can easily miss in my distraction and preoccupation. Everything looks so much more beautiful from His perspective when I consider His view and choose to see things as He sees them.

Sometimes He beckons me to stop and listen, opening my ears to pay attention to things I can't hear with all the noise that surrounds me. At times, He invites me to a nearby bench or green meadow where we can rest for a while.

"Stop and smell the roses while they're in bloom," I hear Him say.

Often He woos me toward streams of living water where He refreshes my soul. I especially love the moments when He pulls me close and whispers sweet nothings, meant for my ears only.

Of course there are times when we walk through valleys. He's never closer to me than in those dark but cherished times.

As hard as it is to admit, and as much as I'd love to think I've always kept in step with Him, it hasn't always been the case. There are times when I get excited and carried away on my own path of exploration. If I'm completely honest, sometimes it's because I just want to do my own thing. I have my own path in mind. The Lord is inclined to meander and enjoy the walk. It's me who's more prone to wander, lag behind, stray from the path, or run ahead of Him.

A friend I've walked with for several years once said, "As we take this walk of faith in step with the Spirit, He often changes our course. When we give Him the script of our lives, it's likely that He will. Each step we take leads us to the next one and the next one, and many times we end up not at all at the place we thought. This is exciting, because that's when we know the Spirit is on the move."

Let's just say that walking with Jesus is never more enjoyable as when we take His nail-scarred, loving hand and keep in step with Him.

Survival Tip

> **Go for a prayer walk.** There's nothing like meeting with the Lord in the beauty of His creation. Go for a walk and enjoy His companionship. Take a friend with you and direct your conversation to things of the Lord. Meet the Lord in your garden. Find a body of water and sit by it, allowing the living water to refresh your body, mind, and soul. Let Him lead you beside still waters. Stop and rest somewhere along the way and read or recite Psalm 23 as a prayer. Write about your "walk" experience. Take to heart what Deuteronomy 31:6–8 says: *"For the Lord your God goes with you; he will never leave you nor forsake you."*

Mary and Me

As I've nurtured my walk with the Lord, I have frequently connected with Mary, the Mother of Jesus. Like her, I've taken time to process, pray, and ponder the things of God and treasure them in my heart (Luke 2:19, 51).

Mary and I connect on so many levels. Like Mary, I've had a personal encounter with the Lord as a teenager. We both know what it is to have our souls pierced (Luke 2:35). We also know what it is to watch a son suffer and die. And we know what it is to turn our mess into a message of hope that will ripple through the generations to come (Luke 1:46–50).

Like in Mary's life, time and time again the Lord has shown up in unexpected ways, stepping into my ordinary life on an ordinary day and extending extraordinary invitations that have led me to unforeseen circumstances.

The Lord has asked both of us to do the impossible, made possible only by Him, the One who works best in impossible situations.

In the context of these impossible situations, Mary's example has helped me identify and overcome two significant fears that I'm sure we can all relate to.

The first is my fear of inadequacy. At times I've wrestled with my identity in Christ. Like Mary, I've been greatly troubled at His words and wondered what kind of greeting and invitation He's extending to me. I've questioned the Lord's calling in my life. I have felt like He's chosen the wrong person.

So I've used Mary's words: *"How will this be?"* (Luke 1:34) And I go on to explain all the reasons why this cannot be, giving Him every excuse as to why I can't possibly do what He's asking of me. That's when the rest of my deepest fears and inadequacies come pouring out, including the fear of failure, rejection, and not-enough-ness.

Through Mary's example, I've learned that it's not who I am but Whose I am. I'm not simply favoured but highly favoured, chosen, and called (Luke 1:28, 30). It's not about what I cannot do, but what Christ can do in and through me. Nothing is impossible with God! (Luke 1:37) It's not about what lies ahead, but about my humble obedience and simple faith in the fulfillment of His promises (Luke 1:38).

Which leads me to my second fear: the unknown. The fear of the unknown is a very real thing. It is debilitating, paralyzing, and stifling. Sadly, if we give in to it, we'll never know the good that can come out of it. We will never know what could have been if only we hadn't given in to our fears.

I could never have guessed where the Lord would lead me to fulfill my calling: church conflict, burnout, ministry to pastoral couples dealing with all kinds of personal challenges, painful ministry transitions, the demands of hurting churches full of hurting people, and perhaps most profound of all, the death of my own nineteen-year-old son after a year of battling leukemia.

Through each challenge, I've learned the importance of turning my misery into ministry.

Mary has taught me the importance of demonstrating a simple willingness to comply with God's plan, whether I understand it or not. None of us knows what the future holds, but we know Who holds the future.

Mary has shown me the importance of surrounding myself with those who come alongside, encourage, listen, and speak into my life. Those who "get it" or "get me." People like Elizabeth was for Mary (Luke 1:36–56). Mary's journey reminds me that the Lord is not only with me, but He's empowered me with His Holy Spirit (Luke 1:35).

As I ponder all the treasures my heart has stored up, my thoughts are transported to another place in time when a young teenaged mother embraced her infant son for the first time before laying him in a manger.

In the same heartbeat, another scene floods my soul: that same mother embracing her adult son at the foot of a cross.

Mary could never have known where her calling would lead her, but through her example I am given the courage to face my own fears. Perhaps what Mary has taught me most is that being called really isn't about me at all; it's about the glory of God.

> *My soul glorifies the Lord and my spirit rejoices in God my Savior, for he has been mindful of the humble state of his servant. From now on all generations will call me blessed, for the Mighty One has done great things for me—holy is his name. His mercy extends to those who fear him, from generation to generation.*
> —Luke 1:46–50

Survival Tip

Allow God to turn your ordinary into the extraordinary. It's humbling when God chooses to use us, but He does—in spite of ourselves. That's what He finds pleasure in. That's where His glory is most profoundly demonstrated. There are so many characters in the Bible we can learn from, which is why I've included so many of my own biblical mentors throughout this book. In each case, God stepped into their ordinary lives and did something extraordinary. Who are some of your biblical mentors? What have you learned from their example? Can you think of a time when God stepped into your ordinary life and did something extraordinary? Remember: *"Nothing is impossible for God!"* (Luke 1:37, CEV)

Flourishing in Times of Drought

It had been a long drive through the badlands of the Holy Land. The sun was beating down on us as we filed in line toward what looked to be a hole in the ground. We weren't given any indication as to where we were going. All I knew was that it had been a long wait in the hot, dry, dusty land. It occurred to me why foot-washing was so important in Jesus's day.

As I waited for my turn to descend, a fluorescent pink flowering bush caught my eye. Smack dab in the middle of this barren land, the beautiful plant grew out of the crevice of a rock. I was surprised that it was living at all, much less flowering. It wasn't merely surviving; it was thriving!

Once at the bottom of a narrowly winding iron staircase, my spiritual eyes were opened. I thought back to my flowering friend, and suddenly the words of Jeremiah sprang to life:

> *But blessed is the one who trusts in the Lord, whose confidence is in him. They will be like a tree planted by the water that sends out its roots by the stream. It does not fear when heat comes; its leaves are always green. It has no worries in a year of drought and never fails to bear fruit.*
>
> —Jeremiah 17:7–8

A drought is defined as an extended period when a region notes a deficiency in its water supply, whether surface or underground water. Droughts can last for months or years or be declared after as few as fifteen days. Nearly every part of our country experiences drought or periods of reduced rainfall.

Similarly, based on personal experience, I knew that droughts in our lives can be caused by a wide variety of things: a difficult time of hardship, trial, crisis, discouragement, disillusionment, the death of a loved one, the loss of a friendship, depression, illness, loneliness, burnout, etc. I could think of many times in my life when, as a result of some of these experiences, I felt like I was all dried up and had nothing left to give. Can you relate?

I take consolation in the fact that several characters in the Bible experienced drought, both physical and spiritual. Abraham and Sarah experienced the drought called infertility. Moses led the children of Israel through forty years in the wilderness. Then there's Elijah, who endured three and a half years in a drought that left him high and dry. Jesus spent forty days of testing in the desert before commencing His earthly ministry.

As I considered Jeremiah 17:7–8, the implications became clear. God doesn't just want us to survive, but thrive during seasons of drought. He wants us to bear fruit, but how?

In my research, I've learned that the key, according to agriculturalists, is planning for drought through water conservation. That way, there's less of a chance of getting caught unprepared in dry years.

This principle made sense as I applied it to my own life. Water conservation is definitely the key to thriving. Living water, that is! I was more thankful than ever that I learned to dig my roots down deep in my relationship with the Lord—before the droughts hit!

Survival Tip —

> **Dig your roots down deep into living water.** As we read in Psalm 1:1–3, *"Blessed is the one… whose delight is in the law of the Lord, and who meditates on his law day and night. That person is like a tree planted by streams of water, which yields its fruit in season and whose leaf does not wither—whatever they do prospers."* God's restorative power is readily available as we plant ourselves in the soil of His love, send out our roots by the stream of living water, and bask in the Son's light. The result is a fruitful life, even in times of drought. The key is not to wait for the drought to hit before we invest in the abundant life that can be ours today. How has the Lord used His Word to refresh your spirit? What kind of fruit have you borne, even in times of drought? How has the Lord allowed you to prosper as you've given Him priority in your life and ministry?

The importance of nurturing, cultivating, and growing in our relationship with the Lord is the most important element of our Christian life. It fuels our faith, nourishes our soul, renews our mind, and restores our joy. When we root ourselves deep into the soil of His love, we flourish with everlasting fruit (Colossians 2:7). And it's all ours for the investing!

May we aspire to radiate the beauty of our Lord, just as Moses did on Mount Sinai (Exodus 34:29–30). More importantly, may we seek to look more like our beautiful Saviour as we meet with Him daily in the presence of His holiness!

Straight from the Father's Heart

For this reason, since the day we heard about you, we have not stopped praying for you. We continually ask God to fill you with the knowledge of his will through all the wisdom and understanding that the Spirit gives, so that you may live a life worthy of the Lord and please him in every way: bearing fruit in every good work, growing in the knowledge of God, being strengthened with all power according to his glorious might so that you may have great endurance and patience, and giving joyful thanks to the Father, who has qualified you to share in the inheritance of his holy people in the kingdom of light.
—Colossians 1:9–12

Biblical Mentor
David (Psalms of David)

When I think of a character in the Bible who nurtured a vibrant, thriving walk with God, it's David, a man after God's own heart (Acts 13:22). David tapped into his close-knit relationship with the Lord for confidence, hope, and joy throughout his life.

We can gain a wealth of insights into the heart of God as we look to David's shepherd's heart example.

Recognize the need for authenticity. David was real and honest with the Lord. He kept it real. He told it like it was. That authenticity allowed him to express himself openly with the King of the universe in a personal relationship.

We see evidence of the intimacy he and the Lord shared throughout the psalms. Psalm 63 is a beautiful example of his genuine heart of worship:

> *You, God, are my God, earnestly I seek you; I thirst for you, my whole being longs for you, in a dry and parched land where there is no water. I have seen you in the sanctuary and beheld your power and your glory. Because your love is better than life, my lips will glorify you. I will praise you as long as I live, and in your name I will lift up my hands.*
>
> —Psalm 63:1–4

We can learn much from his example when it comes to pouring out our hearts to God in full disclosure (Psalm 62:8).

Experience the joy of intimacy. David, the shepherd boy, knew the Lord as *his* Shepherd (Psalm 23). He was fully aware of how fully known He was by the Creator of his heart (Psalm 139). He knew how essential it was to draw near to the heart of God.

We reap the benefits of the intimacy he shared with the Lord today through many of his psalms. Psalm 8 invites us to the hills where he first fell in love with the Lover of his soul:

> *When I consider your heavens, the work of your fingers, the moon and the stars, which you have set in place, what is mankind that you are mindful of them, human beings that you care for them?*
>
> —Psalm 8:3

Exemplify teachability. Through David we learn the value of many biblical truths. Truths like trusting in the Lord, delighting ourselves in the Lord, committing our way to the Lord, and being still and waiting patiently for Him (Psalm 37:3–7). We read about the benefits of praise, forgiveness, healing, redemption, satisfaction, and renewal (Psalm 103). We learn of the worth of God's Word in terms of reviving the soul, making wise the simple, giving joy to the heart, giving light to the eyes, warning God's servant, and of great reward (Psalm 19:7–11).

Realize the power of dependency. More often than not David sought the counsel of the Lord. Time and again we see him inquiring of the Lord (1 Samuel 23:4, 30:8, 2 Samuel 2:1, 5:19, 5:23). He saw the importance of depending upon the Lord for his decisions, his hope (Psalm 42:11), his joy (Psalm 51:12), his refuge (Psalm 18), and his strength (1 Samuel 30:6).

David knew the value of encouraging himself in the Lord and recognized the power in numbers. His dependency upon God also came through in his friendship with his soulmate, Jonathan, who also encouraged him in the Lord (1 Samuel 23:16).

Know the freedom of humility. In 2 Samuel 12:1–14, we read of a heartrending scene between David and the prophet Nathan. Talk about humility! And thank God for accountability that brings about true repentance.

Here, a deeper level of humility is displayed as he humbles himself before His Maker by acknowledging his sinful state. David understood the importance of true confession. He knew repentance was a key factor in his relationship with the Lord.

We read his humble prayer in Psalm 51:10– 2, which says,

Create in me a pure heart, O God, and renew a steadfast spirit within me. Do not cast me from your presence or take your Holy Spirit from me. Restore to me the joy of your salvation and grant me a willing spirit, to sustain me.

Like David, may we be men and women after God's own heart.

KEEP ON KEEPING ON

Long before you held this book in your hands, I held it in my heart. It was conceived there several years ago. From time to time I'd open the computer file where my notes were safely stored. As the Lord triggered memories and my thoughts percolated, I began adding to the growing list of scriptures and subtitles, just as the Lord impressed them upon my heart.

Who knew that it would take a year of seclusion amid a pandemic to provide me with the opportunity to go public with it all? It wasn't until then that I understood why the Lord had lain Jeremiah 30:2 upon my heart in January 2020: *"This is what the Lord, the God of Israel, says: 'Write in a book all the words I have spoken to you.'"*

Looking back with 20/20 vision, it all makes sense to me now.

If I'm completely honest, I welcomed the pandemic as a gift—a reprieve, if you will. It gave me the necessary time to lock myself away in my house and remain in social isolation, out of the spotlight of public ministry, to reflect upon my forty years in ministry. It was also the perfect opportunity to consider my journey with the Lord. He has been my Strength, my Comforter, my Healer, my Provider, my Redeemer, my Wonderful Counsellor, and my Guide every step of the way.

> *The Lord [my] God has blessed [me] in all the work of [my] hands. He has watched over [my] journey through this vast wilderness. These forty years the Lord [my] God has been with [me], and [I] have not lacked anything.*
> —Deuteronomy 2:7

This is my testimony. I am not the same person today as I was forty years ago when I entered full-time ministry. Nor will you be as your journey unfolds. That's not a bad thing.

In the meantime, wherever we live and serve the Lord, we can look forward to that glorious day when all that we are and everything we've done will be exposed. As we humbly and vulnerably stand before the throne of grace, before our Maker, we will see Him for who He is and ourselves for who He created us to be. On that day, we will be complete. Our hearts will be mended, relationships will be whole, and we will see how He has worked all things together for our good and His glory.

Dear friends, now we are children of God, and what we will be has not yet been made known. But we know that when Christ appears, we shall be like him, for we shall see him as he is.

—1 John 3:2

… in a flash, in the twinkling of an eye, at the last trumpet. For the trumpet will sound, the dead will be raised imperishable, and we will be changed.

—1 Corinthians 15:52

By His grace, He will give us all we need to thrive, not merely survive, this extraordinary calling He's invited us to share. With this in mind, I close with this prayer over your heart, straight from the heart of God:

May the Lord answer you when you are in distress; may the name of the God of Jacob protect you. May he send you help from the sanctuary and grant you support from Zion. May he remember all your sacrifices and accept your burnt offerings. May he give you the desire of your heart and make all your plans succeed. May we shout for joy over your victory and lift up our banners in the name of our God.

May the Lord grant all your requests.

Now this I know: the Lord gives victory to his anointed. He answers him from his heavenly sanctuary with the victorious power of his right hand. Some trust in chariots and some in horses, but we trust in the name of the Lord our God.

—Psalm 20:1–7

God bless you as you serve our God and King.

Bible Study

DEEPER INTO THE
HEART OF GOD

Chapter One: Learning to Live Your Private Life in Public

1. Read Philippians 1:6. Consider the good work He started in you. Write out your personal testimony. How have you seen evidence of God's good work being completed in your life? Who is someone you could share your testimony with?
2. Read and make a list of the spiritual gifts (Romans 12:6–8, 1 Corinthians 12:8–10, Ephesians 4:11–16, 1 Peter 4:11). Prayerfully consider those you believe apply to you. How can you put your gifts to practice within the body of believers?
3. Read 2 Peter 1:3–8. What has God given us? What does Peter suggest we add to our faith? Why is it important to make every effort to add these things? List some of the great and precious promises God has given you in His Word. Which one(s) can you claim for yourself?
4. 1 Samuel 16:7 says, *"The Lord does not look at the things people look at. People look at the outward appearance, but the Lord looks at the heart."* Why is this biblical truth important as you serve the Lord in public ministry?
5. Read Psalm 139. List the intimate ways the Lord knows you. Write out this psalm and insert your name. Make it a personal prayer.

Chapter Two: Fortifying Your Marriage in a Broken World

1. Based upon Ecclesiastes 4:9–12, list the benefits of two versus one. What does that look like in today's society? What can you do to strengthen the cord of three strands in your marriage?

2. Ephesians 5:31 says, *"For this reason a man will leave his father and mother and be united to his wife, and the two will become one flesh."* What does it mean to leave and cleave? And why is it so important?

3. Read the book of Ruth. Why do you think Ruth was so devoted to her mother-in-law, Naomi? List some of the character qualities you see in Boaz throughout the story. What lessons can you glean from this story that will help you fortify your marriage?

4. Read 1 Timothy 3:11. Why are these character traits important? How are they beneficial to a ministry marriage?

5. Look up and write the following verses in your own words. Why are these principles so important? How can you apply them to your marriage?
   a. Matthew 19:6
   b. Ephesians 5:22
   c. Hebrews 13:4
   d. 1 Peter 4:8
   e. Ephesians 4:3
   f. Ephesians 4:26

Chapter Three: Making Family a Priority When Ministry Calls

1. Proverbs 24:3–4 says, *"By wisdom a house is built, and through understanding it is established; through knowledge its rooms are filled with rare and beautiful treasures."* What foundational principles have you put into place in your family? In what ways can you seek wisdom, understanding, and knowledge?

2. Deuteronomy 6:4–9 offers ways to impress God's truth upon your children. What are some of the ways in which you have instilled God's Word in their hearts? Why is it so important to preach what we practice and not merely practice what we preach?

3. Read Psalm 145:4–7, 11–13. Consider your spiritual heritage, whether blood relatives or spiritual mentors. How has the faith been passed on to you? How can you pass on God's great deeds to the next generation?

4. Read Ecclesiastes 3:1–8 to better understand the balance of life. Using Solomon's wisdom, how do you balance family and ministry? What causes you to become unbalanced? Which verses have been used to get you back on track? How do you know when a sacrifice of the family for ministry or vice versa needs to be made?

5. Psalm 127:1 tells us, *"Unless the Lord builds the house, the builders labor in vain. Unless the Lord watches over the city, the guards stand watch in vain."* Write this verse in your own words. How does the Lord build a house? Why is it in vain otherwise?

Chapter Four: Fulfilling Your Calling Without Burning Out

1. We read in 2 Corinthians 11:3, *"But I am afraid that just as Eve was deceived by the serpent's cunning, your minds may somehow be led astray from your sincere and pure devotion to Christ."* How does Satan distract us and get us spinning on the treadmill of life and ministry? How does this feed into burnout? What can you do to better enable you to devote time and attention to the Lord?
2. Many things can drive us to burnout. One of them is people-pleasing. Read the following verses. What does each reference have to say about people-pleasing versus God-pleasing? What do you learn about what it is to please God?
    a. Galatians 1:10
    b. Proverbs 29:25
    c. 1 Thessalonians 2:4
    d. Romans 12:1
    e. Psalm 118:8
    f. 2 Timothy 2:15
    g. Colossians 3:23
    h. Ephesians 6:7
    i. 1 Peter 5:2–4
3. Read Matthew 11:28–29. Why is it important to respond to the Lord's invitation to rest? What kind of rest is He referring to? What is the result of exchanging our burdens for the Lord's? What burdens do you need to put down at His feet?
4. Read Isaiah 40:31. What are the benefits of waiting upon the Lord? How could this verse benefit you personally?
5. Read Psalm 23. Consider times in your life when the Good Shepherd has made you lie down in green pastures. How has He restored your soul?
6. Matthew 6:33 says, *"But seek first his kingdom and his righteousness, and all these things will be given to you as well."* What are the benefits of putting God first in your life and ministry? What do you need to say "no" to in order to say "yes" to what God's calling you to do?

Chapter Five: Finding Joy in the Journey When Transitions Are Tough

1. Genesis 12:1 says, *"The Lord had said to Abram, 'Go from your country, your people and your father's household to the land I will show you.'"* Have you ever packed up everything you owned to head for an unknown destination? Describe what that was like. What lessons did you learn along the way? Take some time this week to read Abraham's journey of faith found in Genesis 12–25. Note the things that stand out to you. Ask yourself why they stood out.
2. Read Luke 9:57–62. What applicable principles do you learn from this passage?
3. Read Proverbs 3:5–6. How has the Lord directed your path as you've trusted in Him? Which scriptures has the Lord used to guide you?
4. Read 1 Samuel 7:12. An Ebenezer refers to a time when God helped. Similarly, in Joshua 4 the Lord instructs the Israelites to gather twelve stones and set them up in remembrance of His faithfulness. Where on your journey have you set up Ebenezers or memorials?
5. Take some time to document your journey of faith. How has the Lord been faithful to you as you've followed in His steps?

Chapter Six: Moving through Hurt to Become a Wounded Healer

1. What can we learn about pain and healing from passages like Psalm 55:12–18 and Psalm 118:5–9? What makes pain inflicted by a fellow believer more painful than that of an unbeliever?
2. Read James 4. What causes fights and quarrels among us? What part does submission play?
3. Read aloud Ephesians 4:32. Why is forgiveness so important? What harm can bitterness do? Describe a time in your life when you've experienced the healing power of forgiveness. How does God use our wounds to bring healing to others? How does that bring you comfort?
4. Proverbs 4:23 says, *"Above all else, guard your heart, for everything you do flows from it."* What do you think this means? Why is important to guard your heart above all else? In what ways can we guard our hearts wisely? How can we better discern with whom we can share our hearts?
5. Read Romans 12:18–19. What does it mean when it says, *"as far as it depends on you, live at peace with everyone"*? How can we do that effectively? Why is it important to leave room for God's wrath? Describe a time when it depended upon

you to keep the peace. How did that situation work out? Did you feel peace, even if it didn't work to preserve that relationship?

Chapter Seven: Building Relationships that Provide Support

1. Look up the following scriptures and list the one-anothers you find. Then identify which one-another you value most and why. Which one could you work on?
    a.   John 15:12
    b.   Romans 12:10
    c.   Romans 12:16
    d.   Romans 14:19
    e.   Romans 15:7
    f.   Romans 15:14
    g.   Galatians 5:13
    h.   Galatians 6:2
    i.   Ephesians 4:32
    j.   Ephesians 5:21
    k.   Philippians 2:13
    l.   Colossians 3:13
    m.   Thessalonians 4:18
    n.   Thessalonians 5:11
    o.   Hebrews 10:24–25
    p.   James 5:16
    q.   1 Peter 4:9
    r.   1 Corinthians 1:3–4
2. Read Romans 12:10–16. What are some of the qualities to look for in seeking out a godly community? Why is it so important to find a support system in ministry? How do you find someone who's safe?
3. Read Hebrews 10:24–25. What is the importance of fellowship? How have others spurred you on toward love and good deeds? How have you been encouraged? Why is it so important to encourage one another *"all the more"* as we await the coming of our Saviour?
4. Proverbs 27:17 says, *"As iron sharpens iron, so one person sharpens another."* In your own words, what does this mean? How have you experienced this in your own life and ministry?
5. Read Colossians 1:9–12. What did Paul pray for this group of believers? Why did he pray this way? What did he hope the outcome of his prayers would be?

Chapter Eight: Growing through Challenges that Teach Lasting Lessons

1. Read Hebrews 12:1–13. What is the purpose of discipline? How does considering Him help you not to grow weary and lose heart? How does focusing on the Lord encourage your heart when you face challenges? Take some time to consider Him right now.
2. Read 1 Peter 1:6, 7. Peter speaks of suffering grief in all kinds of trials. List some of the grief and trials you've experienced. Why are we able to rejoice in them? What is the value that comes from trials? What kind of hope does that give you?
3. Proverbs 17:3 says, *"The crucible for silver and the furnace for gold, but the Lord tests the heart."* How and why does the Lord test our hearts?
4. Read 2 Timothy 1:13–14. What is the good deposit that has been entrusted to you? Why is it important to guard it with the help of the Holy Spirit?
5. Read Psalm 18:25–36. How does this passage encourage your heart?

Chapter Nine: Recognizing God's Blessings When Your Vision Is Obstructed

1. List some of the promises of God. What promises have you been the recipient of? What was the context of your receiving them? How have they been a blessing to you?
2. Read Jeremiah 30–31 and highlight all the "I will…" passages. Which one applies to your present situation or a situation you've faced?
3. Acts 20:35 tells us to remember *"the words the Lord Jesus himself said: 'It is more blessed to give than to receive.'"* How is this so? When have you experienced this kind of boomerang blessing?
4. Read Psalm 103:1–5. According to these verses, what are the benefits the Lord has given us? Why is it important not to forget them?
5. Read Philippians 1:9–11. How does love abound in your life? What can you do to increase your knowledge and depth of insight? This passage speaks of being filled with the fruit of righteousness. What does that look like in your life?
6. Read Galatians 22:23. What fruit of the Spirit do you need to nurture in your life to produce the fruit of righteousness? Who is someone you can pass this blessing to?

Chapter Ten: Nurturing Your Soul Thrive, Not Just Survive

1. Read John 15:5. What is the importance of abiding in the vine?

2. Read Psalm 19:7–11. List the benefits of God's Word mentioned in this passage. How have you experienced each one in your life and ministry?

3. We read in 1 Thessalonians 1:2–3, *"We always thank God for all of you and continually mention you in our prayers. We remember before our God and Father your work produced by faith, your labor prompted by love, and your endurance inspired by hope in our Lord Jesus Christ."* How do these verses apply to and encourage you in your relationship with the Lord?

4. According to Deuteronomy 30:20, what are three vital components to nurturing a vibrant relationship with the Lord? What are some of the ways you can put these three components into practice?

5. Read Jeremiah 17:7–8. What does it mean to put your confidence in the Lord? What are the benefits of trusting in the Lord? Why is it important to invest in a healthy relationship with the Lord before a drought hits?

Suggested Reading

Chapter One

Robert Boyd Munger, *My Heart, Christ's Home* (Downers Grove, IL: InterVarsity Press, 1954).

Don and Katie Fortune, *Discover Your God-Given Gifts* (Grand Rapids, MI: Chosen Books, 1987).

Robert S. McGee, *The Search for Significance: Seeing Your True Worth through God's Eyes* (Nashville, TN: W Publishing Group, 2003).

Carol Kent, *Tame Your Fears, and Transform Them into Faith, Confidence, and Action* (Colorado Springs, CO: NavPress, 2003).

Donna Partow, *Becoming a Vessel God Can Use* (Minneapolis, MN: Bethany House Publishers, 2004).

Chapter Two

Bill and Pam Farrell, *Men Are Like Waffles, Women Are Like Spaghetti: Understanding and Delighting in Your Differences* (Eugene, OR: Harvest House, 2001).

John Gray, *Men Are from Mars, Women Are from Venus: A Practical Guide for Improving Communication and Getting What You Want in Your Relationships* (New York, NY: HarperCollins, 1994).

Willard F. Harley, Jr., *His Needs, Her Needs: Building an Affair-Proof Marriage* (Grand Rapids, MI: Revell, 2011).

Chapter Three

Stormie Omartian, *The Power of a Praying Parent* (Eugene, OR: Harvest House Publishers, 1995).

Deborah Shaw Lewis, with Gregg Lewis, *Motherhood Stress* (Grand Rapids, MI: Zondervan, 1992).

Chapter Four

Charles E. Hummel, *Tyranny of the Urgent* (Wheaton, IL: Crossway Books, 1997).

Mark Buchanan, *The Rest of God: Restoring Your Soul by Restoring Sabbath* (Nashville, TN: Thomas Nelson, 2006).

Susie Larson, *Your Sacred Yes: Trading Life-Draining Obligation for Freedom, Passion, and Joy* (Minneapolis, MN: Bethany House Publishers, 2015).

Charles R. Swindoll, *A Man of Heroism and Humility: Elijah* (Nashville, TN: Word Publishing, 2000).

Patricia H. Sprinkle, *Women Who Do Too Much: Stress and the Myth of the Superwoman* (New York, NY: Harper Paperbacks, 1992).

Geri Scazzero with Peter Scazzero, *I Quit!* (Grand Rapids, MI: Zondervan, 2010).

Dr. Henry Cloud and Dr. John Townsend, *Boundaries: When to Say YES, When to Say NO to Take Control of Your Life* (Grand Rapids, MI: Zondervan, 1992).

Chapter Five

Beth Moore, *Believing God* (Nashville, TN: Broadman & Holman Publishers, 2004).

Evelyn Christenson, *Lord Change Me!* (Wheaton, IL: Victor Books, 1977).

Carol Kent, *A New Kind of Normal: Hope-Filled Choices When Life Turns Upside Down* (Nashville, TN: Thomas Nelson, 2007).

Chapter Six

Larry Crabb, *The Safest Place on Earth* (Nashville, TN: Word Publishing, 1999).

Andy Stanley, *Enemies of the Heart: Breaking Free from the Four Emotions that Control You* (Colorado Springs, CO: Multnomah Books, 2011).

Anne Graham Lotz, *Wounded by God's People* (Grand Rapids, MI: Zondervan, 2013).

Chapter Seven

Florence Littauer, *Silver Boxes: The Gift of Encouragement* (Dallas, TX: Word Incorporated, 1989).

Chapter Eight

Jill Briscoe, *Heart Strings: Finding a Song When You've Lost Your Joy* (Wheaton, IL: Tyndale House Publishers, 1997).

Gary Smalley, *Joy that Lasts* (New York, NT: Harper Paperbacks, 1988).

Chapter Nine

Gary Smalley and John Trent, *The Blessing* (New York, NY: Pocket Books, 1986).

Chapter Ten

Elizabeth George, *A Woman After God's Own Heart* (Eugene, OR: Harvest House Publishers, 1997).

Peter Scazzero, *Emotionally Healthy Spirituality, Updated Edition* (Grand Rapids, MI: Harper Collins Publishers, 2017).

Richard J. Foster, *Celebration of Discipline: The Path to Spiritual Growth* (Grand Rapids, MI: Harper Collins Publishers, 1978).

ABOUT THE AUTHOR

Born and raised in Toronto, Ontario, Canada, Lisa Elliott had an unquenchable longing to know God from a young age. She accepted Jesus as her Saviour at camp when she was fifteen years old and graduated from Ontario Bible College (Tyndale) with her Bachelor of Religious Education in 1985. While there, she met the love of her life, David. For the last forty years, they have served the Lord faithfully in a wide variety of roles in full-time pastoral ministry. Together they have raised four children (three on earth and one now in heaven). Their tribe continues to increase as in-laws—and most recently as grandparents to four precious grandchildren (so far).

Also a gifted speaker, Lisa's ministry, Straight from the Heart, has impacted the lives of men and women across the nation at conferences, retreats, camps, and special events for three decades. She has made appearances on *100 Huntley Street*, Christian radio, webinars, and podcasts.

Additionally, Lisa is an award-winning author of *The Ben Ripple: Choosing to Live through Loss with Purpose* and *Dancing in the Rain: One Family's Journey through Grief and Loss*. She is a long-standing contributor to *Just Between Us* magazine and writes a monthly blog for Word Alive Press titled Straight from the Heart. Other contributions of Lisa's are found in *Good Ground* devotional app, Scripture Union's online devotional, *theStory, Hot Apple Cider with Cinnamon*, and *Good Grief People*.

Lisa's love for the Lord is contagious and her passion to share the life-changing truths and principles of God's Word is inspiring. Her transparency, authenticity, and often humorous approach will inspire you to live the abundant life to the fullest!

You can contact Lisa at lisakelliott22@gmail.com, check out her blog at www.wordalivepress.ca/blogs, and follow her on Facebook (https://www.facebook.com/Lisa-Elliott-Straight-from-the-Heart-SpeakerAuthor-370667793001091). Her website is: lisaelliottstraightfromtheheart.wordpress.com

The Ben Ripple: Choosing to Live through Loss with Purpose

"Ben's life is producing eternal ripples."

—Moira Brown, 100 Huntley Street

On August 12, 2008, Lisa Elliott received the phone call that changed her life forever. It was from her husband, David, on his way to the hospital emergency with their 18-year-old son Ben who was subsequently diagnosed with Acute Lymphoblastic Leukemia. After a one year and one week valiant battle, Ben was promoted to his heavenly home. Throughout his life, but even throughout his death, Ben's Christlike attitude became an inspiration for thousands around the world who followed updates Lisa posted on a Facebook blog entitled, "Prayer for Benjamin Elliott". It was appropriately re-titled, "The Ben Ripple" upon his death.

This is not just an ordinary "journal", but a victorious and candid "journey" of one faith-filled mother who sought to use her story for the glory of God through her pain, loss and grief. It provides validation for those dealing with a family crisis, hope and inspiration for those who are grieving losses, and practical help for those desiring to come alongside those needing comfort.

Dancing in the Rain: One Family's Journey through Grief and Loss

"[*Dancing in the Rain*] is a chronicle of a spiritual journey, a decisive choosing to find and experience God in brokenness and ultimately live again with new inner strength, renewed hope, and joyful purpose."
—Margaret Gibb
Founder and Director of Women Together

We all know what it is to face storms in our lives. The question is, how do you deal with them when they come?

- How do you keep your head above water when the undertow of crisis pulls you under?
- How do you keep your faith afloat amid loss and disappointment?
- How do you keep your hope from drowning in depression?
- How do you weather the storms as they break into the safe shelter of your home?
- How do you find an anchor during times of change?
- How do you live the abundant life when the life is sucked out of you?

Lisa Elliott invites you into the living room of her heart in the aftermath of the biggest storm she ever faced. Let her take you by the hand as she and her family candidly share their journey of hope. You will find invaluable insights that will help you to dance in the rain!